I0831896

United We Stand, Divided We Fall.

THE PROTOCOLS

OF THE MEETINGS OF THE

LEARNED ELDERS OF ZION

WITH

PREFACE AND EXPLANATORY NOTES

Translated from the Russian Text by

VICTOR E. MARSDEN

Formerly Russian Correspondent of "The Morning Post"

1934

The Protocols of Zion
ISBN 1-58509-015-8

Republished 1999 by
The Book Tree
Post Office Box 724
Escondido, CA 92033

COVER: SERGIUS A. NILUS, FIRST PUBLISHER OF "THE PROTOCOLS" 1901

INDEX:

INTRODUCTION

The Book Tree specializes in publishing rare, hard to find, and, often times, controversial books. In reissuing what is probably the most controversial book in history, *The Protocols of the Learned Elders of Zion*, The Book Tree has no agenda. We are not a "hate group," nor are we connected or affiliated with any such organization.

It is claimed that this book contributed to the deaths of many people, and we do not argue this point. After careful study we have concluded and publicly state that we do not endorse this book as being valid except, if anything, by coincidence alone. Even after overwhelming proof surfaced that proved it was a forgery, Henry Ford, of the Ford Motor Company, continued to print it in the early 20th century based on coincidence (a strong coincidence to Ford) – but on nothing more than that. As far as we can tell, there was no master plan made by Jewish leaders to rule the world as outlined in this book. People were misled and mistakenly believed it.

Although it is an unquestionable forgery to most everyone, we still offer this book in the same way we publish and offer a book called *Malleus Malificarum*, which also contributed to the deaths of thousands of innocent people (accused of witchcraft). We do not support what *The Protocols* claims any more than we support the burning of "witches" at the stake. Some people still believe there are witches and they should die, based on a Bible scripture that was misinterpreted (or even forged) during the time of King James. Some also believe in the message of *The Protocols*, which is to the best of our knowledge an unquestionable and fraudulent hoax – a forgery. We offer both of these books – not in support of their messages – but as a tool for people to understand how nations and people can be duped into thinking and doing insane things. It is sometimes referred to as mass hysteria.

A number of these books (*The Protocols*) are being used in college classrooms, and it seems clear that professors are using it as an educational tool – they are not preaching hate with it. Nor are we trying to preach hate by offering it. We at The Book Tree were unaware of the evidence that proves conclusively that *The Protocols* is a hoax, and had taken a neutral stand in the Introduction to a previous edition, saying people should read the book and decide for themselves. We extend our apologies for being unaware of this evidence, and now support those who claim it to be a hoax.

How do we know that it is? A Russian court examined all the evidence and used various (non-Jewish) experts to rule that it was in 1993. Approximately 175 excerpts, over 60% of the book, are said to almost precisely match French satirist Maurice Joly's novel from 1864 entitled, *Dialogues in Hell Between Machiavelli and Monttesquieu*. If this is true, and we take it on good authority that it is (having seen some examples), then we stand by those who have exposed it as a forgery. A known forger and German anti-Semite named Hermann Goedsche (aka Sir John Retcliffe) took Joly's *Dialogues* and adapted them into what eventually became *The Protocols*. The Russian secret police then found it useful as a propaganda tool on a number of levels.

There are those few who are still adamant that *The Protocols* is genuine. They are free to read this book as a matter of choice and form their own opinions, while keeping in mind the conclusions of the publisher, myself, and various experts. At the same time, The Book Tree is not a believer in the suppression of information. A number of groups are trying to ban this book in America, and it seems they have succeeded in doing so in Germany. For the first time in the history of publishing, a bookseller has posted a disclaimer from another party besides the publisher (the Anti-Defamation League), as part of the information about the book on the Internet, and it will seemingly remain there. Two companies posted the disclaimer, one refused (Border's Books). Will this practice soon be allowed in stores – for outside groups to post notices next to any book they do not like? With such a thing happening, where does one draw the line? This may have set a precedent toward suppressing other types of information that may not be so clear cut, and legal groups supporting free speech have begun to question these actions. One in particular (the EFF) has said, "This is the beginning of a slippery slope." At the same time, we have come to agree with the ADL's conclusion about the origin of the book, and understand their concern. But we do not agree that this or any other book should be banned.

Because of this belief (in the freedom of the press and the First Amendment), The Book Tree is being cast into the light of being an anti-Semitic hate group. Not once have we ever stated that *The Protocols* was a genuine and believable document. Contrary to what the President of the American Jewish Committee implied in a letter to the CEO of Barnes and Noble, released on the news services on March 21, 2000, The Book Tree is not a hate group. We are a balanced company that is willing to publish all sides of any issue. He said to Barnes and Noble, "Your sale of these materials indirectly adds to the coffers of hate groups," immediately after The Book Tree was mentioned as a publisher.

All people have a God-given right to read and investigate what they wish. There is much to be learned from this book by examining it closely. Plutarch once said, "To make no mistakes is not in the power of man, but from their errors and mistakes the wise and good learn wisdom for the future." It is our hope that past mistakes will not be repeated, and we believe that open dialogue and education is the key (rather than suppression). Another famous philosopher once said, "If we do not learn from our past mistakes, then we are doomed to repeat them." Those who believed *The Protocols* made a terrible mistake. But society as a whole has evolved beyond witch burnings and the systematic murder of Jewish people. Instead of covering up or suppressing the books which contributed to such things, we believe they should be made available and studied.

Paul Tice

ERRATUM:

At the bottom of page 151, the last sentence should read: "Through the Press we have gained the power to influence while remaining ourselves in the shade; thanks to the Press we have got the *gold* in our hands, notwithstanding that we have had to gather it out of oceans of blood and tears.

PREFACE

Victor E. Marsden.

The author of this translation of the famous PROTOCOLS was himself a victim of the Revolution. He had lived for many years in Russia and was married to a Russian lady. Among his other activities in Russia he had been for a number of years Russian Correspondent of the *Morning Post,* a position which he occupied when the Revolution broke out, and his vivid descriptions of events in Russia will still be in the recollection of many of the readers of that journal. Naturally he was singled out for the anger of the Soviet. On the day that Captain Cromie was murdered by Jews, Victor Marsden was arrested and thrown into the Peter-Paul Prison, expecting every day to have his name called out for execution. This, however, he escaped, and eventually he was allowed to return to England very much of a wreck in bodily health. However, he recovered under treatment and the devoted care of his wife and friends. One of the first things he undertook as soon as he was able was this translation of the Protocols. Mr. Marsden was eminently well qualified for the work. His intimate acquaintance with Russia, Russian life and the Russian language on the one hand, and his mastery of a terse literary English style on the other, placed him in a position of advantage which few others could claim. The consequence is that we have in his version an eminently readable work, and the subject-matter is somewhat formless, Mr. Marsden's literary touch reveals the thread running through the twenty-four Protocols. The Summary placed at the head of each is Mr. Marsden's own, and will be found very useful in acquiring a comprehensive view of its scope.

It may be said with truth that this work was carried out at the cost of Mr. Marsden's own life's blood. He told the writer of this Preface that he could not stand more than an hour at a time of his work on it in the British Museum, as the diabolical spirit of the matter which he was obliged to turn into English made him positively ill.

Mr. Marsden's connection with the *Morning Post* was not severed by his return to England, and he was well enough to accept the post of special correspondent of that journal in the suite of H. R. H. The Prince of Wales on his Empire tour. From this he returned with the Prince, apparently in much better health, but within a few days of his landing he was taken suddenly ill, and died after a very brief illness. His sudden death is still a *mystery*.

May this work be his crowning monument! In it he has performed an immense service to the English-speaking world, and there can be little doubt that it will take its place in the first rank of the English versions of "THE PROTOCOLS of the Meetings of the LEARNED ELDERS OF ZION."

PART I

A SELECTION OF THE ARTICLES (1920-22)

published by

Mr. Henry Ford's paper

THE DEARBORN INDEPENDENT

THE JEWISH QUESTION — FACT OR FANCY

(IV)

The chief difficulty in writing about the Jewish Question is the supersensitiveness of Jews and non-Jews concerning the whole matter. There is a vague feeling that even to openly use the word "Jew," or to expose it nakedly to print, is somehow improper. Polite evasions like "Hebrew" and "Semite," both of which are subject to the criticism of inaccuracy, are timidly essayed, and people pick their way gingerly as if the whole subject were forbidden, until some courageous Jewish thinker comes straight out with the good old word "Jew," and then the constraint is relieved and the air cleared. The word "Jew" is not an epithet; it is a name, ancient and honorable, with significance for every period of human history, past, present and to come.

There is extreme sensitiveness about the public discussion of the Jewish Question on the part of Gentiles. They would prefer to keep it in the hazy borderlands of their thought, shrouded in silence. Their heritage of tolerance has something to do with their attitude, but perhaps *their instinctive sense of the difficulty involved has more to do with it. The principal public Gentile pronouncements upon the Jewish Question are in the manner of the truckling politician or the pleasant after-dinner speaker; the great Jewish names in philosophy, medicine, literature, music and finance are named over, the energy, ability and thrift of the race are dwelt upon, and everyone goes home feeling that a difficult place has been rather neatly negotiated. But nothing is changed thereby. The Jew is not changed.* The Gentile is not changed. *The Jew still remains the enigma of the world.*

Gentile sensitiveness on this point is best expressed by the desire for silence — "Why discuss it at all?" is the attitude. Such an attitude is itself a proof that there is a problem which we would evade if we could. "Why discuss it at all?" — the keen thinker clearly sees in the implications of such a question, the existence of a problem whose discussion or suppression will not always be within the choice of easy-going minds.

Is there a Jewish Question in Russia? Unquestionably, in its most virulent form. Is it necessary to meet that Question in Russia? Undoubtedly, meet it from every angle along which light and healing may come.

Well, the percentage of the Jewish population of Russia is just one per cent more than it is in the United Sates. The majority of the Jews themselves are not less well-behaved in Russia han they are here; they lived under restrictions which do not exist here; yet in Russia their genius has enabled them to attain a degree of power which has completely baffled the Russian mind. Whether you go to Rumania, Russia, Austria or Germany, or anywhere else that the Jewish Question has come to the forefront as a vital issue, you will discover that the principal cause is the outworking of the Jewish genius to achieve the power of control.

Here in the *United States* it is the fact of this remarkable minority — a sparse Jewish ingredient of *three per cent* in a nation of 110,000,000 — attaining in 50 years a degree of control that would be impossible to a ten times larger group of any other race, that creates the Jewish Question here. Three per cent of any other people would scarcely occasion comment, because we could not meet with a representative of them wherever we went in high places — in the innermost secrecy of the councils of the Big Four at Versailles; in the supreme court; in the councils of the White House; in the vast dispositions of world finance — wherever there is power to get or use. *Yet we meet the Jew everywhere in the upper circles, literally everywhere there is power. He has the brains, the initiative, the penetrative vision which almost automatically projects him to the top, and as a consequence he is more marked than any other race.*

And that is where the Jewish Question begins. It begins in very simple terms — *How does the Jew so habitually and so resistlessly gravitate to the highest places? What puts him there? Why is he put there? What does he do there? What does the fact of his being there mean to the world?*

That is the Jewish Question in its origin. From these points it goes on to others, and whether the trend becomes pro-Jewish or anti-Semitic depends on the amount of prejudice brought to the inquiry, and whether it becomes pro-Humanity depends on the amount of insight and intelligence.

The use of the word Humanity in connection with the word Jew usually throws a side-meaning which may not be intended. *In this connection it is usually understood that the humanity ought to be shown toward the Jew. There is just as great an obligation upon the Jew to show his humanity toward the whole race. The Jew has been too long accustomed to think of himself as exclusively the claimant on the humanitarianism of society; society has a large claim against him that he cease his exclusiveness, that he cease exploiting the world, that he cease making Jewish groups the end and all of his gains, and that he begin to fulfill, in a sense his exclusiveness has never yet enabled him to fulfill, the ancient prophecy that through him all the nations of the earth should be blessed.*

The Jew cannot go on forever filling the role of suppliant for the world's humanitarianism; *he must himself show that quality to a society which seriously suspects his higher and more powerful groups of exploiting it with a pitiless rapacity which in its wide-flung and long drawn-out distress may be described as an economic program against a rather helpless humanity. For it is true that society is as helpless before the well-organized extortions of certain financial groups, as huddled groups of Russian Jews were helpless against the anti-Semitic mob. And as in Russia, so in America, it is the poor Jew who suffers for the delinquencies of the rich exploiter of his race.*

This series of articles is already being met by an organized barrage by mail and wire and voice, every single item of which carries the wail of persecution. One would think that a heartless and horrible attack were being made on a most pitiable and helpless people — until one looks at the letterheads of the magnates who write, and at the financial ratings of those who protest and at the membership of the organizations whose responsible heads hysterically demand retraction. And always in the background there is the threat of boycott, a threat which has practically sealed up the colums of every publication in America against even the mildest discussion of the Jewish Question.

The Jewish Question in America cannot be concealed forever by threats against publications, nor by the propagandist publication of matter extremely and invariably favorable to everything Jewish. It is here and it cannot be twisted into something else by the adroit use of propaganda, nor can *it be forever silenced by threats. The Jews of the United States can best serve themselves and their fellow-Jews all over the world by letting drop their far too ready cry of "anti-Semitism," by adopting a franker tone than that which befits a helpless victim, and by seeing what the Jewish Question is and how it behooves every Jew who loves his people to help solve it.*

There has been used in this series the term "International Jew". It is susceptible of two interpretations: one, the Jew wherever he may be; the other, the Jew who exercises international control. The real contention of the world is with the latter and his satellites, whether Jew or Gentile.

Now, this international type of Jew, this grasper after world-control, this actual possessor and wielder of world-control is a very unfortunate connection for his race to have. The most unfortunate thing about the international Jew, from the standpoint of the ordinary Jew, is that the international type is also a Jew. And the significance of this is that the type does not grow anywhere else than on a Jewish stem. There is no other racial nor national type which puts forth this kind of person. It is not merely that there are a few Jews among international financial controllers; it is that these world controllers are exclusively Jews. That is the phenomenon which creates an unfortunate situation for those Jews who are not and never shall be world-controllers, who are the plain people of the Jewish race. If world-control were mixed, like the control, say, of the biscuit business, then the occasional Jews we might find in those higher financial altitudes would not constitute the problem at all; the problem would then be limited to the existence of world-control in the hands of a few men, of whatever race or lineage they might be. *But since world-control is an ambition which has only been achieved by Jews, and not by any of the methods usually adopted by would-be world conquerors, it becomes inevitable that the question should center in that remarkable race.*

This brings another difficulty: in discussing this group of world-controllers under the name of Jews (and they are Jews), it is not always possible to stop and distinguish the group of Jews that is meant. The candid reader can usually determine that, but the Jew who is in a state of mind to be injured is sometimes pained by reading as a charge against himself what was intended for the upper group. "Then why not discuss the upper group as financiers and not as Jews?" may be asked. Because they are Jews. It is not to the point to insist that in any list of rich men there are more Gentiles than Jews; we are not talking about merly rich men who have, many of them, gained their riches by serving a System, *we are talking about those who Control — and it is perfectly apparent that merely to be rich is not to control. The world-controlling Jew has riches, but he also has something much more powerful than that.*

The international Jew, as already defined, *rules not because he is rich, but because in a most marked degree he possesses the commercial and masterful genius of his race, and avails himself of a racial loyalty and solidarity the like of which exists in no other human group. In other words, transfer to-day the world-control of the international Jew to the hands of the highest commercially talented group of Gentiles, and the whole fabric of world-control would eventually fall to pieces, because the Gentile lacks a certain quality, be it human or divine, be it natural or acquired, that the Jew possesses.*

This, of course, the modern Jew denies. There is a new position taken by the modernists among the Jews which constitutes a denial that the Jew differs from any other man except in the matter of religion. "Jew" they say is not a racial designation, but a religious designation like "Episcopalian", "Catholic," "Presbyterian." This is the argument used in newspaper offices in the Jews' protests against giving the Jewish designation to those of their people who are implicated in crime — "You don't give the religious classifications of other people who are arrested," the editor is told, "why should you do it with Jews?" *The appeal to religious tolerance always wins, and is sometimes useful in diverting attention from other things.*

Well, if the Jews are only religiously differentiated from the rest of the world, the phenomenon grows stranger still. For the rest of the world is interested less in the Jew's religion than in anything else that concerns him. There is really nothing in his religion to differentiate the Jew from the rest of mankind, as far as the moral content of that religion is concerned, and if there were he would have overcome that by the fact that his Jewish religion supplies the moral structure for both of the other great religions. Moreover, it is stated that there are among English speaking nations, 2,000,000 *Jews who acknowledge their race and not their religion, while* 1,000,000 *are classed as agnostic — are these any less Jews than the others?* The world does not think so. The authoritative students of human differences do not think so. An Irishman who grows indifferent to the Church is still an Irishman, and it would seem to be equally true that a Jew who grows indifferent to the Synagogue is still a Jew. He at least feels that he is, and so does the non-Jew.

A still more serious challange would arise if this contention of the modernists were true, for it would necessitate the explanation of these world-controlling Jews by their religion. We should have to say, "They excel through their religion," and then the problem would turn on the religion whose practice should bring such power and prosperity to its devotees. But another fact would intervene, namely, that *these world-controlling Jews are not notably religious;* and still another fact would hammer for recognition, namely, *the most devout believers and most obedient followers of the Jewish religion are the poorest among the Jews.* If you want Jewish orthodoxy, the bracing morality of the Old Testament, you will find it, not among the successful Jews, who have Unitarianized their religion to the same extend that the Unitarians have Judaized their Christianity, but among the poor in the side streets who still sacrifice the Saturday business for their Sabbath keeping. *Certainly their religion has not given them world-control; instead, they have made their own sacrifices to keep it inviolate against modernism.*

Of course, if the Jew differs from the rest of mankind only when he is in full accord with his religion, the question becomes very simple. Any criticism of the Jew becomes sheer religious bigotry and nothing else! And that would be intolerable. But it would be the consensus of thoughtful opinion that the *Jew differs less in his religion than anything else. There is more difference between the two great branches of Christianity, more conscious difference, than between any branch of Christianity and Judaism.*

So that, the contention of certain modernists notwithstanding, the world will go on thinking of the Jew as a member of a race, a race whose persistence has defeated the utmost efforts made for its extermination, a race that has preserved itself in virility and power by the observance of those natural laws the violation of which has mongrelized so many nations, a race which has come up out of the past with the two great moral values which may be reckoned on monotheism and monogamy, a race which to-day is before us as the visible sign of an antiquity to which all our spiritual wealth harks back. Nay, the Jew will go on thinking of himself as the member of a people, a nation, a race. And all the mixture and intermixture of thought or faith or custom cannot make it otherwise. *A Jew is a Jew and as long as he remains within his perfectly unassailable traditions, he will remain a Jew.* And he will always have the right to feel that to be a Jew is to belong to a superior race.

These world-controlling Jews at the top of affairs, then, are there by virtue of, among other things, certain qualities which are inherent in their Jewish natures. Every Jew has these qualities even if not in the supreme sense, just as every Englishman has Shakespeare's tongue but not in Shakespeare's degree. *And thus it is impracticable, if not impossible, to consider the international Jew without laying the foundations broadly upon Jewish character and psychology.*

We may discount at once the too common libel that this greater form of Jewish success is built upon dishonesty. It is impossible to indict the Jewish people or any other people on a wholesale charge. No one knows better than the Jew how widespread is the notion that Jewish methods of business are all unscrupulous. There is no doubt a possibility of a great deal of unscrupulousness existing without actual legal dishonesty, but it is altogether possible that the reputation the Jewish people have long borne in this respect may have had other sources than actual and persistent dishonesty.

We may indicate one of these possible sources. The Jew at a trade is naturally quicker than most other men. They say there are other races which are as nimble at a trade as is the Jew, but the Jew does not live much among them. In this connection one may remember the famous joke about the Jew who went to Scotland.

Now, it is human nature for the slower man to believe that the quicker man is too deft by far, and to become suspicious of his deftness. Everybody suspects the "sharper" even though his sharpness be entirely honest. The slower mind is likely to conceive that the man who sees so many legitimate twists and turns to a trade, may also see and use a convenient number of illegitimate twists and turns. Moreover, there is always the ready suspicion that the one who gets "the best of the bargain" gets it by trickery which is not above board. Slow, honest, plain-spoken and straight-dealing people always have their doubts of the man who gets the better of it.

The Jews, as the records for centuries show, were a keen people in trade. They were so keen that many regarded them as crooked. And so the Jew became disliked for business reasons, not all of which were creditable to the intelligence or initiative of his enemies.

Take, for example, the persecution which Jew merchants once suffered in England. In older England the merchant class had many easy-going traditions. One tradition was that a respectable tradesman would never seek business but wait for it to come to him. Another tradition was that to decorate one's store window with lights or colors, or to display one's stock of goods attractively in the view of the public, was a contemptible and underhanded method of tempting a brother tradesman's customers away from him. Still another tradition was that it was strictly unethical and unbusinesslike to handle more than one line of goods. If one sold tea, it was the best reason in the world why he should not sell teaspoons. As for advertising, the thing would have been so brazen and bold that public opinion would have put the advertiser out of business. The proper demeanor for a merchant was to seem reluctant to part with his goods.

One may readily imagine what happened when the Jewish merchant bustled into the midst of this jungle of traditions. He simply broke them all. In those days tradition had all the force of a divinely promulgated moral law and in consequence of his initiative the Jew was regarded as a great offender. A man who would break those trade traditions would stop at nothing! The Jew was anxious to sell. If he could not sell one article to a customer, he had another on hand to offer him. The *Jews' stores became bazaars,* forerunners of our modern department stores, and the old English custom of one store for one line of goods was broken up. The Jew went after trade, pursued it, persuaded it. He was the originator of "a quick turnover and small profits". He *originated the installment plan.* The one state of affairs he could not endure was business at a standstill, and to start it moving he would do anything. He was *the first advertiser* — in a day when even to announce in the public prints the location of your store was to intimate to the public that you were in financial difficulties, were about to go to the wall and were trying the last desperate expedient to which no self-respecting merchant would stoop.

It was as easy as child's play to connect this energy with dishonesty. The Jew was not playing the game, at least so the staid English merchant thought. As a matter of fact he was playing the game to get it all in his own hands — which he has practically done.

The Jew has shown that same ability ever since. His power of analyzing the money currents amounts to an instinct. His establishment in one country represented another base from which the members of his race could operate. Whether by the natural outworking of innate gifts, or the deliberate plan of race unity and loyalty, all Jewish trading communities had relations, and as these trading communities increased in wealth, prestige and power, as they formed relations with governments and great interests in the countries where they operated, they simply put more power into the central community wherever it might be located, now in Spain, now in Holland, now in England. Whether by intention or not, they became more closely allied than the branches of one business could be, because the cement of racial unity, the bond of racial brotherhood cannot in the very nature of things exist among the Gentiles as it exists among the Jews. *Gentiles never think of themselves as Gentiles, and never feel that they owe anything to another Gentile as such. Thus they have been convenient agents of Jewish schemes at times and in places when it was not expedient that the Jewish controllers should be publicly known; but they have never been successful competitors of the Jew in the field of world-control.*

From these separated Jewish communities went power to the central community where the master bankers and the master analysts of conditions lived. And back from the central community flowed information of an invaluable character and assistance wherever needed. *It is not difficult to understand how, under such a condition, the nation that did not deal kindly with the Jews was made to suffer, and the nation that yielded to them their fullest desire was favored by them.* And it is credibly stated that they have made certain nations feel the power of their displeasure.

This system, if it ever existed, *exists in greater power today. It is to-day, however, threatened as it has never been. Fifty years ago, international banking, which was mostly in control of the Jews as the money brokers of the world, was on top of business. It exercised the super-control of governments and finance everywhere. Then came that new thing, Industry, which expanded to a degree unguessed by the shrewdest prophets and analysts. As Industry gathered strength and power it became a powerful money magnet, drawing the wealth of the world in its train, not, however, merely for the sake of possessing the money, but of making it work. Production and profit on production, instead of loans and interest on loans, became the master method for a time. The war came, in which the former broker-masters of the world had undoubtedly their large part. And now the two forces, Industry and Finance, are in a struggle to see whether Finance is again to become the master, or creative Industry. This is one of the elements which is bringing the Jewish Question to the bar of public opinion.*

DEARBORN INDEPENDENT - ISSUE OF JUNE 12, 1920.

DOES A DEFINITE JEWISH WORLD PROGRAM EXIST?

(VIII)

In all the explanations of anti-Jewish feeling which modern Jewish spokesmen make, *these three* alleged *causes are commonly given* — these three and no more: *religious prejudice, economic jealousy, social antipathy. Whether the Jew knows it or not, every Gentile knows that on his side of the Jewish Question no religious prejudice exists.* Economic jealousy may exist, at least to this extent, that his uniform success has exposed the Jew to much scrutiny. A few Jewish spokesmen seek to turn this scrutiny by denying that the Jew is pre-eminent in finance, but this is loyalty in extremity. *The finances of the world are in control of Jews; their decisions and their devices are themselves our economic law.* But because a people excels us in finance is no sufficient reason for calling them to the bar of public judgment. If they are more intellectually able, more persistently industrious than we are, if they are endowed with faculties which have been denied us as an inferior or slower race, that is no reason for our requiring them to give an account of themselves. Economic jealousy may explain some of the anti-Jewish feeling: it cannot account for the presence of the Jewish Question except as the hidden causes of Jewish financial success may become a minor element of the larger problem. And as for social antipathy — there are many more undesirable Gentiles in the world than there are undesirable Jews, for the simple reason that there are more Gentiles.

None of the Jewish spokesmen to-day mention the political cause, or if they come within suggestive distance of it, they limit and localize it. It is not a question of the patriotism of the Jew, though this too is very widely questioned in all the countries. You hear it in England, in France, in Germany, in Poland, in Russia, in Rumania, — and, with a shock, you hear it in the United States. Books have been written, reports published and scattered abroad, statistics skillfully set forth for the purpose of showing that the Jew does his part for the country in which he resides; and yet the fact remains that in spite of these most zealous and highly sponsored campaigns, the opposite assertion is stronger and lives longer. The Jews who did their duty in the armies of Liberty, and did it doubtless from truehearted love and allegiance, have not been able to overcome the impression made upon officers and men and civilians by those who did not.

But that is not what is here meant as the political element in the Jewish Question. To understand why the Jew should think less of the nationalities of the world than do those who comprise them is not difficult. *The Jew's history is one of wandering among them all.* Considering living individuals only, there is no race of people now upon the planet who have lived in so many places, among so many peoples as have the Jewish masses. *They have a clearer world-sense than any other people, because the world has been their path. And they think in world terms more than any nationally cloistered people could.* The Jew can be absolved if he does not enter into national loyalties and prejudices with the same intensity as the natives; the Jew has been for centuries a cosmopolitan. While under a flag he may be correct in the conduct required of him as a citizen or resident, inevitably he has a view of flags which can hardly be shared by the man who has known but one flag.

The political element inheres in the fact that the Jews form a nation in the midst of the nations. Some of their spokesmen, particularly in America, deny that, but the genius of the Jew himself has always put these spokesmen's zeal to shame. *And why this fact of nationhood should be so strenuously denied is not always clear.* It may be that when Israel is brought to see that her mission in the world is not to be achieved by means of the Golden Calf, her very cosmopolitanism with regard to the world and her inescapable nationalistic integrity with regard to herself will together prove a great and serviceable factor in bringing about human unity, which the total Jewish tendency at the present time is doing much to prevent. *It is not the fact that the Jews remain a nation in the midst of the nations; it is the use made of that inescapable status, which the world has found reprehensible.* The nations have tried to reduce the Jew to unity with themselves; attempts toward the same end have been made by the Jews themselves; but destiny seems to have marked them out to continuous nationhood. Both the Jews and the World will have to accept that fact, find the good prophecy in it, and seek the channels for its fulfillment.

Theodor Herzl, one of the greatest of the Jews, was perhaps the farthest-seeing public exponent of the philosophy of Jewish existence that modern generations have known. And he was never in doubt of the existence of the Jewish nation. Indeed, he proclaimed its existence on every occasion. He said, "*We are a people — One people.*"

He clearly saw that what he called the Jewish Question was political. In his introduction to "The Jewish State" he says, "I believe that I understand anti-Semitism, which is really a highly complex movement. I consider it from a Jewish standpoint, yet without fear or hatred. I believe that I can see what elements there are in it of vulgar sport, of common trade jealousy, of inherited prejudice, of religious intolerance and also of pretended self-defense. I think the Jewish Question is no more a social than a religious one, notwithstanding that it sometimes takes these and other forms. *It is a national question, which can only be solved by making it a political world-question* to be discussed and controlled by the civilized nations of the world in council."

Not only did Herzl declare that the Jews formed a nation, but when questioned by Major Evans Gordon before the British Royal Commission on Alien Immigration in August, 1902, Dr. Herzl said: "I will give you my definition of a nation, and you can add the adjective 'Jewish.' A nation is, in my mind, an historical group of men of a recognizable cohesion held together by a common enemy. That is in my view a nation. *Then if you add to that the word 'Jewish' you have what I understand to be the Jewish nation.*"

Also, in relating the action of this Jewish nation to the world, Dr. Herzl wrote: "When we sink, we become a revolutionary proletariat, the subordinate officers of the revolutionary party; when we rise there rises also our terrible power of the purse."

This view, which appears to be the true view in that it is the view which has been longest sustained in Jewish thought, is brought out also by Lord Eustace Percy, and re-published, apparently with approval, by the Canadian *Jewish Chronicle.* It *will repay a careful reading*:

"*Liberalism and Nationalism, with a flourish of* trumpets, threw open the doors of the ghetto and offered equal citizenship to the Jew. The Jew passed out into the Western World, saw the power and the glory of it, used it and enjoyed it, laid his hand indeed upon the nerve centers of its civilization, guided, directed and exploited it, and then — refused the offer * * * Moreover — and this is a remarkable thing — the Europe of nationalism and liberalism, of scientific government and democratic equality is more intolerable to him than the old oppressions and persecutions of despotism * * * In the increasing consolidation of the western nations, it is no longer possible to reckon on complete toleration * * *

"In a world of completely organized territorial sovereignties he (the Jew) has only two possible cities of refuge: he must either pull down the pillars of the whole national state system or he must create a territorial sovereignity of his own. In this perhaps lies the explanation both of Jewish Bolshevism and of Zionism, for at this moment Eastern Jewry seems to hover uncertainly between the two.

"In Easten Europe Bolshevism and Zionism often seem to grow side by side, just as Jewish influence molded Republican and Socialist thought throughout the nineteenth century, down to the Young Turk revolution in Constantinople hardly more than a decade ago — *not because the Jew cares for the positive side of radical philosophy, not because he desires to be a partaker in Gentile nationalism or Gentile democracy, but because no existing Gentile system of government is ever anything but distasteful to him*".

All that is true, and Jewish thinkers of the more fearless type always recognize it as true. *The Jew is against the Gentile scheme of things. He is, when he gives his tendencies full sway, a Republican as against the monarchy, a Socialist as against the republic, and a Bolshevist as against Socialism.*

What are the causes of this disruptive activity? First, his *essential lack of democracy. Jewish nature is autocratic. Democracy is all right for the rest of the world, but the Jew wherever he is found forms an aristocracy of one sort or another. Democracy is merely a tool of a word which Jewish agitators use to raise themselves to the ordinary level in places where they are oppressed below it; but having reached the common level they immediately make efforts for special privileges, as being entitled to them — a process of which the late Peace Conference will remain the most startling example. The Jews to-day are the only people whose special and extraordinary privileges are written into the world's Treaty of Peace. But more of that at another time.*

NO ONE NOW PRETENDS TO DENY, except a few spokesmen who really do not rule the thought of the Jews but are set forth for the sole benefit of influencing Gentile thought, that the socially and economically disruptive elements abroad in the world to-day are not only MANNED but also MONEYED by Jewish interests. For a long time this fact was held in suspense owing to the vigorous denial of the Jews and the lack of information on the part of those agencies of publicity to which the public had looked for its information. But now the facts are coming forth. Herzl's words are being proved to be true—"when we sink, we become a revolutionary proletariat, the subordinate officers of the revolutionary party" — and these words were first published in English in 1896, or 24 years ago.

Just now these tendencies are working in two directions, one for the tearing down of the Gentile states all over the world, the other for the establishment of a Jewish state in Palestine. The latter project has the best wishes of the whole world, but it is far from having the best wishes of the whole, or even the larger part of Jewry. The Zionist party makes a great deal of noise, but it is really an unrepresentative minority. It can scarcely be designated as more than an usually ambitious colonization scheme. * *It is doubtless serving, however, as a very useful public screen for the carrying on of secret activities. International Jews, the controllers of the world's governmental and financial power, may meet anywhere, at any time, in war time or peace time, and by giving out that*

* NOTE: The statements indicated are those of non-Zionist Jews. The real Jewish program is that program which is executed. It was the Zionist program that was followed by the Peace Conference. It must therefore be regarded as the official program.

they are only considering the ways and means of opening up Palestine to the Jews, they easily escape the suspicion of being together on any other business. The Allies and enemies of the Gentile nations at war thus met and were not molested. *It was at a Zionist conference — the sixth, held in 1903 — that the recent war was exactly predicted, its progress and outcome indicated, and the relation of the Jews to the Peace Treaty outlined.*

That is to say, though Jewish nationalism exists, its enshrinement in a state to be set up in Palestine is not the project that is engaging the whole Jewish nation now. The Jews will not move to Palestine just yet; it may be said that they will not move at all merely because of the Zionist movement. *Quite another motive* will be the cause of the exodus out of the Gentile nations, when the time for that exodus fully comes.

As Donald A. Cameron, late British Consul-General at Alexandria, a man fully in sympathy with Zionism and much quoted in the Jewish press, says: "The Jewish immigrants (into Palestine) will tire of taking in one another's washing at three per cent, of winning one another's money in the family, and their sons will hasten by train and steamer to win 10 per cent in Egypt * * * *The Jew by himself in Palestine will eat his head off; he will kick his stable to pieces*". *Undoubtedly the time for the exodus — at least the motive for the exodus — is not yet here.*

The political aspect of the Jewish Question which is now engaging at least three of the great nations — France, Great Britain and the United States — has to do with matters of the present organization of the Jewish nation. Must it wait until it reaches Palestine to have a State, or is it an organized State now? Does Jewry know what it is doing? *Has it a* "foreign policy" with regard to the *Gentiles? Has it* a department which is executing that *foreign* policy? *Has this Jewish State, visible or invisible, if it* exists, *a head?* Has it a *Council* of State? And if *any* of these things is so, who is aware of it?

The first impulsive answer of the Gentile mind would be, "No" to all these questions — it is a Gentile habit to answer impulsively. *Never having been trained in secrets or invisible unity, the Gentile immediately concludes that such things cannot be, if for no other reason than that they have not crossed his path and advertised themselves.*

The questions, however, answered thus, require some explanation of the circumstances which are visible to all men. *If there is no deliberate combination of Jews in the world, then the control which they have achieved and the uniformity of the policies which they follow must be the simple result, not of deliberate decisions, but of a similar nature in all of them working out the same way.* Thus, we might say that as a love for adventure on the water drove the Britisher forth, so it made him the world's great colonist. Not that he deliberately sat down with himself and in formal manner resolved that he would become a colonizer, but the natural outworking of his genius resulted that way. But would this be a sufficient account of the British Empire?

Doubtless the Jews have the genius to do, wherever they go, the things in which we see them excel. But does this account for the relations which exist between the Jews of every country, for their world councils, for their amazing foreknowledge of stupendous events which break with shattering surprise on the rest of the world, for the smoothness and preparedness with which they appear, at a given time in Paris, with a world program on which they all agree?

The world has long suspected — at first only a few, then the secret departments of the governments, next the inellectuals among the people, now more and more the common people themselves — that not only are *the Jews a nation distinct from all the other nations* and mysteriously unable to sink their nationality by any means they or the world may adopt to this end, *but that they also constitute a state; that they are nationally conscious, not only, but consciously united for a common defense and for a common purpose.* Revert to Theodor Herzl's definition of the Jewish nation, as held together by a common enemy, *and then reflect that this common enemy is the Gentile world. Does this people which know itself to be a nation remain loosely unorganized in the face of that fact? It would hardly be like Jewish astuteness in other fields. When you see how closely the Jews are united by various organizations in the United States, and when you see how with practiced hand they bring those organizations to bear as if with tried confidence in their pressure, it is at least not inconceivable that what can be done within a country, — can be done, or has been done. between all the countries where the Jews live.*

At any rate, in the *American Hebrew of June* 25, 1920, Herman Bernstein writes thus: "About a year ago a representative of the Department of Justice submitted to me a copy of the manuscript of 'The Jewish Peril' by Professor Nilus, and asked for my opinion of the work. He said that the manuscript was a translation of a Russian book published in 1905 which was later suppressed. The manuscript was supposed to contain 'protocols' of the Wise Men of Zion and was supposed to have been read by Dr. Herzl at a secret conference of the Zionist Congress at Basle. He expressed the opinion that the work was probably that of Dr. Theodor Herzl . . . . He said that some American Senators who had seen the manuscript were amazed to find that so many years ago a scheme ha been elaborated by the Jews which is now being carried out, and that Bolshevism had been planned years ago by Jews who sought to destroy the world".

This quotation is made merely to put on record the fact that it was a representative of the Department of Justice of the United States Government, who introduced this document to Mr. Bernstein, and expressed a certain opinion upon it, namely, "that the work was probably that of Dr. Theodor Herzl". Also that "some American Senators" were amazed to note the comparison between what a publication of the year 1905 proposed and what the year 1920 revealed.

The incident is all the more preoccupying because it occured by action of the representative of a government who to-day is very largely in the hands of, or under the influence of, Jewish interests. It is more than probable that as soon as the activity became known, the investigator was stopped. But it is equally probable that whatever orders may have been given and apparently obeyed, the investigation may not have stopped.

The United States Government was a little late in the matter, however. At least for other world powers had preceded it, some by many years. *A copy of the Protocols was deposited in the British Museum and bears on it the stamp of that institution, "August* 10, 1906". The notes themselves probably date from 1896, or the year of the utterances previously quoted from Dr. Herzl. The first Zionist Congress convened in 1897.

The document was published in England recently under auspices that challeged attention for it, in spite of the unfortunate title under which it appeared. Eyre and Spotiswoode are the appointed printers to the British Government, and it was they who brought out the pamphlet. It was as if the Government Printing Office at Washington should issue them in this country. While there was the usual outcry by the Jewish press, the London *Times* in a review pronounced all the Jewish counter-attacks as "unsatisfactory".

The Times noticed what will probably be the case in this country also that the Jewish defenders leave the text of the protocols alone, while they lay heavy emphasis on the fact of their anonymity. When they refer to the sub-

stance of the document at all there is one form of words which recurs very often — "it is the work of a criminal or a madman."

The protocols, without name attached, appearing for the most part in manuscripts here and there, laboriously copied out from hand to hand, being sponsored by no authority that was willing to stand behind it, assiduously studied in the secret department's of the governments and passed from one to another among higher officials, have lived on and on, increasing in power and prestige by the sheer force of their contents. A marvelous achievement for either a criminal or a madman! The only evidence it has is that which it carries within it, and that internal evidence is, as the London *Times* points out, the point on which attention is to be focused, and the very point from which Jewish effort has been expended to draw us away.

The interest of the Protocols at this time is their bearing on the questions: Have the Jews an organized world system? What is its policy? How is it being worked?

These questions all receive full attention in the Protocols. *Whosoever was the mind that conceived them possessed a knowledge of human nature, of history and of statecraft which is dazzling in its brilliant completeness, and terrible in the objects to which it turns its powers. Neither a madman nor an intentional criminal, but more likely a super-mind mastered by devotion to a people and a faith could be the author, if indeed one mind alone conceived them. It is too terribly real for fiction, too well-sustained for speculation, too deep in its knowledge of the secret springs of life for forgery.*

Jewish attacks upon it thus far make much of the fact that it came out of Russia. *That is hardly true. It came by way of Russia. It was incorporated in a Russian book published about* 1905 *by a Professor Nilus, who attempted to interpret the Protocols by events then going forward in Russia.* This publication and interpretation gave it a Russian tinge which has been useful to Jewish propagandists in this country and England, because these same propagandists have been very successful in establishing in Anglo-Saxon mentalities a certain atmosphere of thought surrounding the idea of Russia and Russians. One of the biggest humbugs ever foisted on the world has been that foisted by Jewish propagandists, principally on the American public, with regard to the temper and genius of the truly Russian people. So, to intimate that the Protcols are Russian, is partially to discredit them.

The internal evidence makes it clear that the Protocols were not written by a Russian, nor originally in the Russian language, nor under the influence of Russian conditions. But they found their way to Russia and were first published there. *They have been found by diplomatic officers in manuscript in all parts of the world. Whereever Jewish power is able to do so, it has suppressed them, sometimes under the supreme penalty.*

Their persistence is a fact which challenges the mind. Jewish apologists may explain that persistence on the ground that the Protocols feed the anti-Semitic temper, and therefore are preserved for that service. *Certainly there was no wide nor deep anti-Semitic temper in the United States to be fed or that felt the greed for agreeable lies to keep itself alive. The progress of the Protocols in the United States can only be explained on the ground that they supply light and give meaning to certain previously observed facts, and that this light and meaning is so startling as to give a certain standing and importance to these otherwise unaccredited documents. Sheer lies do not live long, their power soon dies. These Protocols are more alive than ever.* They have penetrated higher places than ever before. They have compelled a more serious attitude to them than ever before.

The Protocols would not be more worthy of study if they bore, say, the name of Theodor Herzl. *Their anonymity does not decrease their power any more than the omission of a painter's signature detracts from the art value of a painting. Indeed, the Protocols are better without a known source.* For if it were definitely known that in France or Switzerland in the year 1896, or thereabouts, a group of International Jews, assembled in conference, drew up a program of world conquest it would still have to be shown that. such program was more than a mere vagary, that it was confirmed at large by efforts to fulfill it. *The Protocols are a World Program — there is no doubt anywhere of that. Whose program, is stated within the articles themselves. But as for outer confirmation, which would be the more valuable — a signature, or six signatures, or twenty signatures, or a 25-year unbroken line of effort fulfilling that program?*

The point of interest for this and other countries is not that a "criminal or a madman" conceived such a program, but that, when conceived, this program found means of getting itself fulfilled in its most important particulars. *The document is comparatively unimportant; the conditions to which is calls attention are of a very high degree of importance.*

DEARBORN INDEPENDENT — ISSUE OF JULY 10, 1920

AN INTRODUCTION TO THE JEWISH PROTOCOLS

(X)

The documents most frequently mentioned by those who are interested in the theory of Jewish World Power rather than in the actual operation of that power in the world to-day, are those 24 documents known as "The Protocols of the Learned Elders of Zion."

The Protocols have attracted much attention in Europe, having become the centre of an important *storm of opinion in England only recenly, but discussion of them in the United States has been limited.* These are the documents concerning which the Department of Justice was making inquiries more than a year ago, and which were given publication in London by Eyre and Spottiswoode, the official printers to the British Government.

Who it was that first entitled these documents with the name of the "Elders of Zion" is not known. It would be possible without serious mutilation of the documents to remove all hint of Jewish authorship, and yet retain all the main points of most comprehensive program for world subjugation that has ever come to public knowledge.

Yet it must be said that thus to eliminate all hint of Jewish authorship would be to bring out a number of contradictions which do not exist in the Protocols in their present form. *The purpose of the plan revealed in the Protocols is to undermine all authority in order that a new authority in the form of autocracy may be set up. Such a plan could not emanate from a ruling class which already possessed authority, although it might emanate from anarchists. But anarchists do not avow autocracy as the ultimate condition they seek. The authors might be conceived as a company of French Subversives such as existed at the time of the French Revolution and had the infamous Duc d'Orleans as their leader, but this would involve a contradiction between the fact that those Subversives have passed away, and the fact that the program announced in these Protocols is being steadily carried out, not only in France, but throughout Europe, and very noticeably in the United States.*

In their present form which bears evidence of being their original form, there is no contradiction. The allegation of Jewish authorship seems essential to the consistency of the plan.

If these documents where the forgeries which Jewish apologists claim them to be, the forgers would probably have taken pains to make Jewish authorship so clear that their anti-Semitic purpose could easily have been detected. *But only twice is the term "Jew" used in them. After one has read much further than the average reader usually cares to go into such matters, one comes upon the plans for the establishment of the World Autocrat, and only then it is made clear of what lineage he is to be.*

But all through the documents there is left no doubt as to the people against whom the plan is aimed. It is not aimed against aristocracy as such. It is not aimed against capital as such. It is not aimed against government as such. Very definite provisions are made for the enlistment of aristocracy, capital and government for the execution of the plan. *It is aimed against the people of the world who are called "Gentiles."* It is the frequent mention of "Gentiles" that really decides the purpose of the documents. Most of the destructive type of "liberal" *plans aim at the enlistment of the people as helpers; this plan aims at the degeneration of the people in order that they may be reduced to confusion of mind and thus manipulated. Popular movements of a "liberal" kind are to be encouraged, all the disruptive philosophies in religion, economies, politics and domestic life are to be sown and watered, for the purpose of so disintegrating social solidarity that a definite plan, herein set forth, may be put through without notice, and the people then molded to it when the fallacy of these philosophies is shown.*

The formula of speech is not, "We Jews will do this", but "The Gentiles will be made to think and do these things". With the exception of a few instances in the closing Protocols, the only distinctive racial term used is "Gentiles".

To illustrate: the first indication of this kind comes in the first Protocol in this way:

"The great qualities of the people — honesty and frankness — are essentially vices in politics, because they dethrone more surely and more certainly than does the strongest enemy. These qualities are attributes of Gentile rule; we certainly must not be guided by them."

And again:

"On the ruins of the hereditary aristocracy of the Gentiles we have set up the aristocracy of our educated class, and over all the aristocracy of money. We have established the basis of this new aristocracy on the basis of riches, which we control, and on the science guided by our wise men".

Again:

"We will force up wages, which however will be of no benefit to workers, for we at the same time will cause a rise in the prices of prime necessities, pretending that this is due to the decline of agriculture and of cattle raising. We will also artfully and deeply undermine the sources of production by instilling in the workmen ideas of anarchy and encourage them in the use of alcohol, at the same time taking measures to drive all the intellectual forces of the Gentiles from the land".

(A forger with anti-Semitic malice might have written this any time within the last five years, but these words were in print at least 14 years ago according to British evidence, a copy having been in the British Museum since 1906, and they were circulated in Russia a number of years prior.)

The above point continues: "*That the true situation shall not be noticed by the Gentiles prematurelly we will mask it by a pretended effort to serve the working classes and promote great economic principles, for which an active propaganda will be carried on through our economic theories*".

These quotations will illustrate the style of the Protocols in making reference to the parties involved. It is "we" for the writers, and "Gentiles" for those who are being written about. This is brought out very clearly in the Fourteenth Protocol:

"In this divergence between the Gentiles and ourselves in ability to think and reason is to be seen clearly the seal of our election as the chosen people, as higher human beings, in contrast with the Gentiles who have merely instinctive and animal minds. They observe, but they do not foresee, and they invent nothing (except perhaps material things). It is clear from this that nature herself predestined us to rule and guide the world".

This, of course, has been the Jewish method of dividing humanity from the earliest times. The world was only Jew and Gentile; all that was not Jew was Gentile.

The use of the word Jew in the Protocol may be illustrated by this passage in the eighth section:

"For the time being, until it will be safe to give responsible government positions to our brother Jews, we shall entrust them to people whose past and whose characters are such that there is an abyss between them and the people".

This is the practice known as using: *"Gentile fronts" which is extensively practiced in the financial world to-day in order to cover up the evidences of Jewish control. How much progress has been made since these words were written is indicated by the occurence at the San Francisco convention when the name of Judge Brandeis was proposed for President. It is reasonably to be expected that the public mind will be made more and more familiar with idea of Jewish occupancy — which will be really a short step from the present degree of influence which the Jew exercise — of the highest office in the government.* There is no function of the American Presidency in which the Jews have not already secretly assisted in a very important degree. Actual occupancy of the office is not necessary to enhance their power, but to promote certain things which parallel very closely the plans outlined in the Protocols now before us.

Another point which the reader of the Protocols will notice is that the tone of exhortation is entirely absent from these documents. *They are not propaganda.* They are not efforts to stimulate the ambitions or activity of those to whom they are addressed. *They are as cool as a legal paper and as matter-of-fact as a table of statistics.* There is none of the "Let us rise, my brothers" stuff about them. There is no "Down with the Gentiles" hysteria.

These Protocols, if indeed they were made by Jews and confided to Jews, or if they do contain certain principles of a Jewish World Program, were certainly not intended for the firebrands but for the carefully prepared and tested initiates of the higher groups.

Jewish apologists have asked, "Is it conceivable that if there were such a world program on the part of the Jews, they would reduce it to writing and publish it?" But there is no evidence that these Protocols were ever uttered otherwise than in spoken words by those who put them forth. The Protocols as we have them are apparently the notes of lectures which were made by someone who heard them. Some of them are lengthy; some of them are brief. The assertion which has always been made in connection with the Protocols since they have become known is that they are the notes of lectures delivered to Jewish students presumably somewhere in France or Switzerland. The attempt to make them appear to be of Russian origin is absolutely forestalled by the point of view, the references to the times and certain grammatical indications.

The tone certainly fits the supposition that they were originally lectures given to students, *for their purpose is clearly not to get a program accepted but to give information concerning a program which is represented as being already in process of fulfillment.* There is no invitation to join forces or to offer opinions. Indeed it is specifically announced that neither discussion nor opinions are desired. ("While preaching liberalism to the Gentiles, we shall hold our own people and our own agents in unquestioning obedience." "The scheme of administration must emanate from a single brain * * * Therefore, we may *know* the plan of action, but we must not *discuss* it, lest we destroy its unique character * * * The inspired work of our leader therefore must not be thrown before a crowd to be torn to pieces, or even before a limited group.")

Moreover, taking the Protocols at their face value, it is evident that the program outlined in these lecture notes was not a new one at the time the lectures were given. There is no evidence of its being of recent arrangement. There is almost the tone of a tradition, or a religion, in it all, as if it had been handed down from generation to generation through the medium of specially trusted and initiated men. There is no note of new discovery or fresh enthusiasm in it, but the certitude and calmness of facts long known and policies long confirmed by experiment.

This point of the age of the program is touched upon

at least twice in the Protocols themselves. In the First Protocol this paragraph occurs:

"Already in ancient times we were the first to shout the words, 'Liberty, Equality, Fraternity', among the people. These words have been repeated many times since by unconscious poll-parrots, flocking from all sides to this bait, with which they have ruined the prosperity of the world and true personal freedom * * * The presumably clever and intelligent Gentiles did not understand the symbolism of the uttered words; did not observe their contradiction in meaning; did not notice that in nature there is no equality * * * ".

The other reference to the program's finality is found in the Thirteenth Protocol:

"Questions of policy, however, are permitted to no one except those who have *originated the policy* and have directed it *for many centuries."*

Can this be a reference to a secret Jewish Sanhedrin, self-perpetuating within a certain Jewish caste from generation to generation?

Again, it must be said that the originators and directors here referred to cannot be at present any ruling caste, for all that the program contemplates is directly opposed to the interests of such a caste. It cannot refer to any national aristocratic group, like the Junkers of Germany, for the methods which are proposed are the very ones which would render powerless such a group. *It cannot refer to any but a people who have no government, who have everything to gain and nothing to lose, and who can keep themselves intact amid a crumbling world. There is only one group that answers that description.*

Again, a reading of the Protocols makes it clear that the speaker himself was not seeking for honor. There is a complete absence of personal ambition throughout the document. All plans and purposes and expectations are merged in the future of Israel, which future, it would seem, can only be secured by the subtle breaking down of certain world ideas held by the Gentiles. *The Protocols speak of what has been done, what was being done at the time these words were given, and what remained to be done. Nothing like them in completeness of detail, in breadth of plan and in deep grasp of the hidden springs of human action has ever been known. They are verily terrible in their mastery of the secrets of life, equally terrible in their consciousness of that mastery.* Truly they would merit the opinion which Jews have recently cast upon them, that they were the work of an inspired madman, were it not that what is written in the Protocols in words is also written upon the life of today in deeds and tendencies.

The criticisms which these Protocols pass upon the Gentiles for their stupidity are just. It is impossible to disagree with a single item in the Protocols' description of Gentile mentality and veniality. Even the most astute of the Gentile thinkers have been fooled into receiving as the motions of progress what has only been insinuated into the common human mind by the most insidious systems of propaganda.

It is true that here and there a thinker has arisen to say that science so-called was not science at all. It is true that here and there a thinker has arisen to say that the so-called economic laws both of conservatives and radicals were not laws at all, but artificial inventions. It is true that occasionally a keen observer has asserted that the recent debauch of luxury and extravagance was not due to the natural impulses of the people at all, but was systematically stimulated, foisted upon them by design. It is true that a few have discerned that more than half of what passes for "public opinion" is mere hired applause and booing and has never impressed the public mind.

But even with these clues here and there, for the most part disregarded, there has never been enough continuity and collaboration between those who were awake, to follow all the clues to their source. The chief explanation of the hold which the Protoocols have had on many of the leading statesmen of the world for several decades is that they explain whence all these false influences come and what their purpose is. They give a clue to the modern maze. *It is now time for the people to know.* And whether the Protocols are judged as proving anything concerning the Jews or not, they constitute an education in the way the masses are turned about like sheep by influences which they do not understand. *It is almost certain that once the principles of the Protocols are known widely and understood by the people, the criticism which they now rightly make of the Gentile mind will no longer hold good.*

It is the purpose of future articles in this series to study these documents and to answer out of their contents all the questions that may arise concerning them.

Before that work is begun, one question should be answered — *"Is there likelihood of the program of the Protocols being carried through to success?" The program is successful already. In many of its most important phases it is already a reality. But this need not cause alarm, for the chief weapon to be used against such a program, both in its completed and uncompleted parts is clear publicity. Let the people know. Arousing the people, alarming the people, appealing to the passions of the people is the method of the plan outlined in the Protocols. THE ANTIDOTE IS MERELY ENLIGHTENING THE PEOPLE.*

That is the only purpose of these articles. Enlightenment dispels prejudice. *It is as desirable to dispel the prejudice of the Jew as of the Gentile. Jewish writers too frequently assume that the prejudice is all on one side. The Protocols themselves ought to have the widest circulation among the Jewish people, in order that they may check those things which are bringing suspicion upon their name.*

DEARBORN INDEPENDENT —ISSUE OF JULY 24, 1920.

HOW THE "JEWISH QUESTION" TOUCHES THE FARM

(XVI)

Those wonderful documents known as the "Protocols," with their strong grasp of every element of life, have not overlooked *Land*. The Land Program is found in the Sixth Protocol, which is one of the briefest of these documents and may be quoted in full to show now the relation it bears to certain excerpts made in previous articles:

Protocol VI

"We shall soon begin to establish huge monopolies, colossal reservoirs of wealth, upon which even the big Gentile properties will be dependent to such an extent that they will all fall together with the government credit on the day following the political catastrophe. *The economists here present* must carefully weigh the significance of this combination. We must develop by every means the importance of *our super-government,* representing it as the protector and benefactor of all who voluntarily submit to us.

"The aristocracy of the Gentiles as a political force has passed away. We need not take them into consideration. But, *as owners of the land,* they are harmful to us in *that they are independent in their sources of livelihood.*

Therefore, at all costs, *we must deprive them of their land.*

"*The best means to attain this is to increase the taxes and mortgage indebtedness. These measures will keep land ownership in a state of unconditional subordination.* Unable to satisfy their needs by small inheritances, the aristocrats among the Gentiles will burn themselves out rapidly.

"At the same time it is necessary to encourage trade and industry vigorously and especially speculation, the function of which is to act as a counterpoise to industry. Without speculation, industry *will cause private capital to increase and tend to improve the condition of Agriculture BY FREEING THE LAND FROM INDEBTEDNESS FOR LOANS* by the land banks. *It is necessary for industry to deplete the land both of laborers and capital,* and, through speculations, *transfer all the money of the world into our hands,* thereby *throwing the Gentiles into the ranks of the proletariat.* The Gentiles will then bow before us to obtain the right to existence.

"*To destroy Gentile industry, we shall,* as an incentive to this speculation, *encourage among the Gentiles a strong demand for luxuries, all enticing luxuries.*

"We will *force up wages,* which however will be of *no benefit to workers,* for *we will at the same time cause a rise in the prices of prime necessities, pretending that this is due to the decline of agriculture and of cattle raising.* We will also artfully and deeply undermine the sources of production by *instilling in the workmen ideas of anarchy,* and encourage them in the use of alcohol, at the same time taking measures to drive all the intellectual forces of the Gentiles from the land.

"That the true situation shall not be noticed by the Gentiles prematurely, we will mask it by a pretended effort to serve the working classes and promote great economic principles, for which an active propaganda will be carried on *through our economic theories.*"

The local and passing element in this is "the aristocracy of the Gentiles." That is to say, the program is not entirely fulfilled by the passing of aristocrats. Jewry goes on just the same. Its program stretches far. *Jewry will retain such kings as it desires, as long as it desires them. Probably the last throne to be vacated will be the British throne because what to the British mind is the honor of being Jewry's protector and therefore the inheritor of the blessing which that attitude brings, is to the Jewish mind the good fortune of being able to use a world-wide empire for the furtherance of Jewry's purpose. Each has served the other and the partnership will probably last until Jewry gets ready to throw Britain over, which Jewry can do at almost any time. There are indications that it has already started on this last task.*

But the permanent elements in this Protocol are the *Land*, the *Jews*, and the *Gentiles*. A word of explanation may be necessary on this inclusion of the Gentiles as permanent: the Protocols do not contemplate the extermination of the Gentiles, nor the making of this world a completely Jewish populated world. The Protocols contemplate a Gentile world ruled by the Jews — the Jews as masters, the Gentiles as hewers of wood and drawers of water, a policy which every Old Testament reader knows to be typically Jewish and the source of divine judgment upon Israel time and again.

Now, look at this whole Program as it concerns the Land.

*"Owners of the land * * * are harmful to us in that they are independent in their sources of livelihood."*

That is a foundation principle of the Protocols. It matters not whether the owners are the "Gentile aristocracy," the peasants of Poland, or the farmers of the United States — land ownership makes the owners *"independent in their sources of livelihood."* And *any* form of independence is fatal to the success of the World Program which is written so comprehensively in the Protocols and which is advancing so comprehensively under Jewish guidance in the world of actual affairs to-day.

Not "tillers" of the land, not "dwellers" on the land, not "tenants," not an "agricultural peasantry", but "*owners* of the land" — this is the class singled out for attention in this Sixth Protocol, *BECAUSE* they are *"independent in their sources of livelihood"*.

Now, there has been no time in the history of the United States when apparently it was more easy for the farmer to own his land than now. Mortgages should be a thing of the past. Everywhere the propaganda of the question tells us that the farmers are growing "rich". And yet there were never so many abandoned farms!

"Therefore, at all costs we must deprive them of their land".

How? *"The best means to attain this is to increase land taxes and mortgage indebtedness"*. High taxes to keep the land at all, borrowed money to finance the tilling of it.

"These measures will keep land ownership in a state of unconditional subordination".

We will leave it to the farmers of the United States to say whether this is working out or not.

And in a future reference to this subject we will show that whenever an attempt is made to enable farmers to borrow money at decent rates, whenever it is proposed to lighten the burden of "mortgage indebtedness" on the farm, Jewish financial influence in the United States steps in to prevent it, or failing to prevent it, mess it all up in the operation.

By increasing the farmer's financial disability on the one hand and by increasing industrial allurements on the other, a very great deal is accomplished. The Protocol says: *"It is necessary for industry to deplete the Land both of laborers and capital."*

Has that been done? Have the farms of the United States been depleted both of laborers and capital? Certainly. Money is harder for the farmer to get than it is for any other man; and as for labor, he cannot get it on any terms.

What is the result of these two influences, the one working on the farm, and the other in the cities? It is precisely what the Protocol says it will be: Increased wages that buy less of the materials of life — "we will at the same time cause a rise in the prices of prime necessities, pretending that this is *due to the decline of agriculture and cattle raising*".

The Jew who set these Protocols in order was a financier, economist and philosopher of the first order. He knew what he was talking about. His operations in the ordinary world of business always indicated that he knew exactly what he was doing. How well this Sixth Protocol has worked and is still working out in human affairs is before the eyes of everyone to see.

Here in the United States one of the most important movements toward real independence of the financial powers has been begun by the farmers. The farmers' strong advantage is that, owning the land, he is independent in his sources of livelihood. The land will feed him whether he pleases International Jewish Financiers or not. His position is impregnable as long as the sun shines and the seasons roll. It was therefore necessary to do something to hinder this budding independence. He was placed under a greater disadvantage than any other business man in borrowing capital. He was placed more ruthlessly than any other producer between the upper and nether stones of a thievish distribution system. Labor was drawn away from the farm. The Jew-controlled melodrama made the farmer a "rube", and Jew-made fiction presented him as a "hick", causing his sons to be ashamed of farm life. *The grain syndicates which operate against the farmer are Jew-controlled.* There is no longer any possibility of doubting, when the facts of actual affairs are put alongside the written Program, that the farmer of the United States has an interest in this Question.

What would this World Program gain if the wage-workers were enslaved and the farmers were allowed to go scot-free? Therefore the program of agricultural interference which has been only partially outlined here.

But this is not all.

Any writer who attempts fully to inform the Gentile mind on the Jewish Question must often feel that the extent of the Protocols' Conspiracy *is so great as to stagger the Gentile mind. Gentiles are not conspirators. They cannot follow a clue through long and devious and darkened channels. The elaborate completeness of the Jewish Program, the perfect co-ordination of its mass of details wearies the Gentile mind. This, really more than the daring of the Program itself, constitutes the principal danger of Program being fulfilled. Gentile mental laziness is the most powerful ally the World Program has.*

For example: after citing the perfectly obvious coincidence and most probable connection between the Protocols and the observable facts with reference to the farm situation, the writer is compelled to say, as above, "*But this is not all*". *And it is a peculiarity of Gentile psychology that the Gentile reader will feel that it ought to be all because it is so complete. This is where the Jewish mind out-maneuvers the Gentile mind.*

Gentiles may do a thing for one reason: the Jew often does the same thing for three or four reasons. The Gentile can understand thus far why Jewish financiers should seek control of the land in order to prevent widespread Agricultural Independence which, as Protocol Six says, would be "harmful to us". That reason is perfectly clear.

But there is another. It is found in the Twelfth Protocol. It contemplates nothing less than the playing of City against Country in the great game now being exposed. Complete control over the City by the industrial leverage, and over the Country by the debt leverage, will enable the Hidden Players to move first the Country by saying that the City demands certain things, and then move the City by saying that the Country demands certain things, thus splitting Citizens and Farmers apart and using them against one another.

Look at the plainness and the boldness, yet the calm assurance, with which this plan is broached:

"*Our calculations reach out, especially into the country districts. There we* must necessarily *arouse those interests and ambitions which we can always turn against the city, representing them to the cities as dreams and ambitions for independence on the part of the provinces.* It is clear that the source of this will be precisely the same, and that it will come from us. It will be necessary for us *before we have attained full power* to so arrange matters that, *from time to time, the cities shall come under the influence of opinion in the country districts,* that is, of the majority *prearranged by our agents* * * * "

The preliminaries of the game are here set forth — to *jockey City and Farm against each other,* that in the end the Conspirators may use whichever proves the stronger in putting the Plan over. *In Russia, both schemes have been worked.* The old regime, established in the Cities, was persuaded to lay down power because it was made to believe that the peasants of Russia requested it. Then, when the Bolshevists seized power, they ruled the peasantry on the ground that the Cities wanted it. The cities listened to the Country, now the Country is listening to the Cities.

If you see any attempt made to divide City and Farm into antagonistic camps, remember this paragraph from the Twelfth Protocol. Already the poison is working. Have you never heard that Prohibition was something which the backwoods districts forced upon the cities? Have you never heard that the High Cost of Living was due to extravagant profits of the farmer? — profits which he doesn't get.

One big dent in this Program of World Control could be made if the Citizen and the Farmer could learn each other's mind, not through self-appointed spokesmen, but directly from each other. City and Farm are drifting apart because of misrepresentation of outsiders, and in the widening rift the sinister shadow of the World Program appears.

Let the Farmers look past the "Gentile fronts" in their villages or principal trading points, past them to the real controllers who are hidden.

DEARBORN INDEPENDENT —ISSUE OF SEPT. 4, 1920.

Dr. LEVY, A JEW, ADMITS HIS PEOPLE'S ERROR

(LVI)

A Jew of standing, Dr. Oscar Levy, well known in English literary circles and a lover of his people, has had the honesty and the wisdom to meet the Jewish Question with truth and candor. His remarks are printed in this article as an example of the methods by which Jewry can be saved in the estimation of Twentieth Century Civilization.

The circumstances were these: George Pitt-Rivers, of Worcester College, Oxford, wrote a most illuminating brochure entitled, "The World Significance of the Russian Revolution," which is published and sold for two shillings by Basil Blackwell, Oxford. The book is the result of unprejudiced observation and study and agrees with the statements made in *The Dearborn Independent* about the personnel of Bolshevism. The manuscript was sent to Dr. Oscar Levy, as a representative Jew, and Dr. Levy's letter was subsequently published as a preface to the book.

That the reader may understand the tenor of Mr. Pitt-Rivers's book, section XVI, pp. 39-41, is herewith given in full, and is followed by Dr. Levy's comments. The italics throughout are intended to remind the reader of remarks on similar lines made in this series:

It is not unnaturally claimed by Western Jews that Russian Jewry, as a whole, is most bitterly opposed to

Bolshevism. Now although there is a great measure of truth in this claim, since the prominent Bolsheviks, who are preponderantly Jewish, do not belong to the orthodox Jewish Church, it is yet possible, without laying oneself open to the charge of anti-Semitism, to point to the obvious fact that Jewry, *as a whole,* has, consciously or *unconsciously,* worked for and promoted an international economic, material despotism which, with Puritanism as an ally, has tended in an ever-increasing degree to crush national and spiritual values out of existence and substitute the ugly and deadening machinery of finance and factory. It is also a fact that Jewry, as a whole, strove every nerve to secure and heartily approved of the overthrow of the Russian monarchy, which they regarded as their most formidable obstacle in the path of their ambitions and business pursuits. All this may be admitted, as well as the plea that, individually or collectively, most Jews may heartily detest the Bolshevik regime, yet it is still true that the whole weight of Jewry was in the revolutionary scales against the czar's government. It is true their apostate brethren, who are now riding in the seat of power, may have exceeded their orders; that is disconcerting, but it does not alter the fact. It may be that the Jews, often the victims of their own idealism, have always been instrumental in bringing about the events they most heartily disapprove of; that perhaps is the curse of the Wandering Jew.

Certainly it is from the Jews themselves that we learn most about the Jews. It is possible that only a Jew can understand a Jew. Nay, more, it may be that only a Jew can save us from the Jews, a Jew who is great enough, strong enough — for greater racial purity is a source of strength in the rare and the great — and inspired enough to overcome in himself the life-destructive vices of his own race. It was a Jew who said, "Wars are the Jews' harvest"; but no harvest so rich as civil wars. A Jew reminds us that the French Revolution brought civil emancipation for the Jews in Western Europe. Was it a *Jew* who inspired Rousseau with the eighteenth century idea of the sameness of man according to nature? Dr. Kallen, a Zionist author, writes: "Suffering for 1,000 years from the assertion of their difference from the rest of mankind, they accepted eagerly the escape from suffering which the eighteenth century assertion of the sameness of all men opened to them .... They threw themseles with passion into the republican emancipating movements of their fellow subjects of other stocks." It was a Jew, Ricardo, who gave us the nineteenth century ideal of the sameness of man according to machinery. And without the Ricardian gospel of international capitalism, we could not have had the international gospel of Karl Marx. Moses Hess and Disraeli remind us of the particularly conspicuous part played by Jews in the Polish and Hungarian rebellions, and in the republican uprising in Germany of '48. Even more conspicuous were they in the new internationalism logically deducible from the philosophy of Socialism. This we were taught by the Jew Marx, and the Jew Ferdinand Lasalle, and they but developed the doctrine of the Jew David Ricardo.

It was Weininger, a Jew — and also a Jew hater — who explained why so many Jews are naturally Communists. Communism is not only an international creed, but it implies the abnegation of real property, especially property in land, and Jews, being international, have never acquired a taste for real property; they prefer money. Money is an instrument of power, though eventually, of course, Communists claim that they will do away with money — when their power is sufficiently established to enable them to command goods, and exercise despotic sway without it. Thus the same motives prompt the Jew Communist and his apparent enemy, the financial Jew. When owners of real property in times of economic depression feel the pinch of straightened circumstances, it is the Jewish usurers who become most affluent and who, out of goodness of their hearts, come to their assistance — at a price.

To these and other statements, Dr. Levy, as a Jew, made this reply:

Dear Mr. Pitt-Rivers:

When you first handed me your MS. on *The World Significance of the Russian Revolution,* you expressed a doubt about the propriety of its title. After a perusal of your work, I can assure you, with the best of consciences, that your misgivings were entirely without foundation.

No better title than *The World Significance of the Russian Revolution* could have been chosen, for no event in any age will finally have more significance for our world than this one. We are still too near to see clearly this Revolution, this portentous event, *which was certainly one of the most intimate and therefore least obvious, aims of the world-conflagration, hidden as it was at first by the fire and smoke of national enthusiasms and patriotic antagonisms.*

It was certainly very plucky of you to try and throw some light upon an event which necessarily must still be enveloped in mist and mystery, and I was even somewhat anxious, lest your audacity in treating such a dangerous subject would end in failure, or what is nearly the same, in ephemeral success. No age is so voracious of its printed offspring as ours. There was thus some reason to fear lest you had offered to this modern Kronos only another mouthful of his accustomed nourishment for his immediate consumption.

I was, I am glad to report, agreeably surprised — surprised, though not by the many new facts which you give, and which must surprise all those who take an interest in current events — facts, I believe, which you have carefully and personally collected and selected, not only from books, but from the lips and letters of Russian eye-witnesses and sufferers, from foes as well as from friends of the great Revolution.

What I appreciate more than this new light thrown on a dark subject, more than the conclusion drawn by you from this wealth of facts, is the psychological insight which you display in *detecting the reasons why a movement so extraordinarily bestial and so violently crazy as the Revolution was able to succeed and finally to overcome its adversaries.* For we are confronted with two questions which need answering and which, in my opinion, you have answered in your pamphlet. These questions are: (1) How has the Soviet Government, *admittedly the government of an insignificant minority,* succeeded not only in maintaining but in strenghtening its position in Russia after two and a half years of power? and (2) Why has the Soviet Government, in spite of its outward bestiality and brutal tyranny, succeeded in gaining the sympathies of an increasing number of people in this country? . .

You rightly recognize that there is an ideology behind it and you clearly diagnose it as an ancient ideology. There is nothing new under the Sun, *it is even nothing new that this Sun rises in the East . . . .*

For Bolshevism is a religion and a faith. How could these half-converted believers ever dream to vanquish the "Truthful" and the "Faithful" of their own creed, these holy crusaders, who had gathered round the Red Standard of the Prophet Karl Marx, and who fought under the daring guidance of *experienced officers of all latter-day revolutions — the Jews?*

I am touching here on a subject which, to judge from your own pamphlet, is perhaps more interesting to you than any other. In this you are right. *There is no race in the world more enigmatic, more fatal, and therefore more interesting than the Jews.*

Every writer, who, like yourself, is oppressed by the aspect of the present and embarrassed by his anxiety for the future, MUST try to elucidate the Jewish Question and its bearing upon our Age.

For the question of the Jews and their influence on the world past and present, cuts to the root of all things, and should be discussed by every honest thinker, however bristling with difficulties it is, however complex the subject as well as the individuals of this Race may be.

For the Jews, as you are aware, are a sensitive Community, and thus very suspicious of any Gentile who tries to approach them with a critical mind. They are always inclined — and that on account of their terrible experiences — to denounce anyone who is not with them as against them, as tainted with "medieval" prejudice, as an intolerant Antagonist of their Faith and of their Race.

Nor could or would I deny that there is some evidence, some prima facie evidence of this antagonistic attitude in your pamphlet. You point out, and with fine indignation, *the great danger that springs from the prevalence of Jews in finance and industry and from the preponderance of Jews in rebellion and revolution.* You reveal, and with great fervor, *the connection between the Collectivism of the immensely rich international Finance* — the Democracy of cash values, as you call it — *and the international Collectivism of Karl Marx and Trotsky* — the Democracy of and by decoycries . . . And all this evil and misery, the economic as well as the political, you trace back to one source, to one "*fons et origo malorum*" — the Jews.

Now other Jews may vilify and crucify you for these outspoken views of yours; I myself shall abstain from joining the chorus of condemnation! I shall try to understand your opinions and your feelings, and having once understood them — as I think I have — I can defend you from the unjust attacks of my often too impetuous Race. But first of all, I have to say this: *There is scarcely an event in modern Europe that cannot be traced back to the Jews. Take the Great War that appears to have come to an end, ask yourself what were its causes and its reasons: you will find them in nationalism. You will at once answer that nationalism has nothing to do with the Jews, who, as you have just proved to us, are the inventors of the international idea.* But no less than Bolshevist Ecstasy and Financial Tyranny can National Bigotry (if I may call it so) *be finally followed back to a Jewish source* — are not they the inventors of the Chosen People Myth, and is not this obsession part and parcel of the political credo of every modern nation, *however small and insignificant it may be?* And then think of the history of nationalism. It started in our time and as a reaction against Napoleon; Napoleon was the antagonist of the French Revolution; the French Revolution was the consequence of the German Reformation; the German Reformation was based upon a crude Christianity; this kind of Christianity was invented, preached and propagated by the Jews; THEREFORE the Jews have made this war!.. Please do not think this a joke; it only seems a joke, and behind it there lurks a gigantic truth, and it is this, *that all latter-day ideas and movements have originally sprung from a Jewish source,* for the simple reason, that the Semitic idea has finally conquered and entirely subdued this *only apparently irreligious universe of ours.*

...There is no doubt that the Jews regularly go one better or worse than the Gentile in whatever they do, there is no further doubt that *their influence to-day justifies a very careful scrutiny, and cannot possibly be viewed without serious alarm.* The great question, however, is whether the Jews are conscious or unconscious malefactors. I myself am firmly convinced that they are unconscious ones, but please do not think that I wish to exonerate them on that account... A conscious evildoer has my respect, for he knows at least what is good; an unconscious one — well, he needs the charity of Christ — a charity which is not mine — to be forgiven for not knowing what he is doing. But there is in my firm conviction not the slightest doubt that these revolutionary

Jews do not know what they are doing; that they are more unconscious sinners than voluntary evildoers.

I am glad to see that this is not an original observation of mine, but that you yourself have a very strong foreboding about the Jews being the victims of their own theories and principles. On page 39 of your pamphlet you write: "It may be that the Jews have always been instrumental in bringing about the events that they most heartily disapprove of; that maybe is the curse of the Wandering Jew". If I had not the honor, as well as the pleasure, of knowing you personally, if I were not strongly aware of your passionate desire for light and your intense loathing of unfairness, this sentence, and this sentence alone, which tells the truth, will absolve you in my eyes from the odious charge of being a vulgar anti-Semite.

No, you are not a vulgar, you are a very enlightened, critic of our Race. *For there is an anti-Semitism, I hope and trust, which does the Jews more justice than any blind philo-Semitism,* than does that merely sentimental "Let-them-all-come Liberalism" which in itself is nothing but the Semitic Ideology over again. *And thus you can be just to the Jews, without being "romantic" about them.*

You have noticed with alarm that the *Jewish elements provide the driving forces for both Communism and capitalism,* for the material as well as the spiritual ruin of this world. But then you have at the same time the profound suspicion that the reason of all this extraordinary behavior may be the intense Idealism of the Jew. In this you are perfectly right. The Jew, if caught by an idea, never thinks any more in watertight compartments, as do the Teuton and Anglo-Saxon peoples, whose right cerebral hemisphere never seems to know what its left twin brother is doing; he, the Jew, like the Russian, at once begins to practice what he preaches, he draws the logical conclusion from his tenets, he invariably acts upon his accepted principles. It is from this quality, no doubt, that springs his mysterious force — that force which you no doubt condemn, but which you had to admire even in the Bolshevists. And we must admire it, whether we are Jews or whether we are Christians, for have not these modern Jews remained true to type, is there no parallel for them in history, do they not go to the bitter end even in our day? . . .

Who stirred up the people during the late war in Germany? Who pretended to have again the truth, *that* truth about which Pontius Pilate once shrugged his shoulders? Who pleaded for honesty and cleanliness in Politics, *that* honesty which brings a smile to the lips of any experienced Pro-consul of to-day? Writers, who were mostly Jews: Fried, Fernau, Latzko, Richard Grelling — the author of "J'accuse". Who was killed and allowed himself to be killed for these very ideas and principles? Men and women of the Jewish Race: Haase, Levine, Luxemburg, Landauer, Kurt Eisner, the Prime Minister of Bavaria. From Moses to Marx, from Isaiah to Eisner, in practice and in theory, in idealism and in materialism, in philosophy and in politics, they are to-day what they have always been: passionately devoted to their aims and to their purposes, and ready, nay, eager, to shed their last drop of blood for the realization of their visions.

"But these visions are all wrong", will you reply. . . . "Look where they have led the world to. Think, that they have now had a fair trial of 3,000 years' standing. How much longer are you going to recommend them to us and to inflict them upon us? And how do you propose to get us out of the morass into which you have led the world so disastrously astray?"

To this question I have only one answer to give, and it is this: "You are right". This reproach of yours, which — I feel it for certain — is at the bottom of your anti-Semitism, is only too well justified, and upon this common ground I am quite willing to shake hands with you and defend you against any accusation of promoting Race Hatred: *If you are anti-Semite, I, the Semite, am an anti-Semite too, and a much more fervent one than even you are . . . We (Jews) have erred, my friend, we have most grievously erred. And if there was truth in our error 3,000, 2,000, nay, 100 years ago, there is now nothing but falseness and madness, a madness that will produce an even greater misery and an even wider anarchy. I confess it to you, openly and sincerely, and with a sorrow, whose depth and pain an ancient Psalmist, and only he, could moan into this burning universe of ours . . . We who have posed as the saviours of the world, we who have even boasted of having given it "the" Saviour, we are today nothing else but the world's seducers, its destroyers, its incendiaries, its executioners* . . We who have promised to lead you to a new Heaven, we have finally succeeded in landing you into a new Hell . . . There has been no progress, least of all moral progress . . . And it is just our Morality, which has prohibited all real progress, and — what is worse — which even stands in the way of every future and natural reconstruction in this ruined world of ours . . . I look at this world, and I shudder at its ghastliness; I shudder all the more as I know the spiritual authors of all this ghastliness . . . .

But its authors themselves, unconscious in this as in all they are doing, know nothing yet of this startling revelation. *While Europe is aflame, while its victims scream, while its dogs howl in the conflagration, and while its very smoke descends in darker and even darker shades upon our Continent, the Jews, or at least a part of them and by no means the most unworthy ones, endeavor to escape from the burning building, and wish to retire from Europe into Asia, from the somber scene of our disaster into the sunny corner of their Palestine. Their eyes are closed to the miseries, their ears are deaf to the moanings, their heart is hardened to the anarchy of Europe; they only feel their own sorrows, they only bewail their own fate, they only sigh under their own burdens . . .* They know nothing of their duty to Europe, which looks around in vain for help and guidance, they know nothing even of their own great ancestor to whose heart the appeal of pity was never made in vain: they have become too poor in love, too sick at heart, too tired of battle, and lo! these sons of those who were once the bravest of soldiers are now trying to retire from the trenches to the rear, are now eager to exchange the grim music of the whistling shells with that of the cowbells and vintage songs in the happy plain of Sharon . . .

And yet we are not all Financiers, we are not all Bolshevists, we have not all become Zionists. And yet there is hope, great hope, that this same race which has provided the Evil will likewise succeed in supplying its antidote, its remedy — the Good. It has always been so in the past — was not that fatal Liberalism, which has finally led to Bolshevism — in the very midst of the dark nineteenth century, most strenuously opposed by two enlightened Jews — Friedrich Stahl, the founder of the Conservative Party in Germany, and by Benjamin Disraeli, the leader of the Tory Party in England? *And if these two eminent men had no suspicion yet that their own race and its holy message were at the bottom of that unfortunate upheaval, with which their age was confronted*: how eager, how determined, how passionate will be the opposition of the Disraelis of the future, once they have clearly recognized that they are really fighting the tenets of their own people, and that it was their "Good", their "Love", their "Ideal", that had launched the world into this Hell of Evil and Hatred. A new "Good" as new Love, a true Love, an intelligent Love, a Love that calms and heals and sweetens, will then spring up among the Great in Israel and overcome that sickly Love, that insipid Love, that romantic Love, which has hitherto poisoned all the Strength and all the Nobility of this world. For Hatred is never overcome by Hatred: It is only overcome by

Love, and it wants a new and a gigantic Love to subdue that old and devilish Haterd of to-day. That is our task for the future — a task which will, I am sure, not be shirked by Israel, by that same Israel which has never shirked a task, whether it was for good or whether it was for evil . . .

Yes, there is hope, my friend, for we are still here, our last word is not yet spoken, our last deed is not yet done, our last revolution is not yet made. *This, last Revolution, the Revolution that will crown our revolutionaries, will be the revolution against the revolutionaries.* It is bound to come, and it is perhaps upon us now. The great day of reckoning is near. It will pass a judgment upon our ancient faith, and it will lay the foundation to a new religion. And when that great day has broken, when the values of death and decay are put into the melting-pot to be changed into those of power and beauty, then you, my dear Pitt-Rivers, the descendant of an old and distinguished Gentile family, may be assured to find by your side, and as your faithful ally, at least one member of that Jewish Race, which has fought with such fatal success upon all the spiritual battlefields of Europe.

Yours against the Revolution and for Life ever flourishing,

OSCAR LEVY.

ROYAL SOCIETIES CLUB,
ST. JAMES STREET,
LONDON, S. W.
JULY, 1920.

DEARBORN INDEPENDENT – ISSUE OF APRIL 30, 1921

JEWISH IDEA OF CENTRAL BANK FOR AMERICA

(LIX.)

According to his own statements and the facts, Paul M. Warburg set out to reform the monetary system of the United States, and did so. He had the success which comes to few men, of coming an alien to the United States, connecting himself with the principal Jewish financial firm here, and immediately floating certain banking ideas which have been pushed and manipulated and variously adapted until they have eventuated in what is known as the Federal Reserve System.

When Professor Seligman wrote in the Proceedings of the Academy of Political Science that "the Federal Reserve Act will be associated in history with the name of Paul M. Warburg", a Jewish banker from Germany, he wrote the truth. But whether that association will be such as to bring the measure of renown which Professor Seligman implies, the future will reveal.

What the people of the United States do not understand and never have understood is that while the Federal Reserve *Act* was governmental, the whole Federal Reserve *System* is private. It is an officially created private banking system.

Examine the first thousand persons you meet on the street, and 999 will tell you that the Federal Reserve

System is a device whereby the United States Government went into the banking business for the benefit of the people. They have an idea that, like the Post Office and Custom House, a Federal Reserve Bank is a part of the Government's official machinery.

It is natural to feel that this mistaken view has been encouraged by most of the men who are competent to write for the public on this question. Take up the standard encyclopedias, and while you will find no misstatements of fact in them, you will find no direct statement that the Federal Reserve System is a private banking system; the impression carried away by the law reader is that it is a part of the Government.

The Federal Reserve System is a system of private banks, the creation of a banking aristocracy within an already existing autocracy, whereby a great proportion of banking independence was lost, and whereby it was made possible for speculative financiers to centralize great sums of money for their own purposes, beneficial or not.

That this System was useful in the artificial conditions created by war — useful, that is, for a Government that cannot manage its own business and finances and, like a prodigal son, is always wanting money, and wanting it when it wants it — it has proved, either by reason of its inherent faults or by mishandling, its inadequacy to the problems of peace. It has sadly failed of its promise, and is now under serious question.

Mr. Warburg's scheme succeeded just in time to take care of war conditions, he was placed on the Federal Reserve Board in order to manage his system in practice, and though he was full of ideas then as to how banking could be assisted, he is disappointingly silent now as to how the people can be relieved.

However, this is not a discussion of the Federal Reserve System. General condemnation of it would be stupid. But it is bound to come up for discussion one day, and the discussion will become much freer when people understand that it is a system of privately owned banks, to which have been delegated certain extraordinary privileges, and that it has created a class system within the banking world which constitutes a new order.

Mr. Warburg, it will be remembered, wanted only one central bank. But, because of political considerations, as Professor Seligman tells us, twelve were decided upon. An examination of Mr. Warburg's printed discussions of the subject shows that he at one time considered four, then eight. Eventually twelve were established. The reason was that one central bank, which naturally would be set up in New York, would give a suspicious country the impression that it was only a new scheme to keep the nation's money flowing to New York. As shown by Professor Seligman, quoted in the last number, Mr. Warburg was not averse to granting anything that would allay popular suspicion without vitiating the real plan.

So, while admitting to the Senators who examined him as to his fitness for membership on the Federal Reserve Board — the Board which fixed the policies of the Banks of the Federal Reserve System and told them what to do — that he did not like the 12 district banks idea, he said that his objections to it could "be overcome in an administrative way". That is, the 12 banks could be so handled that the effect would be the same as if there were only one central bank, presumably at New York.

And that is about the way it has resulted, and that will be found to be one of the reasons for the present situation of the country.

There is no lack of money in New York to-day. Motion picture ventures are being financed into the millions. A big grain selling pool, nursed into existence and counseled by Bernard M. Baruch, has no hesitancy whatever in planning for a $100,000,000 corporation. Loew, the Jewish theatrical man, had no difficulty in opening 20 new theaters this year —

But go into the agricultural states, where the real wealth of the country is in the ground and in the granaries, and you cannot find money for the farmer.

It is a situation which none can deny and which few can explain, because the explanation is not to be found along natural lines. Unnatural conditions wear an air of mystery. Here is the United States, the richest country in the world, containing at the present hour the greatest bulk of wealth to be found anywhere on earth — real, ready, available, usable wealth; and yet it is tied up tight, and cannot move in its legitimate channels, because of manipulation which is going on as regards money.

Money is the last mystery for the popular mind to penetrate, and when it succeeds in getting "on the inside" it will discover that the mystery is not in money at all, but in its manipulation, the things which are done "in an administrative way".

The United States has never had a President who gave evidence of understanding this matter at all. *Our Presidents have always had to take their views from financiers.* Money is the most public quantity in the country; it is the most federalized and governmentalized thing in the country; and yet, in the present situation, the United States Government has hardly anything to do with it, except to use various means to get it, just as the people have to get it, from those who control it.

The Money Question, properly solved, is the end of the Jewish Question and every other question of a mundane nature.

Mr. Warburg is of the opinion that different rates of interest ought to obtain in different parts of the country. That they have always obtained in different parts of the same state we have always known, but the reason for it has not been discovered. The city grocer can get money from his bank at a lower rate than the farmer in the next country can get it from his bank. Why the agricultural rate of interest has been higher than any other (when money is obtainable: it is not obtainable now) is a question to which no literary nor oratorical financier has ever publicly addressed himself. It is like the fact of the private business nature of the Federal Reserve System — very important, but no authority thinks it worth while to state. The agricultural rate of interest is of great importance, but to discuss it would involve first an admission, and that apparently is not desirable.

In comparing the present Federal Reserve Law with the proposed Aldrich Bill, Mr. Warburg said:

Mr. Warburg — " . . . . I think that this present law has the advantage of dealing with the entire country and giving them different rates of discount, whereas as Senator Aldrich's bill was drawn, it would have been very difficult to do that, as it provided for one uniform rate for the whole country, which I thought was rather a mistake".

Senator Bristow — "That is, you can charge a higher rate of interest in one section of the country under the present law, than you charge in another section, while under the Aldrich plan it would have been a uniform rate".

Mr. Warburg — "That is correct".

That is a point worth clearing up. Mr. Warburg, having educated the bankers, will now turn his attention to the people, and make it clear *why one class in the country can get money for business that is not productive of real wealth, while another class engaged in the production of real wealth is treated as outside the interest of banking altogether; if he can make it clear also why money is sold to one class or one section of the country at one price, while to another class and in another section it is sold at a different price, he will be adding to the people's grasp of these matters.*

This suggestion is seriously intended. Mr. Warburg has the style, the pedagogical patience, the grasp of the subject which would make him an admirable public teacher of these matters.

What he has already done was planned from the point of view of the interest of the professional financier. It is readily granted that Mr. Warburg desired to organize American finances into a more pliable system. Doubtless in some respects he has wrought important improvements. But he had always the banking house in mind, and he dealt with paper. Now, if taking up a position outside those special interests, he would address himself to the special interests, he would address himself to the wider interests of the people — not assuming that those interest of the people — not assuming that those interests always run through a banking house — he would do still more than he has yet done to justify his feeling that he really had a mission in coming to this country.

Mr. Warburg is not at all shocked by the idea that the Federal Reserve System is really a new kind of private banking control, because in his European experience he saw that all the central banks were private affairs.

In his essay on "American and European Banking Methods and Bank Legislation Compared", Mr. Warburg says: (the italics are ours)

"It may also be interesting to note that, *contrary to a widespread idea, the central banks of Europe are, as a rule, not owned by the governments.* As a matter of fact, neither the English, French, nor German Government owns any stock in the central bank of its country. *The Bank of England is run entirely as a private corporation,* the stockholders electing the board of directors, who rotate in holding the presidency. In France the government appoints the governor and some of the directors. In Germany the government appoints the president and a supervisory board of five members, while the stockholders elect the board if directors".

And again, in his discussion of the Owen-Glass Bill, Mr. Warburg says:

"The Monetary Commission's plan proceeded on the theory of the Bank of England, *which leaves the management entirely in the hands of business men without giving the government any part in the management or control.* The strong argument in favor of this theory is that central banking, like any other banking, is based on 'sound credit', that the judging of credits is a matter of business which should be left in the hands of business men, *and that the government should be kept out of business* . . . . The Owen-Glass Bill proceeds, in this respect, more on the lines of the Banque de France and the German Reichsbank, the presidents and boards of which are to certain extent appointed by the government. *These central banks, while legally private corporations,* are semi-governmental organs inasmuch as *they are permitted to issue the notes of the nation* — particularly where there are elastic note issues, as in almost all countries except England — and inasmuch as *they are the custodians of practically the entire metallic reserves of the country and the keepers of the government funds.* Moreover in questtions of national policy *the government must rely on the willing and loyal co-operation of these central organs.*"

That is a very illuminating passage. It will be well worth the reader's time, especially the reader who has always been puzzled by financial matters, to turn over in his mind the facts here given by a great Jewish financial expert about the central bank idea. Observe the phrases:

(a) "without giving the government any part in the management or control".

(b) "these central banks, while legally private corporations . . . . . are permitted to issue the notes of the nation".

(c) "they are custodians of practically the entire metallic reserves of the nation and the keepers of the government funds".

(d) "in questions of national policy, the government

must rely on the willing and loyal co-operation of these central organs".

It is not now a question whether these things are right or wrong; it is merely a question of understanding that they constitute the fact.

It is specially notable that in paragraph (d) it is a fair deduction that in questions of national policy, the government will simply have to depend not only on the patriotism but also to an extend on the permission and counsel of the financial organizations. That is a fair interpretation: questions of national policy are, by this method, rendered dependent upon the financial corporations.

Let that point be clear, quite regardless of the question whether or not this is the way national policies should be determined.

Mr. Warburg said that he believed in a certain amount of government control — but not too much. He said: "In strengthening the government control, the Owen-Glass Bill therefore moved in the right direction; but it went too far and fell into the other and even more dangerous extreme".

The "more dangerous extreme" was, of course, the larger measure of government supervision provided for, and the establishment of a number of Federal Reserve Banks out in the country.

Mr. Warburg had referred to this before; he had agreed to the larger number only because it seemed to be an unavoidable political concession. It has already been shown, by Professor Seligman, that Mr. Warburg was alive to the necessity of veiling a little here and there, and "putting on" a little yonder, for the sake of conciliating a suspicious public. There was also the story of the bartender and the cash register.

Mr. Warburg thinks he understands the psychology of America. In this respect he reminds one of the reports of Mr. von Bernstorff and Captain Boy-Ed of what the

Americans were likely to do or not to do. In the Political Science Quarterly of December, 1920, Mr. Warburg tells how, on a then recent visit to Europe, he was asked by men of all countries what the United States was going to do. He assured them that America was a little tired just then, but that she would come round allright. And then, harking back to his efforts of placing his monetary system on the Americans, he said:

"I asked them to be patient with us until after the election, and *I cited to them our experiences with monetary reform.* I reminded them how the Aldrich plan had failed because, at that time, a Republican President had lost control of a Congress ruled by a Democratic majority; how the Democrats in their platform damned this plan and any central banking system; and how, *once in full power, the National Reserve Association was evolved, not to say camouflaged, by them into the Federal Reserve System*".

Remembering this play before the public, and the play behind the scenes, this "camouflaging", as Mr. Warburg says, of one thing into another, he undertook to assure his friends in Europe that regardless of what the political platforms said, the United States would do substantially what Europe hoped it would. Mr. Warburg's basis for that belief was, as he said, his experience with the way the central bank idea went through in spite of the advertised objection of all parties. He believes that with Americans it is possible to get what you want if you just play the game skillfully. His experience with monetary reform seems to have fathered that belief in him.

Politicians may be necessary pawns to play in the game, but as members of the government Mr. Warburg does not want them in banking. They are not bankers, he says; they don't understand; banking is nothing for a goverment man to meddle with. He may be good enough for the Government of the United States; he is not good enough for banking.

"In our country", says Mr. Warburg, referring to the United States, "with every untrained amateur a candidate for any office, *where friendship or help in a presidential campaign, financial or political, has always given a claim for political preferment*, where the bids for votes and public favor are ever present in the politician's mind, ... a *direct government management, that is to say, a political management, would prove fatal* .... There can be no doubt but that, as drawn at present (1913), with two cabinet officers members of the Federal Reserve Board, and with the vast powers vested in the latter, the Owen-Glass Bill would bring about direct government management".

And that, of course, in Mr. Warburg's mind, is not only "dangerous", but "fatal".

Mr. Warburg had almost his whole will in the matter. And what is the result?

Turn to the testimony of Bernard M. Baruch, when he was examined with reference to the charge that certain men close to President Wilson had profited to the extent of $60,000,000 on stock market operations which they entered into on the strength of advance information of what the President was to say in his next war note — the famous "leak" investigation, as it was called; one of the several investigations in which Mr. Baruch was closely questioned.

In that investigation Mr. Baruch was laboring to show that he had not been in telephone communication with Washington, especially with certain men who were supposed to have shared the profits of the deals. The time was December, 1916. Mr. Warburg was then safely settled on the Federal Reserve Board, which he had kept quite safe from Government inrusion.

The Chairman — "Of course the records of the telephone company here, the slips, will show the persons with whom you talked".

Mr. Baruch — "Do you wish me to say, sir? I will state who they are".

The Chairman — "Yes, I think you might".

Mr. Baruch — "I called up two persons; one, Mr. Warburg, whom I did not get, and one, Secretary McAdoo, whom I did get — both in reference to the same matter. Would you like to know the matter?"

The Chairman — "Yes, I think it is fair that you should state it".

Mr. Baruch — "I called up the Secretary, because someone suggested to me — *asked me to suggest an officer for the Federal Reserve Bank,* and I called him up in reference to that, and discussed the matter with him, I think, *two or three times,* but it was suggested to me that I make the suggestion, and I did so". (pp. 570-571).

Mr. Campbell — "Mr. Baruch, who asked you for a suggestion for an appointee for the Federal Reserve Bank here?"

Mr. Baruch — "Mr. E. M. House."

Mr. Campbell — "Did Mr. House tell you to call Mr. McAdoo up and make the recommendation?"

Mr. Baruch — "I will tell you exactly how it occured: *Mr. House called me up* and said that there was a vacancy on the Federal Reserve Board, and he said, 'I don't know anything about those fellows down there, and I would like you to make a suggestion'. *And I sugested the name,* which he thought was a very good one, and he said to me, 'I wish you would call up the Secretary and tell him'. I said, 'I do not see the necessity; I will tell you'. 'No', he said, 'I would prefer you to call him up'." (p. 575)

There we have an example of the Federal Reserve "kept out of politics", kept away from government management which would not only be "dangerous", but "fatal".

Barney Baruch, the New York stock plunger, who never owned a bank in his life, was called up by Colonel

E. M. House, the arch-politician of the Wilson Administration, and thus the great Federal Reserve Board was supplied another member.

A telephone call kept within a narrow Jewish circle and settled by a word from one Jewish stock dealer — that, in practical operation, was Mr. Warburg's great monetary reform. Mr. Baruch calling up Mr. Warburg to give the name of the next appointee of the Federal Reserve Board, and calling up Mr. McAdoo, secretary of the United States Treasury, and set in motion to do it by Colonel E. M. House — is it any wonder the Jewish mystery in the American war government grows more and more amazing?

But, as Mr. Warburg has written — "friendship or help in *a presidential campaign*, financial or political, has always given a claim to political preferment". And, as Mr. Warburg urges, this is a country "with every untrained amateur a candidate for office", and naturally, with such men comprising the government, they must be kept at a safe distance from monetary affairs.

As if to illustrate the ignorance thus charged, along comes Mr. Baruch, who quotes Colonel House as saying, "I don't know anything about those fellows down there and I would like you to make a suggestion." It is permissible to doubt that Mr. Baruch correctly quotes Colonel House. It is permissible to doubt that all that Colonel House confessed was his ignorance about "those fellows". There was a good understanding between these two men, too good an understanding for the alleged telephone conversation to be taken strictly at its face value. It is possibly quite true that Mr. House is not a financier, Certainly, Mr. Wilson was not. In the long roll of Presidents only a handful have been, and those who have been have been regarded as most drastic in their proposals.

But this whole matter of ignorance, as charged by Mr. Warburg, sounds like an echo of the Protocols:

"The administrators chosen by us from the masses *will not be persons trained for government,* and consequently they will easily become pawns in our game, played by *our learned and talented counsellors, specialists educated from early childhood to administer world affairs*".

In the Twentieth Protocol, wherein the great financial plan of world subversion and control is disclosed, there is another mention of the rulers' ignorance of financial problems.

It is a coincidence that, while he does not use the term "ignorance", Mr. Warburg is quite outspoken concerning the benighted state in which he found this country, and he is also outspoken about the "untrained amateurs" who are candidates for every office. These, he says, are not fitted to take part in the control of monetary affairs. But Mr. Warbug is. He says so. *He admits that it was his ambition from the moment he came here an alien Jewish-German banker, to change our financial affairs more to his liking.* More than that, he has succeeded; he has succeeded, he himself says, more than most men do in a lifetime; he has succeeded, Professor Seligman says, to such an extent that throughout history the name of Paul M. Warburg and that of the Federal Reserve System shall be united.

DEARBORN INDEPENDENT —ISSUE OF JULY 2, 1921.

JEWISH "KOL NIDRE" and "ELI, ELI" EXPLAINED

(LXXI.)

"I have looked this year and last for something in your paper about the prayer which the Jews say at their New Year. But you say nothing. Can it be you have not heard of the Kol Nidre?"

"Lately in three cities I have head a Jewish religious hymn sung in the public theaters. This was in New York, Detroit and Chicago. Each time the program said 'by request'. Who makes the request? What is the meaning of this kind of propaganda? The name of the hymn is 'Eli.' "

The Jewish year just passed has been described by a Jewish writer in the *Jewish Daily News* as the Year of Chaos. The writer is apparently intelligent enough to ascribe this condition to something besides "anti-Semitism." He says, "the thought that there is something wrong in Jewish life will not down", and when he describes the situation in the Near East, he says, "The Jew himself is stirring the mess". He indicts the Jewish year 5681 on 12 counts, among them being, "mismanagement in Palestine", "engaging in internal warfare", "treason to the Jewish people", "selfishness," "self-delusion". "The Jewish people is a sick people", cries the writer, and when he utters a comfortable prophecy for the year 5682, it is not in the terms of Judah but in terms of "Kol Yisroel" — All Israel — the terms of a larger and more inclusive unity which gives Judah its own place, and its own place only, in the world. The Jewish people are sick, to be sure, and the disease is the fallacy of superiority, with its consequent "foreign policy" against the world.

When Jewish writers describe the year 5681 as the Year of Chaos, it is an unconscious admission that the Jewish people are ripening for a change of attitude. The "chaos" is among the leaders; it involves the plans which are based on the old false assumptions. The Jewish people are waiting for leaders who can emancipate them from the thralldom of their self-seeking masters in the religious and political fields. The enemies of the emancipation of Judah are those who profit by Judah's bondage, and these are the groups that follow the American Jewish Committee and the political rabbis. When a true Jewish prophet arises — and he should arise in the United States — there will be a great sweeping away of the selfish, scheming, heartless Jewish leaders, a general desertion of the Jewish idea of "getting" instead of "making", and an emergence of the true idea submerged so long.

There will also be a separation among the Jews themselves. They are not all Jews who call themselves so today. There is a Tartar strain in so-called Jewry that is absolutely incompatible with true Israelitish raciality; there are other alien strains which utterly differ from the true Jewish; but until now these strains have been held because the Jewish leaders needed vast hordes of low-type people to carry out their world designs. But the Jew himself is recognizing the presence of an alien element; and that is the first step in a movement which will place the Jewish Question on quite another basis.

What the Jews of the United States are coming to

think is indicated by this letter — one among many (the writer is a Jew):

"Gentlemen:

" 'Because you believe in a good cause', said Dr. Johnson, 'is no reason why you should feel called upon to defend it, for by your manner of defense you may do your cause much harm.'

"The above applying to me I will only say that I have received the books you sent me and read both with much interest.

"You are rendering the Jews a very great service, that of saving them *from themselves*.

"It takes courage, and nerve, and intelligence to do and pursue such a work, and I admire you for it."

The letter was accompanied by a check which ordered *The Dearborn Independent* sent to the address of another who bears a distinctively Jewish name.

It is very clear that unity is not to be won by the truth-teller soft-pedaling or suppressing his truth, nor by the truth-hearer strenuously denying that the truth is true, but by both together honoring the truth in telling and in acknowledging it. When the Jews see this, they can take over the work of truth-telling and carry it on themselves. These articles have as their only purpose: First, that the Jews may see the truth for themselves about themselves; second, that non-Jews may see the fallacy of the present Jewish idea and use enough common sense to cease falling victims to it. With both Jews and non-Jews seeing their error, the way is opened for cooperation instead of the kind of competition (not commercial, but moral) which has resulted so disastrously to Jewish false ambitions these long centuries.

Now, as the questions at the beginning of this article: THE DEARBORN INDEPENDENT has heretofore scrupulously avoided even the appearance of criticising the Jew for his religion. The Jew's religion, as most people think of it, is unobjectionable. But when he has carried on campaigns against the Christian religion, and when in every conceivable manner he thrusts his own religion upon the public from the stage of theaters and in other public places, he has himself to blame if the public asks questions.

It is quite impossible to select the largest theater in the United States, place the Star of David high in a beautiful stage heavens above all flags and other symbols, apostrophize it for a week with all sorts of wild prophecy and all sorts of silly defiance of the world, sing hymns to it and otherwise adore it, without arousing curiosity. Yet the Jewish theatrical managers, with no protest from the Anti-Defamation Committee, have done this on a greater or smaller scale in many cities. To say it is meaningless is to use words lightly.

The "Kol Nidre" is a Jewish prayer, named from its opening words, "All vows," (kol nidre). It is based on the declaration of the Talmud:

"He who wishes that his vows and oaths shall have no value, stand up at the beginning of the year and say: 'All vows which I shall make during the year shall be of no value.' "

It would be pleasant to be able to declare that this is merely one of the curiosities of the darkness which covers the Talmud, but the fact is that "Kol Nidre" is not only an ancient curiosity; it is also a modern practice. In the volume of *revised* "Festival Prayers", published in 1919 by the Hebrew Publishing Company, New York, the prayer appears in its fullness:

"All vows, obligations, oaths or anathemas, pledges of all names, which we have vowed, sworn, devoted, or bound ourselves to, from this day of atonement, until the next day of atonement (whose arrival we hope for in happiness) we repent, aforehand, of them all, they shall all be deemed absolved, forgiven, anulled, void and made of no effect; they shall not be binding, nor have any power; the vows shall not be reckoned vows, the obliga-

tions shall not be obligatory, nor the oaths considered as oaths".

If this strange statement were something dug out of the misty past, it would scarcely merit serious attention, but as being part of a *revised* Jewish prayer book printed in the United States in 1919, and as being one of the high points of the Jewish religious celebration of the New Year, it cannot be lightly dismissed after attention has once been called to it.

Indeed, the Jews do not deny it. Early in the year, when a famous Jewish violinist landed in New York, after a triumphant tour abroad, he was besieged by thousands of his East Side admirers, and was able to quiet their cries only when he took his violin and played the "Kol Nidre." Then the people wept as exiles do at the sound of the songs of the homeland.

In that incident the reader will see that (hard as it is for the non-Jew to understand it!) there is a deep-rooted, sentimental regard for the "Kol Nidre" which makes it one of the most sacred of possessions to the Jew. Indefensibly immoral as the "Kol Nidre" is, utterly destructive of all social confidence, yet the most earnest efforts of a few really spiritual Jews have utterly failed to remove it from the prayer books, save in a few isolated instances. The music of the "Kol Nidre" is famous and ancient. One has only to refer to the article "Kol Nidre" in the Jewish Encyclopedia to see the predicament of the modern Jew: he cannot deny; he cannot defend; he cannot renouce. The "Kol Nidre" is here, and remains.

If the prayer were a request for forgiveness for the broken vows of the past, normal human beings could quite understand it. Vows, promise, obligations and pledges are broken, sometimes by weakness of will to perform them, sometimes by reason of forgetfulness, sometimes by sheer inability to do the thing we thought we could do. Human experience is neither Jew nor Gentile in that respect.

But the prayer is a holy advance notice, given in the secrecy of the synagogue, that no promise whatever shall be binding, and more than not being binding is there and then violated before it is ever made.

The scope of the prayer is "from this day of atonement, until the next day of atonement."

The prayer looks wholly to the future, "we repent, aforehand, of them all."

The prayer breaks down the common ground of confidence between men — "the vows shall not be reckoned vows; the obligations shall not be obligatory, nor the oaths considered as oaths".

It requires no argument to show that if this prayer be really the rule of faith and conduct for the Jews who utter it, the ordinary social and business relations are impossible to maintain with them.

It should be observed that there is no likeness here with Christian "hypocrisy", so-called. Christian "hypocrisy" arises mostly from men holding higher ideals than they are able to attain to, and verbally extolling higher principles than their conduct illustrates. That is, to use Browning's figure, the man's reach exceeds his grasp; as it always does, where the man is more than a clod.

But the "Kol Nidre" is in the opposite direction. It recognizes by inference that in the common world of men, in the common morality of the street and the mart, a promise passes current as a promise, a pledge as a pledge, an obligation as an obligation — that there is a certain social currency given to the individual's mere word on the assumption that its quality is kept good by straight moral intention. And it makes provision to drop below that level.

How did the "Kol Nidre" come into existence? It is the cause or the effect of that untrustworthiness with which the Jew has been charged for centuries?

Its origin is not from the Bible but from Babylon, and the mark of Babylon is more strongly impressed on the

Jew than is the mark of the Bible. "Kol Nidre" is Talmudic and finds its place among many other dark things in that many-volumed and burdensome invention. If the "Kol Nidre" ever was a backward look over the failures of the previous year, it very early became a forward look to the deliberate deceptions of the coming year.

Many explanations have been made in an attempt to account for this. Each explanation is denied and disproved by those who favor some other explanation. The commonest of all is this, and it rings in the over-worked note of "persecution": The Jews were so hounded and harried by the bloodthirsty Christians, and so brutally and viciously treated in the name of the loving Jesus (the terms are borrowed from Jewish writers) that they were compelled by wounds and starvation and the fear of death to renounce their religion and to vow that thereafter they would take the once despised Jesus for their Messiah. Therefore, say the Jewish apologists, knowing that during the ensuing year the terrible, bloodthirsty Christians would force the poor Jews to take Christian vows, the Jews in advance announced to God that all the promises they would make on that score would be lies. They would say what the Christians forced them to say, but they would not mean or intend one word of it.

That is the best explanation of all. Its weakness is that it assumes the "Kol Nidre" to have been coincident with times of "persecution," especially in Spain. Unfortunately for this explanation, the "Kol Nidre" is found centuries before that, when the Jews were under no pressure.

In a refreshingly frank article in the Cleveland *Jewish World* for October 11, the insufficiency of the above explanation is so clearly set forth that a quotation is made:

"Many learned men want to have it understood that the Kol Nidre dates from the Spanish Inquisition, it having become necessary on account of all sorts of persecution and inflictions to adopt the Christian religion for appearances' sake. Then the Jews in Spain, gathering in cellars to celebrate the Day of Atonement and pardon, composed a prayer that declared of no value all vows and oaths that they would be forced to make during the year.....

"The learned men say, moreover, that in remembrance of those days when hundreds and thousands of Maranos (secret Jews) were dragged out of the cellars and were tortured with all kinds of torment, the Jews in all parts of the world have adopted the Kol Nidre as a token of faithfulness to the faith and as self-sacrifice for the faith.

"*These assertions are not correct*. The fact is that the formula of Kol Nidre was composed and said on the night of Yom Kippur quite a time earlier than the period of the Spanish Inquisition. We find, for instance, a formula to invalidate vows on Yom Kippur in the prayer book of the Rabbi Amram Goun who lived in the ninth century, about five hundred years before the Spanish Inquisition; although Rabbi Amram's formula is not 'Kol Nidre' but 'Kol Nidrim' ('All vows and oaths which we shall swear from Yom Kippurim to Yom Kippurim will return to us void.')......"

The form of the prayer in the matter of its age may be in dispute; but back in the ancient and modern Talmud is the authorization of the practice: "He who wishes that his vows and oaths shall have no value, stand up at the beginning of the year and say: 'All vows which I shall make during the year shall be of no value.'"

That answers our reader's question. This article does not say that all Jews thus deliberately assassinate their pledged word. It does say that both the Talmud and the prayer book permit them to do so, and tell them how it may be accomplished.

Now, as to the Jewish religious hymn which is being sung "by request" throughout the country: the story of it is soon told.

The name of the hymn is "Eli, Eli"; its base is the first verse of the Twenty-second Psalm, known best in Christian countries as the Cry of Christ on the Cross.

It is being used by Jewish vaudeville managers as their contribution to the pro-Jewish campaign which the Jew-controlled theater is flinging into the faces of the public, from stage and motion picture screen. It is an incantation designed to inflame the lower classes of Jews against the people, and intensify the racial consciousness of those hordes of Eastern Jews who have flocked here.

At the instigation of the New York Kehillah, "Eli, Eli" has for a long time been sung at the ordinary run of performances in vaudeville and motion picture houses, and the notice "By Request" is usually a bald lie. It should be "By Order." The "request" is from Jewish headquarters which has ordered the speeding up of Jewish propaganda. The situation of the theater now is that American audiences are paying at the box office for the privilege of hearing Jews advertise the things they want non-Jews to think about them.

If even a vestige of decency, or the slightest appreciation of good taste remained, the Jews who control the theaters would see that the American public must eventually gag on such things. When two Jewish comedians who have been indulging in always vulgar and often indecent antics, appear before the drop curtain and sing the Yiddish incantation "Eli, Eli," which, of course, is incomprehensible to the major part of the audience, the Jewish element always betrays a high pitch of excitement. They understand the game that is being played: the "Gentiles" are being flayed to their face, and they don't know it; as when a Yiddish comedian pours out shocking invectives on the name of Jesus Christ, and "gets away with it," the Jewish portion of his audience howling with delight, and the "boob Gentiles" looking serenely on and feeling it to be polite to laugh and applaud too!

This Yiddish chant is the rallying cry of race hatred which is being spread abroad by orders of the Jewish leaders. You, if you are a theatergoer, help to pay the expense of getting yourself roundly damned. The Kehillah and the American Jewish Committee which for more than ten years have been driving all mention of Christianity out of public life, under their slogan "This Is Not a Christian Country," are spreading their own type of Judaism everywhere with insolence unparralleled.

"Eli, Eli" is not a religious hymn! It is a racial war cry. In the low cafés of New York, where Bolshevik Jews hang out, "Eli, Eli" is their song. It is the Marseillaise of Jewish solidarity. It has become the fanatical chant of all Jewish Bolshevik clubs; it is constantly heard in Jewish coffee houses and cabarets where emotional Russian and Polish Jews — all enemies to all government — shout the words amid torrential excitement. When you see the hymn in point you are utterly puzzled to understand the excitement it rouses.

And this rallying cry has now been obtruded into the midst of the theatrical world.

The term "incantation" here used is used advisedly. The term is used by Kurt Schindler, who adapted the Yidish hymn to American use. An its effect is that of an incantation.

In translation it is as follows:

"My God, my God, why hast thou forsaken me?
With fire and flame they have burnt us,
Everywhere they have shamed and derided us,
Yet none amongst us has dared depart
From our Holy Scriptures, from our Law.

"My God, my God, why hast thou forsaken me?
By day and night I only yearn and pray,
Anxiously keeping our Holy Scriptures
And praying, Save us, save us once again!
For the sake of our fathers and our father's fathers!

"Listen to my prayer and to my lamenting,
For only Thou canst help, Thou, God, alone,
For it is said, 'Hear, O Israel, the Lord is Our God,
The Lord is One;' "

The words of the hymn are so much resembling a lament that they strangely contrast with the spirit which the hymn itself seems to arouse; its mournful melody inspires a very different spirit among the Jewish hearers than the same sort of melody would inspire among other people. Those who have heard its public rendition can better understand how a hymn of such utterly quiet and resigned tone could be the wild rage of the anarchists of the East Side coffee houses.

The motive, of course, for the singing of the hymn is the reference to non-Jewish people.

"With fire and flame *THEY* have burnt us, everywhere *THEY* have shamed and derided us" Who are "they"? Who but the goyim, the Christians who all unsuspectingly sit near by and who are so affected by the Jewish applause that they applaud too! Truly, in one way of looking at it, Jews have a right to despise the "gentiles."

"*THEY* have burnt us; *THEY* have shamed us," but we, the poor Jews, have been harmless all the while, none among us daring to depart from the Law! That is the meaning of "Eli, Eli." That is why, in spite of its words of religious resignation, it becomes a rallying cry. "They" are all wrong; "we" are all right.

It is possible, of course, that right-minded Jews do not approve all this. They may disapprove of "Kol Nidre" and they may resent the use which the Jewish leaders are making of "Eli, Eli." Let us at least credit some Jews with both these attitudes. But they do nothing about it. These same Jews, however, will go to the public library of their town and put the fear of political or business reprisal in the hearts of the Library Board if they do not instantly remove *The Dearborn Independent* from the library; these same Jews will form committees to coerce mayors of cities into issuing illegal orders which cannot be enforced; these same Jews will give commands to the newspapers under their patronage or control — they are indeed mighty and active in the affairs of the non-Jews. But when it is a matter of keeping "Eli, Eli" out of the theater, or the "Kol Nidre" out of the mouths of those who thus plan a whole year of deception "aforehand," these same Jews are very inactive and apparently very powerless.

The Anti-Defamation Committee would better shut up shop until it can show either the will or the ability to bring pressure to bear on its own people. Coercion of the rest of the people is rapidly growing less and less possible.

The "Kol Nidre" is far from being the worst counsel in the Talmud; "Eli, Eli" is far from being the worst anti-social misuse of apparently holy things. But it will remain the policy of *The Dearborn Independent,* for the present at least, to let all such matters alone except, as in the present case, where the number of the inquiries indicates that a knowledge of the facts has been had at other sources. In many instances, what our inquirers heard was much worse than is stated here, so that this article is by way of being a service to the inquirer to prevent his being misled, and to the Jew to prevent misrepresentation.

DEARBORN INDEPENDENT — ISSUE OF NOV. 5, 1921.

JUDAISM

The Pharisees

Judaism has been described by Moses Mendelssohn, a learned Jew, in this way: — "Judaism is not a religion but a Law religionized." This definition does away effectively with the erroneous belief prevalent among the non-Jews that Judaism is a religion.

In spite of the loud and frequent assertions, made by Jews and Christian divines alike, contending that the Jews were the first monotheists, it is a well proven fact that the high initiates of the Memphis priesthood were monotheists long before the Jews ever went to Egypt.

Judaism would be best described as a rite or compendium of rites, for, if one lends belief to the existence of the Jewish Lawgiver, Moses, one must bear in mind that he first studied among the high initiates of Egypt, and later, became the pupil and son-in-law of black Jethro, the Ethiopian magician whom one might call the Father of Voodooism, name given to the magic practices and rites performed by the negroes.

The closer one studies the history of the Jews, the clearer it appears that they are neither a religious entity nor a nation. The absolute failure of Zionism which was a desperate effort on the part of certain Jewish leaders to bind all the Jews of the world into a national entity, whose territory would have been Palestine, proves the futility of such an effort.

Judaism is not a religion and the Jews are not a nation, but they are a sect with Judaism as a rite.

The obligations and rules of the rite for the Jewish masses are contained in the Talmud and Schulchan Aruk, but the esoteric teachings for the higher initiates are to be found in the Cabala.

Therein are contained the mysterious rites for evocations, the indications and keys to practices for conjuration of supernatural forces, the science of numbers, astrology, etc.

The practical application of the Cabalist knowledge is manifested in the use made of it, through the ages, by Jews to gain influence both in the higher spheres of Gentile life and over the masses. Sovereigns and Popes, both, usually had one or more Jews as astrologers and advisers, and they frequently gave Jews control over their very life by employing them as physicians. Political power was thus gained by Jews in almost every Gentile country alongside with financial power, since Jewish court-bankers manipulated state funds and taxes.

Through the ages also, can be followed the spreading power of the sect, and no more awful example of the devastating and destructive power of the penetration of a secret subversive society has even been witnessed.

With its B'nai B'rith Supreme Council as the directing head, the sect with its members swarming among all nations has become the sovereign power ruling in the councils of all nations and governing their political, economic, religious and educational policies.

In his book "Nicholas II et les Juifs", Netchvolodow explains that "the Chaldean science acquired by many of the Jewish priests, during the captivity of Babylon, gave birth to the sect of the Pharisees whose name only appears in the Holy Scriptures and in the writings of the Jewish historians after the captivity (606 B. C.). The works of the celebrated scientist Munk leave no doubt on the point that the sect appeared during the period of the captivity.

"From then dates the Cabala or Tradition of the Pharisees. For a long time their precepts were only transmitted orally but later they formed the Talmud and received their final form in the book called the "Sepher ha Zohar". [1]

The Pharisees were, as it were, a class whose tendency was to form a kind of intellectual aristocracy among the Jews. At first, they formed a sort of brotherhood, a "haburah", the members being called "haburim" or brothers. They were a subversive element, aiming at the overthrow of the Sadducean Highpriesthood, whose members prided themselves on their aristocracy of blood and birth, to which the Pharisees opposed an aristocracy of learning. The war waged by the latter extends over a long period of time, and the rivalry was bitter. The Pharisees, who, although they professed, as one of their chief tenets, the utmost contempt of the "am haretz" or simple people, did not overlook the fact that they needed their mass support for the attainment of their own aim, and they enlisted it by opposing the Sadducean strictness of the Law in many instances, namely, in the observance of the Sabbath.

The power of the Sadducees fell with the destruction of the Temple by Titus and thenceforth the Pharisaic element held supremacy among the Jews.

Quoting an acknowledged authority on Judaism, Mr. Flavien Brenier, Lt. Gen. Netchvolodow further describes the policy of the sect as follows: [2]

"Before appearing proudly as the expression of Jewish aspirations, The Tradition of the Pharisees had serious difficulties to surmount, the chief of which was the revival of the orthodox faith stimulated in the Jewish people by the Captivity. To the exiles, bemoaning the fall of the Temple of Jerusalem and begging Jehovah to end the misfortunes of their homeland, the revelation that

---

1. Lt. Gen. A. Netchvolodow, Nicholas II et les Juifs, p. 139.
2. Ibid., p. 139 et seq.

Jehovah was only a phantom, entailed not only certain defeat, but also their own exposure to perils the last of which would have been the loss of all authority over Israel.

"The Pharisees then, judging it wiser to capture the confidence of their compatriots by taking the lead of the religious movement, affected a scrupulous observance of the slightest prescriptions of the law and instituted the practice of complicated rituals, simultaneously however cultivating the new doctrine in their secret sanctuaries. These were regular secret societies, composed during the captivity of a few hundred adepts. At the time of Flavius Josephus which was that of their greatest prosperity they numbered only some 6,000 members.

"This group of intellectual pantheists was soon to acquire a directing influence over the Jewish nation. Nothing, moreover, likely to offend national sentiment ever appeared in their doctrines. However saturated with pantheistic chaldeism they might have been, the Pharisees preserved their ethnic pride intact. This religion of Man divinised, which they had absorved at Babylon they conceived solely as applying to the profit of the Jew, the superior and predestined being. The promises of universal dominion which the orthodox Jew found in the Law, the Pharisees did not interpret in the sense of the reign of the God of Moses over the nations, but in that of a material domination to be imposed on the universe by the Jews. The awaited Messiah was no longer the Redeemer of original Sin, a spiritual victor who would lead the world, it was a temporal king, bloody with battle, who would make Israel master of the world and "drag all peoples under the wheels of his chariot". The Pharisees did not ask this enslavement of the nations of a mystical Jehovah, which they continued worshipping in public, only as a consession to popular opinion, for they expected its eventual consummation to be achieved by the secular patience of Israel and the use of human means.

"Monstrously different from the ancient law were such principles as these, but they had nothing one could see, which might have rendered unpopular those who let them filter, drop by drop, among the Jews.

"The admirably conceived organization of the Pharisees did not fail soon to bear fruit.

"One cannot better define its action in the midst of Jewish society before Jesus Christ," said Mr. Flavien Brenier, "than in comparing it with that of the Freemasons in modern society."

"A carefully restricted membership tightly bound, imposing on their members the religion of 'the secret', the Pharisees pursued relentlessly their double aim which was:

"1. The seizure of political power, by the possession of the great political offices (the influence of which was tremendous in the reconstituted Jewish nation) and the conquest of the Sanhedrin (Jewish parliament.)

"2. To modify gradually the conceptions of the people in the direction of their secret doctrine."

The first of these aims was achieved when Hillel, a Pharisee of Babylon who claimed Davidic descent, was elected president of the Sanhedrin. Thus ended the bitter fight between the Pharisees and the Sadducees. Opposed to Hillel was Shammai, a Sadducee, supporter of the Sadducean High Priest who was made Chief Judge of the assembly. The attitude of the two men towards each other is a matter of long record in the Talmud.

Among the most noted Pharisees, after Hillel, are: — Yochanan ben Zakkai, founder of the school of Yamnai, Akibah who, with Bar Cochba, formented the revolt against the Romans under Hadrian, rebellion ending with the order for the dispersion of Jews (132 A. D.) Also Simon ben Yohai, who might be termed the great Magician and Father of the Cabala, lastly Judah the Prince who compiled the Babylonian Talmud. Under these chiefs, the Phariasaic power was definitely established in the Sanhedrin. Those among the Jews who clung to the Sadducean tradition and refused to acknowledge the dominion of the Pharisees, remained as dissidents. Such were the Samaritans and the Karaites who rejected the Talmud.

The second of the aims and its method of attainment is exposed in the so-called Protocols of the Wise Men of Zion so loudly denounced by the descendants of those who devised The Secret Doctrine in Israel, Israel here meaning the Jews as a religious community, most of whom remain quite ignorant of the intricate subversive schemes imputed to them.

The attitude of Jesus Christ to this sect is definitely expressed in the New Testament (see Luke XI and John VIII).

Exoteric Judaism, the Jewish religion as practised in the twentieth century, is based on the Old Testament, and on equally ancient commentaries on it, preserved for ages as oral traditions, and known, as above stated, under the general name of The Talmud. All copies of this book were ordered to be burned by Philip IV, the Fair, King of France, in 1306, but the book survived the holocaust.

We know that the Jewish God is not the father of all men and the ideal of love, justice and mercy, like the Christian God, or even like Ahura-Mazd or Brahma. On the contrary, he is the God of vengeance down to the fourth generation, just and merciful only to his own people, but foe to all other nations, denying them human rights and commanding their enslavement that Israel might appropriate their riches and rule over them.

The following quotations will serve to illustrate this point:—

"And when the Lord thy God shall deliver them before thee; thou shalt smite them and utterly destroy them; thou shalt make no covenant with them, nor show mercy to them." — Deut. VII, 2.

"For thou art an holy people unto the Lord thy God; the Lord thy God hath chosen thee to be a special people unto himself, above all people that are upon the face of the earth." — Deut. VII, 6.

The Talmud comments upon it: "You are human beings, but the nations of the world are not human beings but beasts." Baba Mecia 114, 6.

"On the house of the Goy (non-Jew) one looks as on the fold of cattle." Tosefta, Erubin VIII.

From The Talmud (a prayer said on the eve of Passover, to the present day) "We beg Thee, O Lord, indict Thy wrath on the nations not believing inThee, and not calling on Thy name. Let down Thy wrath on them and inflict them with Thy wrath. Drive them away in Thy wrath and crush them into pieces. Take away, O Lord, all bone from them. In a moment indict all disbelievers. Destroy in a moment all foes of Thy nation. Draw out with the root, disperse and ruin unworthy nations. Destroy them! Destroy them immediately, in this very moment!" — (Pranajtis: Christianus in Talmudae Judeorum, quotations from: Synagoga Judaica, p. 212. Minhagin, p. 23. Crach Chaim 480 Hagah).

"When one sees inhabited houses of the 'Goy' one says, 'The Lord will destroy the house of the proud'. And when one sees them destroyed he says, 'The Lord God of Vengeance has revealed himself' — (The Babylonian Talmud, Berachot 58, 6.)

"Those who do not own Torah and the prophets must all be killed. Who has power to kill them, let him kill them openly with the sword, if not, let him use artifices till they are done away with." — (Schulchan Aruch: Choszen Hamiszpat, 425, 50).

The Jewish Sages soon understood that Christ's way of commenting upon the old Law introduced, instead of hatred toward foreign nations, brotherly feelings and equality of all men in the face of God, thus denying the Jews their privileged position as masters of the world.

At the same time, Christ's reforming the very primitive and rough moral ideas of the Old Testament, deprived the Jews of their very convenient-in-the-battle-of-life, unscrupulous, double morality. Thense the Jewish hatred for the Christian faith is conspicuous in the following quotations from Talmudic sources:—

"The estates of the Goys are like wilderness, who first settles in them has a right to them. (Baba Batra, 14 b.)

"The property of the Goys is like a thing without a master." Schulchan Aruch: Choszen Hamiszpat, 116, 5).

"If a Jew has struck his spade into the ground of the Goy, he has become the master of the whole." (Baba Batra, 55 a.)

In order to enhance the authority of the Old Testament equally recognized by the Christians, while simultaneously augmenting that of the Talmud and the Rabbis, its commentators and authors teach: —

"In the law (the Bible) are things more or less important, but the words of the Learned in the Scripture are always important.

"It is more wicked to protest the words of the rabbis than of Torah" (Miszna, Sanhedryn XI, 3.) "Who changes the words of the rabbis ought to die." (Erubin, 21, b.)

"The decisions of the Talmud are words of the living God. Jehovah himself asks the opinion of earthly rabbis when there are difficult affairs in heaven." (Rabbi Menachen, Comments for the Fifth Book.)

"Jehovah himself in heaven studies the Talmud, standing: he has such respect for that book." (Tr. Mechilla).

To enhance the dignity of religious dogmas the following commandments are given:

"That the Jewish nation is the only nation selected by God, while all the remaining ones are contemptible and hateful.

"That all property of other nations belongs to the Jewish nation, which consequently is entitled to seize upon it without any scruples."

"That an orthodox Jew is not bound to observe principles of morality towards people of other nations, and on the contrary, he even ought to act against morality, if it were profitable for himself or for the interest of Jews in general."

"A Jew may rob a Goy (Goy means unclean, and is the disparaging name for a non-Jew), he may cheat him over a bill, which should not be perceived by him, otherwise the name of God would become dishonoured." (Schulchan Aruch, Choszen Hamiszpat, 348.)

"Should a Goy to whom a Jew owned some money die without his heirs knowing about the debt, the Jew is not bound to pay the debt." (Schulchan Aruch, Choszen Hamiszpat 283, 1.)

"The son of Noah, who would steal a farthing ought to be put to death, but an Israelite is allowed to do injury to a goy; where it is written, Thou shalt not do injury to thy neighbour, is not said, Thou shalt not do injury to a goy." (Miszna, Sanhedryn, 57.)

"A thing lost by a goy may not only be kept by the man who found it, but it is forbidden to give it back to him." (Schulchan Aruch, Choszen Hamiszpat. 266, 1.)

"Who took an oath in the presence of the goys, the robbers, and the custom-house officer, is not responsible." (Tosefta Szebnot, 11.)

"In order to annul marriages, oaths, and promises, a Jew must go to the rabbi, and if he is absent, he must call three other Jews, and say to them that he is sorry to have done it, and they say, 'Thou are allowed to.' (Schulchan Aruch, 2, 1.247.)

The Kol Nidre prayer on the Day of Judgment, that acquits beforehand from the nonfulfilment of all kinds of oaths and vows, is given here.

"All vows, oaths, promises, engagements, and swearing, which, beginning this very day of reconciliation, we intend to vow, promise, swear, and bind ourselves to fulfill, we are sorry for already, and they shall be annulled, acquitted, annihilated, abolished, valueless, unimportant, our vow shall be no vows, and our oaths no oaths at all." (Schulchan Aruch, edit. I, 136).

"If a goy wants a Jew to stand witness against a Jew at the Court of Law, and the Jew could give fair evidence, he is forbidden to do it, but if a Jew wants a Jew to be a witness in a similar case against a Goy, he may do it." (Schulchan Aruch, Choszen Hamiszpat, 28 art, 3 and 4.)

"Should a Jew inform the goyish authorities that another Jew has much money, and the other will suffer a loss through it, he must give him renumeration." (Schulchan Aruch. — Ch. Ha., 338.)

"If there is no doubt that someone thrice betrayed the Jews, or caused that their money passed to the goys, a means and wise council must be found to do away with him."

"Every one must contribute to the expense of the community (Kahal) in order to do away with the traitor." Ibid. 163, 1.)

"It is permitted to kill a Jewish denunciator everywhere.... it is permitted to kill him before he has denounced.... though it is necessary to warn him and say, 'Do not denounce.' But should he say, 'I will denounce,' he must be killed, and he who accomplishes it first will have the greater merit." (Ibid, 388, 10.)

"How to interpret the word 'robbery'. A goy is forbidden to steal, rob, or taken women slaves, etc., from a goy or from a Jew, but he (a Jew) is not forbidden to do all this to a goy." (Tosefta, Aboda Zara, VIII, 5.)

"If a goy killed a goy or a Jew he is responsible, but if a Jew killed a goy he is not responsible." (Ibid,. VIII, 5.)

The authors of the Talmud, having issued this horrible moral code, that acquits all kinds of crimes, in order to make easier the strife with foreigners to their own nation, understood the necessity of keeping its contents a secret and thus legislated:

"To communicate to a goy about our religious relations would be equal to the killing of all the Jews, for if the goys knew what we teach about them, they would kill us openly." (Book of Libbre David, 37.)

"It is forbidden to disclose the secrets of the Law. He who would do it would be as guilty as if he destroyed the whole world." (Jaktu Chadasz, 171, 2). The restrictions and commandments bearing this in view were raised to the dignity of dogmas of faith. It is not astonishing that in face of such prohibitions the secrets of the Talmud have been so little known to other nations, especially to the Western ones, and till the present day, even the most progressive and citizen-like Jews think the disclosure of the principles of the Talmud a proof of the most outrageous intolerance, and an attack on the Jewish religion.

In order to separate the Jewish nation from all others, and thus prevent it from mixing with them, and losing their national peculiarities, a great many precepts of the ritual and rules for every-day life, prejudices and superstitions, the remained of the times of barbarism and obscurity, have been gathered in the Talmud and consecrated as canons. The precepts observed by Eastern Jews till the present day deride even the most simple notions of culture and hygiene. For instance they enjoin:

"If a Jew be called to explain any part of the rabbinic books, he only ought to give a false explanation, that he might not, by behaving differently, become an accomplice in betraying this information. Who will violate this order shall be put to death." (Libbre David, 37.)

"It is forbidden to disclose the secrets of the Law."

"One should and must make false oath, when the goys ask if our books contain anything against them. Then we are bound to state on oath that there is nothing like that." (Szaalot-Utszabot. The book of Jore d'a, 17.)

"Every goy who studies Talmud, and every Jew who helps him in it, ought to die." (Sanhedryn 59 a. Aboda Zora 8-6: Szagiga 13.)

"The ears of the goys are filthy, their baths, houses, countries are filthy." (Tosefta Mikwat, v. 1.)

"A boy-goy after nine years and one day old, and a girl after three years and one day old, are considered filthy." (Pereferkowicz: Talmud t. v., p. 11.)

These principles afford an explanation of the action of governments in excluding Jews from judicial and military positions. They also explain that mysterious phenomenon known as

ANTISEMITISM

PART II

CHAPTER I

HOW THE PROTOCOLS CAME TO RUSSIA

The word "protocol" [1] was used to signify a flyleaf pasted at the top of an official document, bearing either the opening formula or a summary of the contents for convenient reference. The original draft of a treaty was usually pasted on in this way, that the signatories might check the correctness of the engrossed copy before signing. The draft itself being based on the discussion at the conference, the word came to mean also the minutes of the proceedings.

In this instance "the protocols" mean the "draft of the plan of action" of the Jewish leaders. There have been many such drafts at different periods in Jewish history since the dispersion, but few of them have come into general circulation. In all, the principles and morality are as old as the tribe. By way of illustration we give an instance which occured in the fifteenth century.

In 1492, Chemor, chief Rabbi of Spain, wrote to the Grand Sanhedrin, which had its seat in Constantinople, for advice, when a Spanish law threatened expulsion. [2] This was the reply:

---

1. From Greek. **protos** (first) + **kolla** (glue).

2. The reply is found in the sixteenth century Spanish book, **La Silva Curiosa,** by Julio-Iniguez de Medrano (Paris Orry, 1608), on pages 156 and 157, shown in photostat, with the fol-

ESTA CARTA SIGVIENTE FVE hallada por el Ermitaño de Salamanca en los Archiuos de Toledo, buſcando las antiguedades de los Reinos d Eſpaña: y pues ella es ſentida, y notable quiero eſcriuirtela aqui.

CARTA DE LOS IVDIOS d'Eſpaña, a los de Conſtantinopola.

IVdios honrrados, Salud y gracia. Sepades que el Rey d'Eſpaña por pregon publico nos haze boluer Chriſtianos, y nos quitan las haziendas, y las vidas, y nos deſtruyen nueſtras Sinagogas, y nos hazen otras vexaciones, las quales nos tienen confuſos, y inciertos de lo que hemos de hazer. Por la Ley de Moyſen os rogamos, y ſuplicamos tengais por bien de hazer ayuntamiento, y embiarnos con toda breuedad la deliberacion que en ello huuieredes fecho.

CHAMORRA Principe de los Iudios de Eſpaña.

Reſpueſta de los Iudios de Conſtantinopla, a los Iudios de Eſpaña.

AMados hermanos en Moyſen vueſtra carta recibimos, en la qual nos ſignificais los trabajos & mfortunios que padeſceis, de cuyo ſentimiento nos a cabido tanta parte como a'vototros. El pareſcer de los grandes Satrapas, y Rabi es lo ſiguiente.

A lo que dezis que el Rey de España os haze boluer Christianos, que lo hagais pues no podeis hazer otro: A lo que dezis que os mandan quitar vuestras haziendas, hazed vuestros hijos mercaderes, para que poco a poco les quiten las suyas. A lo que dezis que os quitã las vidas, hazed vuestros hijos medicos y boticarios, para que les quiten las suyas. A lo que dezis que os destruyen vuestras Sinagogas, hazed vuestros hijos clerigos y theologos, para que les destruyan sus templos. Y a lo que dezis que os hazen otras vexiciones, procurad que vuestros hijos sean abogados, procuradores, notarios, y consejeros, y que siempre entiendan en negocios de Republicas, para que sujetandolos ganeis tierra, y os podais vengar dellos, y no salgais desta orden que os damos, porque por experiencia vereis que de abatidos, verneis a ser tenidos en algo.

VSSVS FF. Principe de los Iudios de Constantinopla.

LA generosa Marfisa estando triste, y muy afligida por la muerte del pastor Gelido de Riojo. embio vna carta a Iulio, y por ella entre otras cosas le ruega, que no le escriua mas cartas ni versos que traten de amores, porque passó solia, y el mayor consuelo que agora ella tomaua, era en andar solitaria por vn desierto, cantando versos tristes, y lamentables, y escriuiendo diuersos epitaphios por las fuentes y peñas, y sobre las cortezas de los arboles. Assi mismo escriue a Iulio y le ruega mucho que en lugar de las sentidas Empresas, y hermosissimas Deuisas, que otras vezes solia of-

"Beloved brethren in Moses, we have received your letter in which you tell us of the anxieties and misfortunes which you are enduring. We are pierced by as great pain to hear it as yourselves.

The advice of the Grand Satraps and Rabbis is the following:

1. As for what you say that the King of Spain [3] obliges you to become Christians: do it, since you cannot do otherwise.

2. As for what you say about the command to despoil you of your property: make your sons merchants that they may despoil, little by little, the Christians of theirs.

3. As for what you say about making attempts on your lives: make your sons doctors and apothecaries, that they may take away Christians' lives.

4. As for what you say of their destroying your synagogues: make your sons canons and clerics in order that they may destroy their churches.

5. As for the many other vexations you complain of: arrange that your sons become advocates and lawyers, and see that they always mix in affairs of State, that by putting Christians under your yoke you may dominate the world and be avenged on them.

6. Do not swerve from this order that we give you, because you will find by experience that humiliated as you are, you will reach the actuality of power.

(Signed) *Prince of the Jews of Constantinople.*"

The protocols given to the world by Nilus are only the latest known edition of the Jewish leaders programme. The story of how the latter came into general circulation is an interesting one.

---

lowing explanation: "This letter following was found in the archives of Toledo by the Hermit of Salamanca, (while) searching the ancient records of the kingdoms of Spain; and, as it is expressive and remarkable, I wish to write it here."

3. Ferdinand.

In 1884 the daughter of a Russian general, Mlle. Justine Glinka, was endeavoring to serve her country in Paris by obtaining political information, which she communicated to General Orgevskii [4] in St. Petersburg. For this purpose she employed a Jew, Joseph Schorst, [5] member of the Mizraim Lodge in Paris. One day Schorst offered to obtain for her a document of great importance to Russia, on payment of 2,500 francs. This sum being received from St. Petersburg was paid over and the document handed to Mlle. Glinka. [6]

She forwarded the French original, accompanied by a Russian translation, to Orgevskii, who in turn handed it to his chief, General Cherevin, for transmission to the Tsar. But Cherevin, under obligation to wealthy Jews, refused to transmit it, merely filing it in the archives. [7]

Meantime there appeared in Paris certain books on Russian court life [8] which displeased the Tsar, who ordered his secret police to discover their authorship. This was falsefy attributed, perhaps with malicious intent, [9] to Mlle. Glinka, and on her return to Russia she was banished to her estate in Orel. To the *maréchal de noblesse* of this district, Alexis Sukhotin, Mlle. Glinka gave a copy of the Protocols. Sukhotin showed the docu-

---

4. At that time Secretary to the Minister of the Interior, General Cherevin.

5. Alias Schapiro, whose father had been sentenced in London, two years previous, to ten years penal servitude for counterfeiting.

6. Schorst fled to Egypt where, according to French police archives, he was murdered.

7. On his death in 1896, he willed a copy of his memoirs containing the Protocols to Nicholas II.

8. Published under the pseudonym "Count Vassilii", their real author was Mme. Juliette Adam, using material furnished by Princess Demidov-San Donato, Princess Radzivill, and other Russians.

9. Among the Jews in the Russian secret service in Paris was Maniulov, whose odious character is drawn by M. Paléologue, Mémoires.

ment to two friends, Stepanov and Nilus; the former had it printed and circulated privately in 1897; the second, Professor Sergius A. Nilus, published it for the first time in Tsarskoe-Tselo (Russia) in 1901, in a book entitled *The Great Within the Small.* Then, about the same time, a friend of Nilus, G. Butmi, also brought it out and a copy was deposited in the British Museum on August 10, 1906.

Meantime, through Jewish members [10] of the Russian police, minutes of the proceedings of the Basle congress [11] in 1897 had been obtained and these were found to correspond with the Protocols. [12]

In January 1917, Nilus had prepared a second edition, revised and documented, for publication. But before it could be put on the market, the revolution of March 1917 had taken place and Kerenski, who had succeded to power, ordered the whole edition of Nilus's book to be destroyed, In 1924, Prof. Nilus was arrested by the Cheka in Kiev, imprisoned, and tortured; he was told by the Jewish president of the court, that this treatment was meted out to him for "having done them incalculable harm in publishing the Protocols". Released for a few months, he was again led before the G. P. U. (Cheka), this time in Moscow and confined. Set at liberty in February 1926, he died in exile in the district of Vladimir on January 13, 1929.

A few copies of Nilus's second edition were saved and sent to other countries where they were published: in

---

10. Notably Eno Azev and Efrom. The latter, formerly a rabbi, died in 1925 in a monastery in Serbia, where he had taken refuge; he used to tell the monks that the protocols were but a small part of Jewish plans for ruling the world and a feeble expression of their hatred of the gentiles.

11. **Supra,** Part I, 34.

12. The Russian government had learned that at meetings of the B'nai Brith in New York in 1893-94, Jacob Schiff (**supra,** 63, 65) had been named chairman of the committee on the revolutionary movement in Russia.

Germany, by Gottfried zum Beek (1919); in England, by *The Briton* (1920; in France, by Mgr. Jouin in *La Revue Internationale des Sociétés Secrètes,* and by Urbain Gohier in *La Vieille France;* in the United States, by Small, Maynard & Co. (Boston 1920), and by The Beckwith Co. (New York 1921). Later, editions appeared in Italian, Russian, Arabic, and even in Japanese.

Such is the simple story of how these Protocols reached Russia and thence came into general circulation.

Mr. Stephanov's deposition [13] relative to it is here given as corroboration.

"In 1895, my neighbor in the district of Toula, Major (retired) Alexis Sukhotin, gave me a manuscript copy of the *Protocols of the Wise Men of Zion.* He told me that a lady of his acquaintance, whose name he did not mention, residing in Paris, had found it at the house of a friend, a Jew. Before leaving Paris, she had secretly translated it and had brought this one copy to Russia and given it to Sukhotin.

At first I mimeographed this translation, but finding it difficult to read, I resolved to have it printed, making no mention of the date, town, or printer's name. In this I was helped by Arcadii Ippolitovich Kelepovskii, who at that time was chief of the household of Grand Duke Sergius. He gave the document to be printed by the district printing press. This took place in 1897. Sergius Nilus inserted these Protocols in his work and added his own commentary.

(Signed) *Philip Petrovich Stepanov.*"

Formerly Procurator of the Synod of Moscow, Chamberlain, Privy Councillor, and (in 1897) Chief of the Moscow Kurk Railway in the town of Orel. April 17, 1927.

Witnessed by *Prince Dimitri Galitzin.*

President of the Russian Colony of Emigrants at Stari Fontag.

---

13. The translation is the author's; a photostat of the original is appended.

CHAPTER II

HOW AN AMERICAN EDITION WAS SUPPRESSED

There is a saying in several languages that only the truth hurts. Recognizing the fact beneath this expression, one is little surprised at the zeal which certain parties seek to disprove documentary evidence. If the evidence were false, then it would be ignored by those concerned and pass quickly into the realm of forgotten things. *But if the evidence is genuine and open to verification from many angles, then the truth will hurt and thus not be ignored.*

If this reasoning is correct, the violent methods used by the Jews, particularly those affiliated with the Zionist movement, to discredit and suppress the document entitled The Protocols of the Elders of Zion, would alone constitute a proof of its authenticity.

Nilus and Butmi had published the document without comment. Its success was therefore entirely due to:

1. The self-evident character of the document;
2. The logical reasoning expressed in clear, simple terms;
3. The explanation it gives of international politics;
4. The fact that the events predicted in it have actually occurred since.

But if its publishers gave no guarantee of its genuineness, those who have attacked it have failed even more conspicuously to discredit and refute it. To quote a contemporary writer: [1]

"The fact remains that the Protocols have never been refuted, and the futility of the so-called refutations which have appeared, as well as its temporary suppression, have done more to convince the public of its authenticity than the writings of all the anti-Semites put together".

There is plenty of indisputable, documentary evidence which explains the Jewish plan of action, without recourse of the Protocols. Their importance lies in the fact that, published at a definite date, they foretold historical events which have upset the world, that they explained these events by the principles set forth in the work itself: this fact makes it superfluous to enquire whether the author of the Protocols is the Zionist Congress *in corpore,* a member of the congress, or some Jewish (or even Christian) thinker. Their source is of small moment: the facts, the relation of cause and effect, are there; the existence of the work prior to the events foretold in it can never be brought into question, and that is enough.

The first attempt at refutation appeared in 1920, entitled, *The Jewish Bogey and the Forged Protocols of the Learned Elders of Zion,* by a Jew, Lucien Wolf; it was followed by articles in the *Metropolitan* (New York) signed "William Hard". The effect of these articles, contrary to the intention of their authors, was to draw wider public attention to the existence of the Protocols. At the same time in America the Jewish Anti-Defamation League [2] filled the papers with denunciations of the libel from all parts of the country, thus proving how powerful is Jewish organization. One of its members was Louis Marshall, and, as an illustration of its acti-

1. Cf. the works of Jouin, Lambelin and N. H. Webster.

2. This league compelled the Beckwith Co., which subsequently published the Protocols after Putnam's withdrawal, to insert in every copy sold a copy of the Jewish Anti-Defamation League's refutation.

vity, the story of the suppression of the edition of the Protocols which an American publishing house had tried to bring out, is instructive. It shows not only the pressure the Jews can bring to bear on anyone who dares to lift his finger against them, but their own mental attitude of *absolute intolerance* towards others, while demanding of the world complete acquiescence in their schemes.

George Haven Putnam, head of the firm Putnam & Son, New York, after his annual visit to London, brought out in 1920 an American edition of *The Cause of World Unrest.* [3] About the same time, he decided to issue *The Protocols of the Elders of Zion* in book form. Advance notices were released and the book set up and ready to go on the stands about October 15. On the eve of its appearance, Putnam received the following letter from Louis Marshall. [4]

MY DEAR SIR:

As one who believes in those qualities that constitute the true American spirit, I have been greatly disturbed by the accounts given by the newspapers of the outrage to which you were subjected at the meeting held at Erasmus High School in Brooklyn the other evening. Knowing your patriotism, I can only regard the alleged cause, namely, that you had condemned the declaration of independence and were of the opinion that we owed an apology to England for severing our relations with her, as a slander, born of prejudice and ignorance.

I had scarcely finished reading this episode which had thus aroused my indignation, when I found upon my

3. The reproduction in book form of a series of articles which had appeared in the **Morning Post** of London.
4. See ante, ch. V.

table a book, bearing the imprint of your firm, entitled *The Cause of World Unrest,* bound in a flaming red and purporting to be a republication of articles that have recently appeared in the London *Morning Post* with which I had become familiar. To say that I was shocked that your honoured name should be made the vehicle of disseminating among the American people these outpourings of malice, intolerance and hatred, this witches' broth of virulent poison, is merely to confess the poverty of my vocubulary. On opening the book I turned to the publishers' note, which was apologetic and disclaimed responsibility for the publication. It was following by an introduction which made it absolutely clear that the purpose of the book was to charge the Jews with an age-long conspiracy to destroy civilization in order that they might absorb the wealth and power of the world. Thus proclaimed, at length came the stupid drivel intended to support this thesis and calculated to make the Jew repulsive in the eyes of his fellow-men and to exterminate him, not figuratively, but literally, appealing, as it does, to the lowest passions and proceeding upon the same processes that were employed in the Middle Ages for the same object. Then it was the blood accusation, the charge of poisoning wells, of spreading plagues and pestilence, of the desecration of the Host. Now it is pretended conspiracy to overturn the economic system of the world by inciting warfare and revolution.

The slightest knowledge of history, the most elementary capacity for analysis, or even a minute inkling as to what the Jew is and has been, would suffice to stamp this book and the forged *Protocols* on which it is based, as the most stupendous libels in history. These writings are the work of a band of conspirators who are seeking to continue to make the Jew, as he has been in all the centuries, the scapegoat of autocracy. The Protocols bear the hall-mark of the secret agents of the dethroned Russian bureaucracy, and the book which you have published

города и типографiи; сдѣлать это взялся Аркадiй Ипполитовичъ Келепковскiй, состоявшiй тогда чиновникомъ особыхъ порученiй при В.К. Сергiи Александровичѣ; онъ далъ ихъ напечатать въ Губернской Типографiи; это было въ 1897 году. С. А. Нилусъ перепечаталъ эти протоколы полностью въ своемъ сочиненiи со своими комментарiями.

Филиппъ Петровичъ Степановъ, бывшiй прокуроръ Московской Синодальной Конторы, камергеръ, дѣйств. статскiй совѣтникъ, а во время этого изданiя — начальникъ участка службы пути (въ г. Орелъ) Московско-Курской жел. дор.

Подпись руки члена колонiи русских беженцев Степанова Филиппа Петровича (Кор. С.Х.С.) удостоверяю. Старые Футог 17 Априля 1927 года

Председатель Правления Колонии Князь Владимир Голицын

Въ 1895 году мой сосѣдъ по имѣні[ю]
Тульской губ. отставной маіоръ Але
Николаевичъ Сухотинъ передалъ мнѣ
рукописный экземпляръ „Протоко[ловъ]
Сіонскихъ Мудрецовъ." Онъ мнѣ сказ[алъ]
что одна его знакомая дама (не на
мнѣ ее), проживавшая въ Парижѣ,
ихъ у своего пріятеля (кажется изъ
и, передъ тѣмъ, какъ покинуть
Парижъ, тайно отъ него перевела и
и привезла этотъ переводъ, въ одно[мъ]
экземплярѣ, въ Россію и передала э
экземпляръ ему — Сухотину.
Я сначала отпечаталъ его въ ста
экземплярахъ на гектографѣ, н
это изданіе оказалось трудно чи
и я рѣшилъ напечатать его въ к
нибудь типографіи, безъ указанія вре

is a mere babbling reiteration of what the murderers of the Ukraine, of Poland, and of Hungary are urging as justification for the holocausts of the Jews in which they have been engaged. It has been intimated, and there is much to sustain the theory, that the real purpose of these publications in the United States and in England is to arouse sufficient hostility against the Jew to subject them to mob violence and thus to give justification to those who have incited pogroms in Eastern Europe.

I have also observed that, upon the cover of the book to which I am now referring, you are advertising the publication of *The Protocols,* which I unhesitatingly denounce as on their face palpable forgeries. If you were called upon to circulate counterfeit money or forged bonds, you would shrink in horror at the suggestion. What you have done and what you propose to do is, however, in morals, incalculably worse. You are assisting in spreading falsehoods, in uttering libels, the effect of which will be felt for decades to come. You are giving them respectability, whilst the name of the author is shrouded in secrecy. Even Mr. Gwynne does not avow paternity for the book which he has heralded. Much as you may desire to shake off responsibility, therefore, the real responsibility for hurling this bomb, for such it is, prepared though it has been by others, rests upon you. Whoever may read this book and is of such a low type of intelligence as to be influenced by it, will not be apt to draw the fine ethical distinctions with which you are seeking to salve your conscience. As a patriotic American, do you believe that you are contributing to the creation of that spirit of justice and fair-play, of unity and harmony, which is the very foundation of that Americanism for which every good citizen has yearned, when you stimulate hatred and passion by the publication of these dreadful falsehoods? If there should occur in this country, in consequence of those publications and those of Henry Ford, what is earnestly desired by the anti-

Semites with whom you have arrayed yourself, do you suppose that, when the Almighty calls you to a reckoning and asks you whether you have ever borne false witness against your neighbour, you will be guiltless in His eyes because of your publishers' note disavowing responsibility?

I know that you must have been pained, as I was when I read of the treatment to which you were subjected, because of lying accusations directed against you. Are you able to appreciate the pain, the grief, the agony, that you are causing to three millions of your fellow-countrymen and millions of men, women and children in other parts of the world by your participation in the disgraceful and inhuman persecution which is now being insidiously carried on by means of publications in the distribution of which you are now actively engaged? I look upon this as a tragedy.

Louis Marshall.

Major Putnam, still feeling and sincerely believing that he was an independent American, though not a very brave one, for throughout he uses the name of Mr. Gwynne as a screen, answered:

New York, October 15th, 1920.

DEAR MR. MARSHALL:

Your letter of the 13th inst., which has to do with the publication of the volume entitled *World Unrest* and the announcement of the companion volume *The Protocols,* has been read before the members of our publishing board and has received the respectful consideration to which any communication from a citizen of your standing and reputation is assuredly entitled. I am asked by my associates to make report as follows as to our own understanding of the matters in question:

1. We are not prepared to accept your view of the responsibility that attaches to a publishing imprint, or to the association of such imprint with one volume or another. We believe that our own policy in this matter is in accord with that of the leading publishing houses on both sides of the Atlantic. It would be impossible to carry on the business of publishing books of opinion, whether the opinions have to do with the issues of today or with matters of the past, if the publisher was assumed to be in accord with the conclusions arrived at by one author or another. It is the intention to bring into print only such volumes as may present on such issues information that is understood to make an addition to the knowledge of the subject, or conclusions which appear to be entitled to consideration, to analysis, or possibly to refutation.

2. We have on our own catalogue, for instance, volumes expressing almost every phase of theological or religious belief. The list includes some books accepted by the Christian Scientists as fairly representative of their doctrines. In publishing such books we have, of course, no intention of announcing ourselves as upholding the theories of the Christian Scientists any more than in the publication of a volume by a Presbyterian divine we have expressed our acceptance of the Westminster catechism, or in printing a book by an Episcopal friend, we have been prepared to approve the reasonableness of the thirty-nine articles.

3. The volume, *World Unrest,* was, as you will have noted, brought into publication in London at the instance of Mr. Gwynne, the scholarly editor of the *Morning Post.* Your doubtless have knowledge of the journals of England and will realize that the *Post* does not belong to the sensation-monger journals like Bottomley's

John Bull or Hearst's *American*. It is a conservative paper which has the reputation of avoiding sensational material.

Mr. Gwynne had convinced himself that the papers brought into print in the *Post*, and later published under his direction in book form, were deserving of consideration. As we have stated in the publisher's-note, we are not prepared to express any opinion whatsoever in regard to the value of the so-called information presented, or as to the weight of the conclusions arrived at by the writer and endorsed by Mr. Gwynne. The recommendation came to us that, as the Gwynne volume used as a large part of its text the document entitled *The Protocols*, the readers of *World Unrest* would be interested in having an opportunity of examing the full text of *The Protocols*. You have already knowledge of this curious document. It has, it seems, been in print since 1905, and possibly earlier. An edition was published some months back by Eyre & Spottiswoode, conservative law publishers of London. The text that was brought to us in a translation freshly made from the Russian and is accompanied by a record of what is known of the original document. [5]

It is evident that the document has, as you point out, no voucher for authenticity and it is quite possible that it will be found to possess no historic importance. Attention has again been directed to it during the past year simply on the ground, according at least to the understanding of Mr. Gwynne's author and of himself, that certain of the instructions given and policies recommended in *The Protocols* appear to have been carried out by the bolshevik government in Russia. Certain suggestions in *The Protocols* have also been connected with the policies of the Zioists, policies which, according to Mr. Gwynne

---

5. This edition prepared by G. H. Putnam was subsequently published by The Beckwith Company, 299 Madison Avenue, New York.

and some other writers, are causing serious unrest in Palestine, Syria and Arabia.

In presenting *The Protocols* to American readers in a carefully printed edition, we have not the least intention of expressing the view that the documents are authentic, or that they will in the end be considered as possessing historic authority.

Mr. Gwynne takes the ground that neither *World Unrest* or *The Protocols* themselves present charges against the Jews as a whole. They emphasize certain things that have been done, or are alleged to have been done, by certain groups of Jews. It would be as fair to say a record of lynching in Texas or Arkansas, or a record of the attempt of the Bryan group to secure the payment of debts fifty cents on the dollar, was to be considered as a charge against the whole American people.

Mr. Gwynne's associates take the ground that the leading Jews on both sides of the Atlantic, men whose patriotism is unquestioned, ought not to put these documents to one side as of trifling importance. The time may very properly have come at which the charges made as said, only against certain groups of Jews should be analyzed by the Jews whose judgments would be accepted as authoritative by English and American readers. If the charge is unfounded that bolshevism as carried on in Russia has been conducted largely under Jewish direction, the statement ought to be refuted.

I received only yesterday a copy of a monthly entitled *The Brooklyn Anti-Bolshevist*. The magazine undertakes to make "defense of American institutions against the Jewish bolshevist doctrines of Morriss Hillquit and Leon Trotzky." It seems to me that American citizens of the Jewish race (and the group comprises some of the best citizens that we have) might properly interest themselves in making clear to the public that there is no foundation for any charge against the *World Patriotism of the Jewish* race. [6]

I wish very much that you might yourself be interested in preparing a volume that should give consideration to the whole subject matter and particularly, of course, to these publications which have come into print as a result of the world's indignation against the Moscow government.

G. P. Putnam's Sons would be well pleased to associate the imprint of their New York and London Houses with such a volume from the pen of a distinguished jurist like yourself.

One further thought occurs to me: You and I are believers in freedom of speech. We recognize that in war times certain reservations are in order for the sake of the nation, but we hold that, with the necessary reservations as to the rights of an individual, or as to a possible libel upon an individual, it is in order, and, from the point of view of the community, wise, to allow full freedom for platform utterances. If, however, this be true for the spoken word it should logically be applicable also to the word, that comes into print.

In case you may be interested in considering the suggestion of a monograph from your pen to be prepared by yourself, or by some competent authority whom you might be able to interest, I should be ready to keep an appointment for a personal word at such time and place as you might find convenient.

Submitting the suggestion for your consideration, I am, with cordial regards,

Yours faithfully,

George Haven Putnam.

The suggestion of the 'monograph' from Louis Marshall' pen was somewhat ironical. There is no doubt

6. Our italics.

that on October 15, 1920, Major Putnam still felt himself an independant American.

And the binding of *The Protocols* went on as usual.

But on October 29th came one more letter from the president of the American Jewish committee:

New York City, October 29th, 1920.

MY DEAR SIR:

Absence from the city and professional engagements have prevented me from replying earlier to yours of the 15th inst., in which you define your policy regarding the publication of *The Cause of the World Unrest* and your announcement of your intended publication of *The Protocols.*

I cannot accept the theories on which you seek to justify acts which, in all modernation, I sought to characterize in my letter of the 13th inst. You disregard entirely the proposition on which my criticism is based. Nobody can go farther than I do in upholding the freedom of the press and freedom of speech. It has been my privilege to aid in the creation of important precedents in furtherance of these fundamental of liberty. Libel and slander, however, have always been looked upon in American law as abuses of a free press and of free speech and as attacks upon the integrity of the constitutional guarantees that you invoke. Nor do I question the right of any publisher to issue "books of opinion" to whatever subject the opinions may relate. They may be polemical or they may attack the soundness of scientific, political or theological theories or doctrines. No fair-minded man would for a moment venture to find fault because of strictures directed against his cherished doxy.

The Protocols and *The Cause of World Unrest* are not, however, books of opinion. They assume to deal with facts. *The Protocols* purport to be the pronouncements of so-called "Wise Men of Zion". *The Cause of World Unrest* undertakes to charge that the Jews and the Freemasons are together engaged in a conspiracy for the overthrow of civilization and the arrogation by them of world domination. It is these alleged facts that I denounce as falsehoods and as libels criminal in intent and criminal in their operation. *The Protocols,* which are made the basis of the *Cause of World Unrest* and which you properly describe as companion volumes, are so intrinsically false that even Mr. Gwynne concedes that he himself has a serious doubt as to their genuineness. That *The Protocols* are a fabrication similar to those that have appeared in every period of history, appears from every line of that document. I am credibly informed that the manuscript was offered for publication to seven different publishing houses in this country, who refused to have their names connected with it, before Small, Maynard & Co., undertook to issue it to the American public. The author of the *Cause of World Unrest* hides behind anonymity. You yourself speak of the author as being "Mr. Gwynne's author." Apparently even you do not know the pedigree of this incendiary book. Yet you have, I repeat, given it your endorsement by publishing it, even though you disavow responsibility. Your position is that of one who endorses a note to give it currency and at the same time makes a mental reservation against meeting his obligation.

No, Major Putnam, the principle which you seek to establish will not work. Whoever touches pitch is defiled. Whoever retails falsehoods and spreads them, whether it be orally or through the medium of the press, is responsible for those falsehoods. It will not do to say that you have many friends among the Jews whom you respect and that these books are not intended to reflect upon all Jews. The world is not so discriminating. People whose passions are aroused do not differentiate. The forger of *The Protocols* and the mysterious author of *The Cause of World Unrest* make no distinctions. Neither did their prototypes of the middle ages nor the black hundred of modern Russia indulge in such refinements. Troy and Tyre were alike to them.

Do not for a moment misunderstand me, I contend that there are no Jews who are now engaged or who have ever been engaged in a conspiracy such as that charged by you as existing in these books which emerge smoking from your presses. The cry of Bolshevism will not suffice. Your reference to the *Brooklyn Anti-Bolshevist* shows what a sad pass you have reached. To shelter yourself behind the bulwarks of an infamous pasquinade of the guttersnipe variety and to insinuate that because that sheet pretends to defend American institutions "against the Jewish bolshevist doctrines of Morris Hillquit and Leon Trotzky" you may therefore descend to the same depths, is a revelation to me. I had not believed that any real, true American would thus lend himself to the creation of ill-will and malevolence. The fact that out of the mass of Russian Jews there is an infinitesimal percentage who are Bolshevists, affords no justification for laying the sins of Bolshevism at the door of the Jewish people. To say that Bolshevism is a Jewish movement is as ridiculous as to say that the Jews are responsible for capitalism, or because there are Jewish musicians, actors and poets, that music, the drama and poetry are Jewish movements.

I am not a Zionist, and yet I regard the slurs that these books are attempting to make against Zionism to be unworthy. The very Zionists whom these books are attacking have been persecuted by the bolsheviks and have been denounced as counter revolutionists, just as the mass of the Jews of Russia have been pursued as members of the bourgeoisie. I am not a member of the Masonic or of any other secret order, but the attempt in these books to charge Freemasonry with participation in such a conspiracy as is proclaimed almost argues the existence of a pathological condition on the part of the author that betokens mental aberration. When one remembers that fifteen of the presidents of the United States, including George Washington, have been Freemasons, it is unnecessary to go further in condemnation of these volumes which you are pleased to denominate "books of opinion".

I had not believed that a Jew in this country would ever be called upon to occupy the humiliating position of defending his people against the charges such as those which are being spread broadcast through your agency. If ever the time comes when it shall be desirable to answer such books, I am quite sure that it will be unnecessary for me to avail myself of your firm as publishers.

Very truly yours,

Louis Marshall.

Two days later, Putnam bowed before the will of Jewry in the following terms:

November 1st, 1920.

DEAR MR. MARSHALL:

Mr. Gwynne, at whose instance we brought into print the American edition of his volume on *World Unrest,* had taken the ground that the publication of the document known as *The Protocols* might throw light on the organization of the Bolshevists. Their operations have caused grave concern throughout the world and they are, therefore, a matter of legitimate public discussion.

It was his opinion that if it had not been for the apprehension aroused by bolshevism, the document would probably have been permitted to rest in obscurity.

An edition of *The Protocols* was, therefore, published

in London by Eyre & Spottiswoode, law publishers of high standing.

It had seemed to us that the readers of "The World Unrest" were entitled to have the opportunity of examining the complete document (to which frequent references are made in Mr. Gwynne's volume) and we had, therefore, undertaken the publication of a carefully prepared translation by us, which is now nearly in readiness, and has involved a considerable outlay.

We now find, however, that an edition printed in Boston is being distributed as a regular publication. There is no necessity for bringing into print another volume containing substantially the same material. We have decided, therefore, *in deference to the objections raised by yourself, and by my valued friend, Oscar Strauss, not to proceed* [7] with the publication.

I am, Yours very truly

Geo. Haven Putnam.

What had taken place between October 29 and November 1? Putnam wrote to one of the parties interested that so much pressure was brought to bear on him that he had to give up publishing *The Protocols,* and would even be obliged to withdraw unsold copies of *World Unrest.* It is safe to conclude that Putnam's firm was threatened with bankruptcy if it persisted. We understand that Small Maynard & Co. of Boston and The Beckwith Co. of New York and in fact practically *every firm* which *has* published *The Protocols* had difficulties within a year or two. Of course it is said that is purely accidental: but it was just such an "accident" that Putnam wished to avoid!

---

7. Our italics.

CHAPTER III

MORE ATTEMPTS AT REFUTATION
THE LONDON TIMES LENDS A HAND

While the Jews have succeeded in having the Protocols suppressed, entirely in Russia, Poland, Rumania, and other countries in Eastern Europe, and partially in England and America, they have failed in their many ingenious efforts to have them refuted by non-Jews. Indeed the so-called refutations with which their henchmen flooded the press in 1920-21 reveal more of the real nature, workings, and associations of the Jews and their agents than they rebut the evidence of the Protocols.

It is noteworthy that *not one* of these numerous and contradictory refutations bears an *honest, non-Jewish signature.* There is the article of the notorious Princess Radzivill [1] published in the *Jewish Tribune* (New York) for March 11, 1921, and followed by a statement by her

---

1. Princess Catherine Radzivill was convicted of forgery in London on April 30, 1902, the amount involved being £3,000, and was sentenced to two years in prison (London **Times**, April 16, 29, and May 1, 1902). On October 13, 1921, suit was filed against her by the Hotel Embassy, New-York, for failure to pay her bill of $1,239, and on October 30 she was arrested on the instance of the Hotel Shelbourne, New York, on a charge of defrauding the hotel of $352. (**New York World**, Oct. 14 and 31, 1921). Later, she went to live with her friend Mrs. Hurlbut at 506 West 124th Street, New York.

friend, Mrs. Hurlbut. The former [2] makes no mention of Mlle. Glinka and describes the forgery of the protocols by "Golovinskii and a renegade Jew, Manassevich Manuilov, in Paris in 1904". Further on, oblivious of chronology, she states that General Cherevin willed her his memoirs, including the protocols, at the time of his death in 1896. Golovinskii and Manuilov might, it would seem, have saved themselves trouble by procuring a copy of the document, which, according to Mr. Stephanov's testimony, [3] had been printed and privately circulated in 1897.

Another person who wrote against the protocols, A. du Chayla, can hardly be taken more seriously. An article of his appeared on May 14, 1921, in the *Tribune Juive* of Paris; and later, another article on June 13 in the *New York Call,* a violent Communist sheet, besides articles in Soviet publications. Prof. Nilus mentions in one of his books [4] meeting this Frenchman, who then paraded as a devotee of the Russian Orthodox Church. The character of this adventurer is well drawn in the reply his articles drew from a Russian lady, Madame Fermor, which is given in full.

"Lately there appeared in the Russian paper *Poslednii Novosti,* Nos. 331-332 a series of articles by Count Alexander du Chayla, in which he casts doubt on the authenticity of a certain document (*The Protocols of the Elders of Zion*), because obtained by a man who did not inspire confidence.

If the value of a document be based on the credit of the person by whom it its produced, one must also analyze the character of him who discredits it.

---

2. She was one of the Russian Liberals in Paris in 1884 who furnished Mme. Juliette Adam with details of Russin court life. She has since claimed the authorship of the books by "Count Vassilii", really written by Mme. Adam.

3. **Supra,** pp. 99, 100.

4. Entitled **On the Bank of the River of God.**

That is why I am prompted to narrate how I became acqainted with Count du Chayla.

I usually spent the summer on my estate in White Russia, in a village near Moguileff, where there is a famous convent. There, one day, about ten years ago, I was visited by the Superior, the Archimandrite Arsene, who introduced a young man, Count du Chayla. Du Chayla had been sent to the convent to study the Russian language and the Orthodox religion of which he pretended to be a devotee.

Mr. Sabler [5] had invited him to come to Russia and sent him to the celebrated monastery of Optina Poustine, whence he was sent to our monastery to serve as an example of anti-Catholic propaganda.

It must be admitted that he lived up to his character and showed himself more of a Russian Orthodox than the Patriarch himself. Thanks to his zeal, beautifully sculptured angels in the Renaissance style were removed from the chapel of our monastery: du Chayla found them too Catholic. He told me the great joy he felt when he smashed these angels with a hammer. When I reproached him with an act of vandalism, his intolerance betrayed itself in the hatred which he then manifested against the Jews. Many a time I heard him say: "One must have a good pogrom in Russia." One can understand my astonishment when I read in his articles a false accusation of propaganda for pogroms against the White Army, which he now blames, he, who so loudly proclaimed that pogroms were a necessity! It is from him that I heard of the existence of Drumont's books, which he praised eloquently; he used to advise me to read them that I might

---

5. Sabler was Procurator of the Holy Synod at St. Petersburg: he supported Rasputin and other pseudo-mystics and had a disastrous influence on the Russian Church, (Cf. Paléologue, Mémoires, 1927).

understand to what extent the Jews had conquered France. He used to predict that the same fate would overtake Russia, if ever the Jews were granted full civil rights.

Great was my surprise when I read du Chayla's attack on Drumont, whose books he now calls lies. He, who had so much admired Drumont.

As I followed du Chayla's life in Russia, I was amazed to see the extraordinary rapidity of his political and ecclesiastical career. He became an intimate friend of the Bishops known for their Orthodoxy, and he preached the sacred and absolute power of the Russian Monarch and implacable hatred towards all foreigners. We saw du Chayla as an intimate friend of the Bishops Anthony of Volinia and Evlogii of Holm, frequent the famous salon of Countess Ignatieff. As he rose in Russian society, his activities shifted from the religious field: he took up politics, and, as a follower of Count Bobrinsky, leader of the Pan-Slavic Party, he was sent to Austria on a secret mission among the Galicians. He was subsequently arrested for espionage.

After his return to Russia, he directed a violent campaign against the smaller racial groups of the empire, especially against the Poles and Finns. As du Chayla was always in need of money, I recommended him to the president of the commission for the affairs of Finland, Mr. Korevo, who used him for anti-Finish propaganda in the foreign press. At the time of the declaration of war, du Chayla was a student in the theological academy of Petrograd; he was appointed chief of a field hospital organized by Bishop Pitirim and provided with funds from Rasputin. Then I lost sight of him until after the revolution, when I heard of him as an *agent provocateur*, inciting the Cossacks against the White Army. In 1919 du Chayla was tried by court martial and convicted of seditious activities in the pay of the Soviets. The sentence was published in the newspapers of the Crimea.

I was astonished to find his name appended to an

article in a Russian newspaper notorious for its equivocal position concerning the reconstruction of Russia.

(Signed) *Tatiana Fermor.*"

June 9th, 1921 — Paris.

Not satisfied — and rightly so — with these efforts to discredit the Protocols, and yet unable to attach the signature of a noted gentile writer to their denials, the Jews sought another expedient: the seal of approval of one of the best known newspapers would impress the general public. Heretofore the articles had borne the name of private persons: now an official exposure of the protocols was to be published over the signature of the "Correspondent of the London *Times* in Constantinople". The identity of the "correspondent" was not revealed [6], although the most elementary sense of justice would insist on giving full credit to the gentleman who had made such a momentous discovery. Nor is there any evidence of his having been in Constantinople. Anyone who writes to the editor of a newspaper is a correspondent, and the number of lies which gain circulation in this fashion is notorious. The "sensational discovery" with *The Times* [7] thus gave to its readers was that the protocols were a "clumsy plagiarism" of a French book it calls "The Dialogues of Geneva", published in Brussels in 1865.

The "correspondent" tells in an easy, off-hand manner and perfect self-assurance, about meeting in Constantinople a Mr. W., who said: "Read this book through and you will find irrefutable proof that the *Protocols of the Learned Elders of Zion* is a plagiarism".

6. Philip Graves.

7. August 16, 17, 18, 1921: reprint entitled, **The Truth about The Protocols,** 24 pages, is sold at the exorbitant price of one shilling.

So it wasn't the correspondent who deserved the credit for the "sensational discovery" after all; but a "Mr. X, a Russian landowner with English connections": Again, it is a pity that the gentleman should not have given his name and received the large reward which would surely be his, from those who have been so active in suppressing and refuting the Protocols.

Then follows the story of Mr. X, with his views on religion, politics, secret societies, and the rest: this Mr. X. is an old-fashioned gentleman and the reader is ready to believe every word, as reported by "our correspondent". Mr. X. explains how he obtained the copy of the *Geneva Dialogues* from an old Okhrana officer; this establishes the fact that the Russian police had made use of the book to forge the Protocols. In fact the "correspondent" goes on to identify this very copy of the *Geneva Dialogues* as belonging to A. Sukhotin — there is an "A. S." scratched in the back which is conclusive — and from which the protocols were plagiarized and given to Nilus. Parallel passages from the *Dialogues* and the protocols are set opposite each other; and the English reader, never at home in Continental politics, is led into speculations on Napoleon III's relations with the Carbonari, his employment of Corsicans in the police, the employment of Corsicans by the Russian police, the knowledge Corsicans had of the existence of the *Geneva Dialogues*, Joly's purpose in writing them, the influence of Philippe, a Lyons mystic, on the Tsar, and so on, until the reader is completely overwhelmed. When he has reached this state, he is told: "At any rate, the fact of the plagiarism has now been conclusively established, and the legend (of the Protocols) may be allowed to pass into oblivion."

The publication of this news from Constantinople was hailed by all the Jews, whose instant enthusiasm is no less revealing than the following letter from a leading Zionist, which appeared in *The Times* on the same day as the "discovery".

"Editor, *London Times.*

Sir,

Your Constantinople correspondent, who has done a world service in tracking to their source the *Protocols* (for they have been carefully published throughout the world), says: "There is no evidence to show how the *Geneva Dialogues* reached Russia." In your leading article, however, you suggest that the protocols were forged under the auspices of Rachkovski, head of the Russian secret police in Paris. This appears to be the truth. M. A. du Chayla, a French student of theology at St. Petersburg in 1910, who was in 1918 on the staff of the army of the Cossacks of the Don, has testified through the *Tribune Juive* (Paris, May 14, 1921) that Nilus told him that the protocols were sent him from Paris by his friend, Mme. K—, who had received them from General Rachkovskii. M. du Chayla confirms a suggestion of yours, that the courier who brought the ms. from Paris was Alexander Sukhotin. He has seen this very ms., which, being in poor French and varying penmanship, suggests a complex authorship in the Russian police bureau. The fact that the *Geneva Dialogues* have now been bought from an ex-member of it, completes the chain.

That the object of the publicaton of 1905 was to drown the Russian revolution in Jewish blood, I, like you, have asserted. But it appears that there was a previous edition in 1902 in the shape of an appendix to a reprint of a pietistic work by Nilus, and the motive behind this earlier publication throws another curious sidelight upon the old Russian court. For that publication was apparently a move in the game to discredit in favor of Nilus a Lyons mystic, Philippe, of whose power over the Tsar the Grand Duchess Elizabeth disapproved. Knowing that Nilus was designed as Philpe's supplanter, Rachkovskii, it is thought, wished to secure his good graces by providing him with a valuable weapon against Russian liberalism.

I am sorry that your correspondent should conclude with the suggestion that those parts of the protocols not in the *Geneva Dialogues* may possibly have been supplied by Jews who spied on their co-religionists; for this far-fetched hypothesis gives a gleam of hope to the considerable number of organs throughout Europe that live only in the Protocols. Now is your correspondent accurate in thinking that only moral harm has been done by this historic forgery? M. du Chayla offers evidence that it has helped to goad on those countless pogroms in the Ukraine, of whose horrors Western Europe is almost ignorant. As for Nilus, he appears to be a fanatical mystagogue, honest enough except for that theological twist which betrayed itself when, confronted by the suspicion that the Protocols were forged, he replied: "Even if they were, God who could speak through Balaam's ass, could also put the truth in a liar's mouth."

Yours gratefully,

Israel Zangwill".

Far End, East Preston, Sussex, August 18, 1921.

Since then, to some extent, the Protocols have been forgotten. But, *Audeatur et altera pars,* in the words of Max Nordau. [8]*The Times* "correspondent" would convince us that there are similar or identical passages to be found in the Protocols and in the *Dialogues;* and this we readily admit. We go farther: identical passages will be found in earlier Protocols [9] which go back to the days before the dispersion.

By way of illustration, let it be assumed that the Book of Common Prayer used in the Anglican Church were unknown to the Jews. Suppose, then, that a copy of it were secretly obtained by a certain Jew and published,

8. **Supra,** p. 45 (note 25).
9. **Supra,** p. 95.

and that the Jews were shocked by the Anglican doctrine of which they learned in this way for the first time. It would then be easy for another Jew to show that the Book of Common Prayer was a plagiarism: it contains passages copied, word for word, from the Gospels; the Psalms are a transcript from King James' Bible; and so on. And not only that, but there are many parallels to be found in the secular literature. "At any rate", one can imagine the second Jew saying at the end, "the fact of plagiarism has been conclusively established, and we may therefore affirm that no such Book of Common Prayer is used in the worship of the Church of England."

The second Jew would be right in pointing out the parallels in the earlier literature — though his conclusion would be ridiculous — for there is a very real connection: and so it is with the Protocols.

One might have thought that *The Times,* in its desire to publish the truth about the Protocols, would at least have given the correct title of the *Geneva Dialogues,* it is, *Dialogues aux Enfers entre Machiavelli et Montesquieu,* published anonymously in Brussels in 1865. Moreover a minute's search in a library catalogue shows that another book, bearing a similar title, was published some years earlier: namely, *Machiavelli, Montesquieu & Rousseau,* by Jacob Venedey, published by Franz Dunnicker in Berlin in 1850. *The Times,* with its interest in plagiarisms, might have been tempted to glance at this latter volume as also at *The Prince* by Machiavelli and *L'Esprit des Lois* by Montesquieu. Had it done so, its curiosity would have been amply rewarded: passages quoted from the Protocols as plagiarized from the *Dialogues* of 1865, are similar to several [10] in Venedey's book of 1850, and

---

10. For example, the passage referring to Vishnu is found in **Machiavelli, Montesqieu ü Rousseau,** in the **Dialogues,** and in Protocol 12, **infra.**

both Jacob Venedey and Maurice Joly should be branded as plagiarists.

But the resemblance between the Protocols and Venedey's book does not stop with a few parallel passages: the spirit of both is the same; it is revolutionary, whereas the *Dialogues* of 1865 are socialistic and polemical. The anonymous author merely borrowed certain descriptive passages in Venedey to give colour to his argument. [11]

Now hadn't *The Times* better discover a copy of Venedey belonging to a former Okhrana officer, so as to explain how the Russian secret police were able to plagiarize the spirit, as well as a few platitudes and descriptive bits, when forging the Protocols? Its correspondent in Peiping might make that discovery some day? No, the Peiping correspondent (or any other) will be very careful *not* to make *that* discovery, for the simple reason that Venedey was a Jew, whereas *The Times*' point is that the Jews had nothing to do with the drafting of the Protocols. Its argument is that the author of the *Dialogues* was a Corsican; that the Corsicans in the Paris Police preserved the *Dialogues* and gave a copy to the Corsican members of the Russian police, who used it to forge the Protocols: these insidious Corsicans! [12] But what of Venedey?

Jacob Venedey, born in Cologne in May, 1805, was early engaged in revolutionary activities which caused his expulsion from Germany. He settled in Paris, where, in 1835, he edited a paper of subversive character, called *"Le Proscrit"*. Driven from Paris by the police, he moved

---

11. Space does not allow us here to trace the links between Jacob Venedy the **Alliance Israelite Universelle**, Adolphe Crémieux, Maurice Joly, and Jules Janin.

12. It is noteworthy that no Corsican has yet raised a voice of protest against the charges made in **The Times.** Yet it is the **Corsicans** who are the real victims of a libel, not the Jews.

to Havre, until, thanks to the representations of Arago and Mignet, friends of Crémieux, he was allowed to return to the capital. Meanwhile his book, *Romanisme, Christianisme et Germanisme,* won the praise of the French Academy. Venedey was a close friend and associate of Karl Marx. After spending the year 1843-44 in England, the headquarters of continental revolutionaries, he worked in Brussels for the founding, with Marx in 1847, of a secret organization, "The Communist League of Workers" (later the "Société internationale de la Démocratie").

After the February revolution in 1848, Venedey joined Marx in Germany, where he became one of the chiefs of revolutionary committee of Fifty (March, 1848), and was sent as commissar into the Oberland to stand against Hecker. Later elected as member of the Left from Hesse-Homburg, he continued to serve on the Committee of Fifty. It was at this time that he brought out in Berlin his *Machiavelli, Montesquieu & Rousseau,* stressing the views attributed to Machavelli and Rousseau in favor of despotism and oppression. [13]

When order was restored in Germany, Venedey was expelled from Berlin and Breslau. He was an active member of the FreeMasons and affiliated with the Carbonari: [14] he was also closely associated not only with revolutionaries of his day, but (as might be expected) with the leading Jews, the founders of the *Alliance Israelite Universelle.* [15] The latter included men of as different political parties as the reactionary-imperialist Fould, the liberal-conservatice Disraeli, and the communist-revolutionary Marx, and whether living under an empire, a constitutional monarchy, or a republic, all laboured towards a common aim, the establishment of an international Jewish

---

13. Another case of plagiarism at work!
14. Cf. **Die Bauhütte,** Feb. 1871, date of Venedey's death.
15. **Supra,** p. 27.

world power.[16] Prominent among them and in close touch with Venedey, was Adolphe Isaac Crémieux (1798-1880). A Nimes lawyer with an ardent admiration for Napoleon, he became legal adviser to the Bona-

---

16. In his novel **Coningsby** (London, 1844), Disraeli draws a picture from life of the Jews ruling the world from behind thrones as graphic as anything in the protocols of Nilus. (It is expected, that **The Times** will shortly be in a position to establish conclusively that **Coningsby** is a plagiarism of a Byzantine novel of the XVIIth century.) The passage in which Rothschild **(Sidonia)** describes this runs as follows:

"If I followed my own impulse, I would remain here," said Sidonia. "Can anything be more absurd than that a nation should apply to an individual to maintain its credit, its existence as an empire and its comfort as a people; and that individual one to whom its laws deny the proudest rights of citizenship, the privilege of sitting in its senate and of holding land; for though I have been rash enough to buy several estates, my own opinion is that by the existing law of England, an Englishman of Hebrew faith cannot posses the soil."

"But surely it would be easy to repeal a law so illiberal."

"Oh! as for illiberality, I have no objection to it if it be an element of power. Eschew political sentimentality. What I contend is that if you permit men to accumulate property, and they use that permission to a great extent, power is inseparable from that property, and it is in the last degree impolitic to make it in the interest of any powerful class to oppose the institutions under which they live. The Jews, for example, independent of the capital qualities for citizenship which they possess in their industry, temperance, and energy and vivacity of mind, are a race essentially monarchical, deeply religious, and shrinking themselves from converts as from a calamity, are ever anxious to see the religious systems of the countries in which they live, flourish; yet since your society has become agitated in England and powerful combinations menace your institutions, you find the once loyal Hebrew invariably arrayed in the same ranks as the leveller and the latitudinarian, and prepared to support rather than tamely continue under a system which seeks to degrade him. The Tories lose an important election at a critical moment; 'tis the Jews come forward to vote against them. The Church is alarmed at the scheme of a latitudinarian university, and learns with relief

parte family and an intimate of Louis Napoleon with whom he joined in overthrowing the government of Louis Philippe in 1849. A member of the Mizraim Lodge, the Scottish Rite (of which he became Supreme Master on the death of Viennet), he was familiar with all

---

that funds are not forthcoming for its establishment; a Jew immediately advances and endows it. Yet the Jews, Coningsby, are essentially Tories. Toryism indeed is but copied from the mighty prototype which has fashioned Europe. And every generation they must become more powerful and more dangerous to the society which is hostile to them. Do you think that the quiet humdrum persecution of a decorous representative of an English university can crush those who have successively baffled the Pharaons, Nebuchadnezzar, Rome, and the feudal ages, The fact is you cannot destroy a pure race of the Caucasian organization. It is a physiological fact; a simple law of nature, which has baffled Egyptian and Assyrian kings, Roman emperors, and Christian inquisitors. No penal laws, no physical tortures, can effect that a superior race should be absorbed in an inferior, or be destroyed by it. The mixed persecuting races disappear, the pure persecuted race remains. And at this moment, in spite of centuries, or tens of centuries, of degradation, the Jewish mind exercises a vast influence on the affairs of Europe. I speak not of their laws, which you still obey; of their literature, with which your minds are saturated; but of the living Hebrew intellect.

"You never observe a great intellectual movement in Europe in which the Jews do not greatly participate. The first Jesuits were Jews: that mysterious Russian diplomacy which so alarms Western Europe is organized and principally carried on by Jews; that mighty revolution (of 1848) which will be in fact a second and greater Reformation, and of which so little is as yet known in England, is entirely developing under the auspices of Jews, who almost monopolize the professorial chairs of Germany, NEANDAR, Founder of spiritual Christianity, and who is Regius Professor of Divinity in the University of Berlin, is a Jew. Benary, equally famous, and in the same university, is a Jew. Wehl, the Arabic Professor of Heidelberg, is a Jew. Years ago, when I was in Palestine, I met a German student who was accumulating materials for the history of Christianity and studying the genius of the place; a modest and learned man. It was Wehl; then unknown,

new movements; and his influence enabled him to render at least one important service to Jewry by having the Jewish murderers of Father Thomas in Damascus (1841) set at liberty. One of the leaders in the revolution of February 1848, he was appointed minister of justice

---

since become the first Arabic scholar of the day, and the author of the life of Mahomet. But for the German professors of this race, their name is legion. I think there are more than ten at Berlin alone.

"I told you just now that I was going up to town to-morrow, because I always made it a rule to interpose when affairs of state were on the carpet. Otherwise, I never interfere. I hear of peace and war in newspapers, but I am never alarmed, except when I am informed that the sovereigns want treasure; then I know that monarchs are serious.

"A few years back we were applied to by Russia. Now there has been no friendship between the Court of St. Petersburg and my family. It has Dutch connections which have generally supplied it; and our representations in favour of the Polish Hebrews, a numerous race, but the most suffering and degraded of all the tribes, has not been very agreeable to the Czar. However circumstances drew to an approximation between the Romanoffs and the Sidonias. I resolved to go myself to St. Petersburg. I had on my arrival an interview with the Russian Minister of Finance, Count Cancrin; I beheld the son of a Lithuanian Jew. The loan was connected with the affairs of Spain; I resolved on repairing to Spain from Russia. I travelled without intermission. I had an audience immediately on my arrival with the Spanish minister, Senor Mendizabel; I beheld one like myself, the son of a Nuevo Christiano, a Jew of Aragon. In consequence of what transpired at Madrid, I went straight to Paris to consult the President of the French Council; I beheld the son of a French Jew, a hero, an imperial marshal, and very properly so, for who should be military heroes if not those who worship the Lord of Hosts?"

"And is Soult a Hebrew?"

"Yes, and others of the French marshals, and the most famous, Massena, for example; his real name was Mannaseh: but to my anecdote. The consequence of our consultations was that some northern power should be applied to in a friendly and medative capacity. We fixed on Prussia, and the President of the Council made an application to the Prussian minis-

under the provisional government, and used all his political influence in the election of Louis Napoleon to the presidency of the republic. Crémieux hoped in this way to be named Prime Minister and control French policy for a period, as Disraeli did in England somewhat later. Like Disraeli, he had the financial support of the Rothschilds; but when the President chose for his banker another Jew, Fould, and named General Cavaignac premier, Crémieux saw he had lost. Bitterly disappointed, he became so hostile to his former friend that, at the time of the coup d'état in 1851, he was imprisoned at Vincennes. On his release, he identified himself with the enemies of the emperor; these included the communist associates of Marx, Mazzini, Jacob Venedey (already mentioned), Louis Blanc, Ledru Rollin, Pierre Leroux, and a group of socialists, among whom was Maurice Joly. [17]

Joly, some thirty years younger than Crémieux, with an inherited hatred of the Bonapartes, seems to have fallen very largely under his influence. Through Crémieux, Joly became acquainted with communists and their writings. Though, until 1871 when his ambition for a government post turned him into a violent communist, he had not in 1864 gone beyond socialism, he was so impressed with the way they presented their arguments that he could not,

---

ter, who attended a few days after our conference. Count Arnim entered the cabinet, and I beheld a Prussian Jew. So you see, my dear Coningsby, **that the world is governed by very different personages from what is imagined by those who are not behind the scenes** (pp. 249-252).

17. His father was Philippe Lambert Joly, born at Dieppe, Attorney-General of the Jura under Louis-Philippe for ten years. His mother, Florentine Corbara Courtois, was the daughter of Laurent Courtois, paymaster-general of Corsica, who had an inveterate hatred of Napoleon I. Maurice Joly was born in 1831 at Lons-le-Saulnier and educated at Dijon: there he had begun his law studies, but left for Paris in 1849 to secure a post in the Ministry of the Interior under M. Chevreau

if the chance were offered, refrain from imitating. And this chance came in 1864-1865, when his hatred of Napoleon, whetted by Crémieux, led him to publish anonymously in Brussels the *Dialogues aux Enfers entre Machiavelli et Montesquieu.* In this work he tells us [18], "Machiavelli represents the policy of Might, while Montesquieu stands for that of Right: Machiavelli will be Napoleon, who will himself describe his abominable policy". It was natural that he should choose the Italian Machiavelli to stand for Bonaparte, and the Frenchman Montesquieu, for the ideal statesman: it was equally natural that he should put in the mouth of Machiavelli some of the same expressions which Venedey had put in it, and which Joly had admired. His own view was: "Socialism seems to me one of the forms of a new life for the people emancipated from the traditions of the old world. I accept a great many of the solutions offered by sociailsm; but I reject communism, either as a social factor, or as a political institution. Communism is but a school of socialism. In politics, I understand extreme means to gain one's ends — in that at least, I am a Jacobin." [19]

The French authorities, however, penetrated the thinly disguised satire: Joly was arrested and sentenced to two years imprisonment (April, 1865). But the *Dialogues* had pleased Crémieux as much as they had displeased the emperor, and, when his term expired, his Jewish patron rallied to his support: Joly was able to found a legal review, *Le Palais,* with Jules Favre, Desmaret, Leblond, Arago, Berryer, and Adolphe Crémieux as its principal stockholders.

---

and just before the coup d'état. He did not finish his law studies till 1860. Committed suicide in 1878.

18. Maurice Joly: son passé, son programme (autobiography), Paris, 1870.

19. Ibid.

With the fall of Napoleon III, Adolphe Crémieux once more took an open part in politics. Pushing to the front his former secretary, Gambetta, he directed through him the negotiations with Bismarck. Bismarck himself was guided by the Jew Bamberger (1832-1899), a former revolutionary of '48, but who had for years managed the Paris branch of the Jewish bank Bischofsheim & Goldschmidt; he was also a friend of Crémieux. A third Jew in the negotiations was the son of James Rothschild. [20] In this way, care was taken that the treaty should be satisfactory, if not entirely to the signatories, yet at least so to the Alliance Israelite Universelle.

From then (1871) until his death in 1880, as President of the *Alliance Israelite Universelle* and Supreme Master of the Scottish Rite, Crémieux was one of the promoters of the anti-clerical movement following the Franco-Prussian war. His favorite theme was that there should be one cult: speaking at a general assembly of the Alliance he said: "The Alliance is not limited to our cult; it voices its appeal to all cults and wants to penetrate in all religions, as it has penetrated into all countries. Let us endeavour boldly to bring about the union of all cults under one flag of "Union and Progress": such is the motto of humanity." [21]

One cult, one flag. Are the Protocols of Nilus, or the words of Machiavelli in Joly's book or in Venedey's

---

20. Bismarck, who had met the latter's grandfather, knew that Rothschild's real name was Meyer, and regarded him as an "Israelitish citizen of Frankfurt", hence a German subject. To make matters worse, the victor was obliged to discuss the terms of peace with this renegade subject in French, the language of the vanquished, because Rothschild professed not to understand German. — Corti, House of Rothschild, vol. II.

21. Speech made on May 31, 1864; "Union and Progress" was the name given to several revolutionary associations and Masonic lodges. "One cult" is strongly reminiscent of Protocol XVI, infra. Cf. Crémieux, Paris, Capitale des Religions.

Sergius A. Nilus

First Publisher of "The Protocols" 1901

book, anything but an elaborate exposition of the ideas thus briefly expressed by Crémieux? His activities are one of the best examples of Jewish internationalism. Thus the principal attempt to discredit the Protocols leads directly into historical studies which substantiate and illustrate their doctrine in a remarkable and unexpected manner.

CHAPTER IV

TEXT AND COMMENTARY

Of the Protocols themselves little need be said in the way of introduction. The book in which they are embodied was published by Sergyei Nilus in Russia in 1905. A copy of this is in the British Museum, bearing the date of its reception, August 10th, 1906. *All copies that were known to exist in Russia were destroyed by the Kerensky regime, and under his successors the possession of a copy by anyone in Sovietland was crime sufficient to ensure the owner's being shot on sight.* This fact is in itself sufficient proof of the genuineness of the Protocols. The Jewish journals, of course, say that they are a forgery, leaving it to be understood that Professor Nilus, who embodied them in a work of his own, had concocted them for his own purposes.

Mr. Henry Ford, in an interview published in the *New York World*, February 17th, 1921, put the case for Nilus tersely and convincingly thus:

> The only statement I care to make about the PROTOCOLS is that they fit in with what is going on. They are sixteen years old, and they have fitted the world situation up to this time. THEY FIT IT NOW.

Indeed they do!

These Protocols give the substance of addresses delivered to the innermost circle of the Rulers of Zion. They reveal the concerted plan of action of the Jewish Nation developed through the ages and edited by the Elders themselves up to date. Parts and summaries of the plan have been published from time to time during the centuries as the secrets of the Elders have leaked out. The claim of the Jews that the Protocols are forgeries is in itself an admission of their genuineness, for they *never attempt to answer the facts* corresponding to the *threats* which the Protocols contain, and, indeed, the correspondence between prophecy and fulfillment is too glaring to be set aside or obscured. This the Jews well know and therefore evade.

When did the Meetings take place and by whom were the Protocols promulgated?

The answer to these questions is to a certain extent conjectural, but the presumption is strong that they were issued at the First Zionist Congress held at Basle in 1897 under the presidency of the Father of Modern Zionism. the late Theodore Herzl.

Is there any collateral evidence of this?

Yes; and a very striking bit of evidence it is. There has been recently published a volume of Herzl's *Diaries*, a translation of some passages of which appeared in the *Jewish Chronicle* of July 14, 1922. Herzl gives an account of his first visit to England in 1895, and his conversation with Colonel Goldsmid, a Jew brought up as a Christian, an Officer in the English Army, and at heart a Jew Nationalist all the time. Goldsmid suggested to Herzl that the best way of expropriating the English Aristocracy and so destroying their power to protect the people of England was to put excessive taxes on the land. Herzl thought this an excellent idea, and it is now to be found definitely embodied in *Protocol VI!*

The "liberal" victory in the English Election of 1906 (the date of the reception of a copy of the *Protocols* by the British Museum, be it noted), which was essentially a Jewish victory, enabled the Elders to carry their land-taxing policy into practical effect. In consequence, the only option now left to a large proportion of the English

Aristocracy is either to sell their estates to Jews or to to marry their sons to Jewesses.

The above extract from Herzl's *Diary* is an extremely significant bit of evidence bearing on the existence of the Jew World Plot and authenticity of the *Protocols,* but any reader of intelligence will be able from his own knowledge of recent history and from his own experience to confirm the genuineness of every line of them, and it is in the light of this *living* comment that all readers are invited to study Mr. Marsden's translation of this terribly inhuman document.

WHO ARE THE ELDERS?

Who, it may be asked, *are* the Elders of Zion?

The are sometimes called "the Sages of Zion", and their sayings are quoted as gospel by the Jews themselves.

And here is another very significant circumstance. The present successor of Herzl as leader of the Zionist movement, Dr. Weizmann, quoted one of these sayings at the send-off banquet given to Chief Rabbi Hertz on October 6th, 1920. The Chief Rabbi was on the point of leaving for *his* Empire tour—a sort of Jewish answer to the Empire tour of H. R. H. the Prince of Wales. And this is the "saying" of the Sages which Dr. Weizmann quoted;— "A beneficent protection which God has instituted in the life of the Jews is that He has dispersed him all over the world." (Jewish Guardian, Oct. 8th, 1920.)

Now compare this with the last clause but one of *Protocol XI.*

"God has granted to us, His Chosen People, the gift of dispersion, and from this, which appears to all eyes to be our weakness, has come forth all our strength, which has now brought us to the threshold of sovereignty over all the world."

The remarkable correspondence between these passages proves several things. It proves that the Learned Elders exist. It proves that Dr. Weizmann knows all about them. It proves that the desire for a "National Home" in Palestine is only camouflage and an infinitesimal part of the Jew's real object. It proves that the Jews of the world have no intention of settling in Palestine or any separate country, and that their annual prayer that they may all meet "Next Year in Jerusalem" is merely a piece of their characteristic make-believe. It also demonstrates that the Jews are now a world menace, and that the Aryan races will have to domicile them permanently out of Europe.

WHAT ARE THE ELDERS' NAMES? THE THREE HUNDRED.

But what are their names? This is a secret which has not been revealed. They are the Hidden Hand. They are not the "Board of Deputies" (the Jewish Parliament in England) or the "Universal Israelite Alliance" which sits in Paris. But the late Walter Rathenau of the Allgemeiner Electricitaets Gesellschaft has thrown a little light on the subject and doubtless he was in possession of their names, being, in all likelihood, one of the chief leaders himself. Writing in the *Wiener Freie Presse,* December 24th, 1912, he said:

> Three hundred men (Jews, of course), each of whom knows all the others govern the fate of the European continent, and they elect their successors from their entourage.

The Learned Elders are the general officers of these — not three, but — three hundred Fates.

NOTES

I. — "AGENTUR" AND "THE POLITICAL"

There are two words in this translation which are unusual, the word *"Agentur"*, and "political" used as a substantive. *Agentur* appears to be a word adopted from the original and it means the whole body of agents and agencies made use of by the Elders, whether members of the tribe or their Gentile tools.

By "the political" Mr. Marsden means, not exactly the "body politic" but the entire machinery of politics.

II. — The Symbolic Snake of Judaism

Protocol III opens with a reference to the Symbolic Snake of Judaism. In his Epiloge to the 1905 Edition of the Protocols, Nilus gives the following interesting account of this symbol: —

According to the records of secret Jewish Zionism, Solomon and other Jewish learned men already, in 929 B. C., thought out a scheme in theory for a peaceful conquest of the whole universe by Zion.

As history developed, this scheme was worked out in detail and completed by men who were subsequently initiated in this question. These learned men decided by peaceful means to conquer the world for Zion with the slyness of the Symbolic Snake, whose head was to represent those who have been initiated into the plans of the Jewish administration, and the body of the Snake to represent the Jewish people — the administration was always kept secret, *even from the Jewish nation itself*. As this Snake penetrated into the hearts of the nations which it encountered, it undermined and devoured all the non-Jewish power of those States. It is foretold that the Snake has still to finish its work, strictly adhering to the designed plan, until the course which it has to run is closed by the return of its head to Zion and until, by this means, the Snake has completed its round of Europe, and has encircled it — and until, by dint of enchaining Europe, it has encompassed the whole world. This it is to accomplish by using every endeavour to subdue the other countries by an *economical* conquest.

The return of the head of the Snake to Zion can only be accomplished after the power of all the Sovereigns of Europe has been laid low, that is to say, when by means of economic crises and wholesale destruction effected everywhere there shall have been brought about a spiritual demoralization and a moral corruption, chiefly with the assistance of Jewish women masquerading as French, Italians, etc. These are the surest spreaders of licentiousness into the lives of the leading men at the heads of nations.

A map of the course of the Symbolic Snake is shown as follows: — Its first stage in Europe was in 429 B. C., in Greece, where, in the time of Pericles, the Snake first started eating into the power of that country. The second stage was in Rome in the time of Augustus, about 69 B. C. The third in Madrid in the time of Charles V., in 1552 A. D. The fourth in Paris about 1790, in the time of Louis XVI. The fifth in London from 1814 onwards (after the downfall of Napoleon). The sixth in Berlin in 1871 after the Franco-Prussian war. The seventh in St. Petersburg, over which is drawn the head of the Snake under the date of 1881.

All these states which the Snake traversed have had the foundations of their constitutions shaken, Germany, with its apparent power, forming no exception to the rule. In economic conditions England and Germany are spared, but only till the conquest of Russia is accomplished by the Snake, on which at present (i.e., 1905), all its efforts are concentrated. The further course of the Snake is not shown on this map, but arrows indicate its next movement towards Moscow, Kieff, and Odessa.

It is now well known to us to what extent the latter cities form the centres of the militant Jewish race. Constantinople is shown as the last stage of the Snake's course before it reaches Jerusalem. (This map was drawn years before the occurence of the "Young Turk" — *i.e.*, Jewish — Revolution in Turkey.)

III. — The term *"Goyim,"* meaning Gentiles or non-Jews, is used throughout *The Protocols* and is retained by Mr. Marsden. It is a term of offence and contempt and reveals the innermost spirit of Judaism.

PART III

PROTOCOLS

OF THE MEETINGS OF THE LEARNED ELDERS OF ZION

PROTOCOL NO. 1

Right lies in Might. Freedom — an idea only. Liberalism. Gold. Faith. Self-Government. Despotism of Capital. The internal foe. The Mob. Anarchy. Politics *versus* Morals. The Right of the Strong. The Invincibility of Jew-Masonic authority. End justifies Means. The Mob a Blind Man. Political A.B.C. Party Discord. Most satisfactory form of rule-Despotism. Alcohol. Classicism. Corruption. Principles and rules of the Jew-Masonic Government. Terror. "Liberty, Equality, Fraternity." Principle of Dynastic Rule. Annihilation of the privileges of the Goy-Aristocracy (*i.e.*, non-Jew). The New Aristocracy. The psychological calculation. Abstractness of "Liberty." Power of Removal of representatives of the people.

. . . . . . Putting aside fine phrases we shall speak of the significance of each thought: by comparisons and deductions we shall throw light upon surrounding facts.

What I am about to set forth, then, is our system from the two point of view, that of ourselves and that of the *goyim* (*i.e.*, non-Jews).

It must be noted that men with bad instincts are more in number than the good, and therefore the best results in governing them are attained by violence and terrorization, and not by academic discussions. Every man aims at power, everyone would like to become a dictator if only he could, and rare indeed are the men who would not be willing to sacrifice the welfare of all for the sake of securing their own welfare.

What has restrained the beasts of prey who are called men? What has served for their guidance hitherto?

In the beginnings of the structure of society they were subjected to brutal and blind force; afterwards — to Law, which is the same force, only disguised. I draw the conclusion that by the law of nature right lies in force.

Political freedom is an idea but not a fact. This idea one must know how to apply whenever it appears necessary with this bait of an idea to attract the masses of the people to one's party for the purpose of crushing another who is in authority. This task is rendered easier if the opponent has himself been infected with the idea of freedom, *so-called liberalism,* and, for the sake of an idea, is willing to yield some of his power. It is precisely here that the triumph of our theory appears: the slackened reins of government are immediately, by the law of life, caught up and gathered together by a new hand, because the blind might of the nation cannot for one single day exist without guidance, and the new authority merely fits into the place of the old already weakened by liberalism.

In our day the power which has replaced that of the rulers who were liberal is the power of Gold. Time was when Faith ruled. The idea of freedom is impossible of realization because no one knows how to use it with moderation. It is enough to hand over a people to self-government for a certain length of time for that people to be turned into a disorganized mob. From that moment on we get internecine strife which soon develops into battles between classes, in the midst of which States burn down and their importance is reduced to that of a heap of ashes.

Whether a State exhausts itself in its own convulsions, whether its internal discord brings it under the power of external foes — in any case it can be accounted irretrievably lost: *it is in our power.* The despotism of Capital, which is entirely in our hands, reaches out to it a straw that the State, willy-nilly, must take hold of: if not — it goes to the bottom.

Should anyone of a liberal mind say that such reflections as the above are immoral I would put the following questions: — If every State has two foes and if in regard to the external foe it is allowed and not considered immoral to use every manner and art of conflict, as for example to keep the enemy in ignorance of plans of attack and defence, to attack him by night or in superior numbers, then in what way can the same means in regard to a worse foe, the destroyer of the structure of society and the commonweal, be called immoral and not permissible?

Is it possible for any sound logical mind to hope with any success to guide crowds by the aid of reasonable counsels and arguments, when any objection or contradiction, senseless though it may be, can be made and when such objection may find more favour with the people, whose powers of reasoning are superficial? Men in masses and the men of the masses, being guided solely by petty passions, paltry beliefs, customs, traditions and sentimental theorism, fall a prey to party dissension, which hinders any kind of agreement even on the basis of a perfectly reasonable argument. Every resolution of a crowd depends upon a chance or packed majority, which, in its ignorance of political secrets, put forth some ridiculous resolution that lays in the administration a seed of anarchy.

The political has nothing in common with the moral. The ruler who is governed by the moral is not a skilled politician, and is therefore unstable on his throne. He who wishes to rule must have recource both to cunning

ing ourselves in the shade; thanks to the Press we have got and to make-believe. Great national qualities, like frankness and honesty, are vices in politics, for they bring down rulers from their thrones more effectively and more certainly than the most powerful enemy. Such qualities must be the attributes of the kingdoms of the *goyim*, but we must in no wise be guided by them.

Our right lies in force. The word "right" is an abstract thought and proved by nothing. The word means no more than: — Give me what I want in order that thereby I may have a proof that I am stronger than you.

Where does right begin? Where does it end?

In any State in which there is a bad organization of authority, an impersonality of laws and of the rulers who have lost their personality amid the flood of rights ever multiplying out of liberalism, I find a new right — to attack by the right of the strong, and to scatter to the winds all existing forces of order and regulation, to reconstruct all institutions and to become the sovereign lord of those who have left to us the rights of their power by laying them down voluntarily in their liberalism.

Our power in the present tottering condition of all forms of power will be more invisible than any other, because it will remain invisible until the moment when it has gained such strength that no cunning can any longer undermine it.

Out of the temporary evil we are now compelled to commit will emerge the good of an unshakeable rule, which will restore the regular course of the machinery of the national life, brought to naught by liberalism. The result justifies the means. Let us, however, in our plans, direct our attention not so much to what is good and moral as to what is necessary and useful.

Before us is a plan in which is laid down strategically the line from which we cannot deviate without running the risk of seeing the labour of many centuries brought to naught.

In order to elaborate satisfactory forms of action it is necessary to have regard to the rascality, the slackness, the instability of the mob, its lack of capacity to understand and respect the conditions of its own life, or its own welfare. It must be understood that the might of a mob is blind, senseless and unreasoning force ever at the mercy of a suggestion from any side. The blind cannot lead the blind without bringing them into the abyss; consequently, members of the mob, upstarts from the people even though they should be as a genius for wisdom, yet having no understanding of the political, cannot come forward as leaders of the mob without bringing the whole nation to ruin.

Only one trained from childhood for independent rule can have understanding of the words that can be made up of the political alphabet.

A people left to itself *i.e.*, to upstarts from its midst, brings itself to ruin by party dissensions excited by the pursuit of power and honours and the disorders arising therefrom. Is it possible for the masses of the people calmly and without petty jealousies to form judgments, to deal with the affairs of the country, which cannot be mixed up with personal interests? Can they defend themselves from an external foe? It is unthinkable, for a plan broken up into as many parts as there are heads in the mob, loses all homogeneity, and thereby becomes unintelligible and impossible of execution.

It is only with a despotic ruler that plans can be elaborated extensively and clearly in such a way as to distribute the whole properly among the several parts of the machinery of the State: from this the conclusion is inevitable that a satisfactory form of government for any country is one that concentrates in the hands of one responsible person. Without an absolute despotism there can be no existence for civilization which is carried on not by the masses but by their guide, whosoever that person may be. The mob is a savage and displays its savagery at every opportunity. The moment the mob seizes freedom in its hands it quickly turns to anarchy, which in itself is the highest degree of savagery.

Behold the alcoholized animals, bemused with drink, the right to an immoderate use of which comes along with freedom. It is not for us and ours to walk that road. The peoples of the *goyim* are bemused with alcoholic liquors; their youth has grown stupid on classicism and from early immorality, into which it has been inducted by our special agents — by tutors, lackeys, governesses in the houses of the wealthy, by clerks and others, by our women in the places of dissipation frequented by the *goyim*. In the number of these last I count also the so-called "society ladies," voluntary followers of the others in corruption and luxury.

Our countersign is — Force and Make-believe. Only force conquers in political affairs, especially if it be concealed in the talents essential to statesmen. Violence must be the principle, and cunning and make-believe the rule for governments which do not want to lay down their crowns at the feet of agents of some new power. This evil is the one and only means to attain the end, the good. Therefore we must not stop at bribery, deceit and treachery when they should serve towards the attainment of our end. In politics one must know how to seize the property of others without hesitation if by it we secure submission and sovereignty.

Our State, marching along the path of peaceful conquest, has the right to replace the horrors of war by less noticable and more satisfactory sentences of death, necessary to maintain the terror which tends to produce blind submission. Just but merciless severity is the greatest factor of strength in the State: not only for the sake of gain but also in the name of duty, for the sake of victory, we must keep to the programme of violence and make-believe. The doctrine of squaring accounts is precisely as strong as the means of which it makes use. Therefore it is not so much by the means themselves as by the doctrine of severity that we shall triumph and bring all governments into subjection to our super-government. It is enough for them to know that we are merciless for all disobedience to cease.

Far back in ancient times we were the first to cry among the masses of the people the words "Liberty, Equality, Fraternity," words many times repeated since those days by stupid poll-parrots who from all sides round flew down upon these baits and with them carried away the well-being of the world, true freedom of the individual, formerly so well guarded against the pressure of the mob. The would-be wise men of the *goyim,* the intellectuals, could not make anything out of the uttered words in their abstractness; did not note the contradiction of their meaning and inter-relation: did not see that in nature there is no equality, cannot be freedom; that Nature herself has established inequality of minds, of characters, and capacities, just as immutably as she has established subordination to her laws: never stopped to think that the mob is a blind thing, that upstarts elected from among it to bear rule are, in regard to the political, the same blind men as the mob itself, that the adept, though he be a fool, can yet rule, whereas the non-adept, even if he were a genius, understands nothing in the political — to all these things the *goyim* paid no regard; yet all the time it was based upon these things that dynastic rule rested: the father passed on to the son a knowledge of the course of political affairs in such wise that none should know it but members of the dynasty and none could betray it to the governed. As time went on the meaning of the dynastic transference of the true position of affairs in the political was lost, and this aided the success of our cause.

In all corners of the earth the words "Liberty, Equality, Fraternity" brought to our ranks, thanks to our blind agents, whole legions who bore our banners with enthusiasm. And all the time these words were canker-worms at work boring into the well-being of the *goyim*, putting an end everywhere to peace, quiet, solidarity and destroying all the foundations of the *goya* States. As you will see later, this helped us to our triumph; it gave us the possibility, among other things, of getting into our hands the master card — the destruction of the privileges, or in other words of the very existence of the aristocracy of the *goyim*, that class which was the only defense peoples and countries had against us. On the ruins of the natural and genealogical aristocracy of the *goyim* we have set up the aristocracy of our educated class headed by the aristocracy of money. The qualifications for this aristocracy we have established in wealth, which is dependent upon us, and in knowledge, for which our learned elders provide the motive force.

Our triumph has been rendered easier by the fact that in our relations with the men whom we wanted we have always worked upon the most sensitive chords of the human mind, upon the cash account, upon the cupidity, upon the insatiability for material needs of man; and each one of these human weaknesses, taken alone, is sufficient to paralyse initiative, for it hands over the will of men to the disposition of him who has bought their activities.

The abstraction of freedom has enabled us to persuade the mob in all countries that their government is nothing but the steward of the people who are the owners of the country, and that the steward may be replaced like a worn-out glove.

It is this possibility of replacing the representatives of the people which has placed them at our disposal, and, as it were, given us the power of appointment.

PROTOCOL NO. 2

Economic Wars — the foundation of the Jewish predominance. Figure-head government and "secret advisers." Successes of destructive doctrines. Adaptability in politics. Part played by the Press. Cost of gold and value of Jewish sacrifice.

It is indispensable for our purpose that wars, so far as possible, should not result in territorial gains: war will thus be brought on to the economic ground, where the nations will not fail to perceive in the assistance we give the strength of our predominance, and this state of things will put both sides at the mercy of our international *agentur;* which possesses millions of eyes ever on the watch and unhampered my any limitations whatsoever. Our international rights will then wipe out national rights, in the proper sense of right, and will rule the nations precisely as the civil law of States rules the relations of their subjects among themselves.

The administrators, whom we shall choose from among the public, with strict regard to their capacities for servile obedience, will not be persons trained in the arts of government, and will therefore easily become pawns in our game in the hands of men of learning and genius who will be their advisers, specialists bred and reared from early childhood to rule the affairs of the whole world. As is well known to you, these specialists of ours have been drawing to fit them for rule the information they need from our political plans from the lessons of history, from observations made of the events of every moment as it passes. The *goyim* are not guided by practical use of unprejudiced historical observation, but by theoretical routine without any critical regard for consequent results. We need not, therefore, take any account of them — let them amuse themselves until the hour strikes, or live on hopes of new forms of enterprising pastime, or on the memories of all they have enjoyed. For them let that play the principal part which we have persuaded them to accept as the dictates of science (theory). It is with this object in view that we are constantly, by means of our press, arousing a blind confidence in these theories. The intellectuals of the *goyim* will puff themselves up with their knowledge and without any logical verification of them will put into effect all the information available from science, which our *agentur* specialists have cunningly pieced together for the purpose of educating their minds in the direction we want.

Do not suppose for a moment that these statements are empty words: think carefully of the successes we arranged for Darwinism, Marxim, Nietzsche-ism. To us Jews, at any rate, it should be plain to see what a distintegrating importance these directives have had upon the minds of the *goyim*.

It is indispensable for us to take account of the thoughts, characters, tendencies of the nations in order to avoid making slips in the political and in the direction of administrative affairs. The triumph of our system, of which the component parts of the machinery may be variously disposed according to the temperament of the peoples met on our way, will fail of success if the practical application of it be not based upon a summing up of the lessons of the past in the light of the present.

In the hands of the States of to-day there is a great force that creates the movement of thought in the people, and that is the Press. The part played by the Press is to keep pointing out requirements supposed to be indispensable, to give voice to the complaints of the people, to express and create discontent. It is in the Press that the triumph of freedom of speech finds its incarnation. But the *goyim* States have not known how to make use of this force; and it has fallen into our hands. Through the Press we have gained the power to influence while remain-
exist. It proves that Dr. Weizmann knows all about

the *gold* in our hands, notwithstanding that we have had to gather it out of oceans of blood and tears. But it has paid us, though we have sacrificed many of our people. Each victim on our side is worth in the sight of God a thousand *goyim*.

PROTOCOL NO. 3

The Symbolic Snake and its significance. The instability of the constitutional scales. Terror in the palaces. Power and ambition. Parliaments "talkeries," pamphlets. Abuse of power. Economic slavery. "People's Rights." Monopolist system and the aristocracy. The Army of Mason-Jewry. Decrescence of the *Goyim*. Hunger and rights of capital. The mob and the coronation of "The Sovereign Lord of all the World." The fundamental precept in the programme of the future Masonic national schools. The secret of the science of the structure of society. Universal economic crisis. Security of "ours" (*i.e.,* our people, Jews). The despotism of Masonry — the kingdom of reason. Loss of the guide. Masonry and the great French Revolution. The King-Despot of the blood of Zion. Causes of the invinsibility of Masonry. Part played by secret masonic agents. Freedom.

To-day I may tell you that our goal is now only a few steps off. There remains a small space to cross and the whole long path we have trodden is ready now to close its cycle of the Symbolic Snake, by which we symbolize our people. When this ring closes, all the States of Europe will be locked in its coil as in a powerful vice.

The constitution scales of these days will shortly break down, for we have established them with a certain lack of accurate balance in order that they may oscillate incessantly until they wear through the pivot on which they turn. The *goyim* are under the impression that they have welded them sufficiently strong and they have all along kept on expecting that the scales would come into equilibrium. But the pivots — the kings on their thrones — are hemmed in by their representatives, who play the fool, distraught with their own uncontrolled and irresponsible power. This power they owe to the terror which has been breathed into the palaces. As they have no means of getting at their people, into their very midst, the kings on their thrones are no longer able to come to terms with them and so strengthen themselves against seekers after power. We have made a gulf between the far-seeing Sovereign Power and the blind force of the people so that both have lost all meaning, for like the blind man and his stick, both are powerless apart.

In order to incite seekers after power to a misuse of power we have set all forces in opposition one to another, breaking up their liberal tendencies towards independence. To this end we have stirred up every form of enterprise, we have armed all parties, we have set up authority as a target for every ambition. Of States we have made gladiatorial arenas where a host of confused issues contend. . . . A little more, and disorders and bankruptcy will be universal. . . . . .

Babblers inexhaustible have turned into oratorical contests the sittings of Parliament and Administrative Boards. Bold journalists and unscrupulous pamphleteers daily fall upon executive officials. Abuses of power will put the final touch in preparing all institutions for their overthrow and everything will fly skyward under the blows of the maddened mob.

All people are chained down to heavy toil by poverty more firmly than ever they were chained by slavery and serfdom; from these, one way and another, they might free themselves, these could be settled with, but from want they will never get away. We have included in the constitution such rights as to the masses appear fictitious and not actual rights. All these so-called "People's Rights" can exist only in idea, an idea which can never be realized in practical life. What is it to the proletariat labourer, bowed double over his heavy toll, crushed by his lot in life, if talkers get the right to bable, if journalists get the right to scribble any nonsense side by side with good stuff, once the proletariat has no other profit out of the constitution save only those pitiful crumbs which we fling them from our table in return for their voting in favour of what we dictate, in favour of the men we place in power, the servants of our *agentur* . . . . Republican rights for a poor man are no more than a bitter piece of irony, for the necessity he is under of toiling almost all day gives him no present use of them, but on the other hand robs him of all guarantee of regular and certain earnings by making him dependent on strikes by his comrades or lockouts by his masters.

The people under our guidance have annihilated the aristocracy, who were their one and only defence and foster-mother for the sake of their own advantage which is inseparably bound up with the well-being of the people. Nowadays, with the destruction of the aristocracy, the people have fallen into the grips of merciless money-grinding scoundrels who have laid a pitiless and cruel yoke upon the necks of the workers.

We appear on the scene as alleged saviours of the worker from this oppression when we propose to him to enter the ranks of our fighting forces — Socialists, Anarchists, Communists — to whom we always give support in accordance with an alleged brotherly rule (of the solidarity of all humanity) of our *social masonry*. The aristocracy, which enjoyed by law the labour of the workers, was interested in seeing that the workers were well fed, healthy and strong. We are interested in just the opposite — in the deminution, the *killing out of the* GOYIM. Our power is in the chronic shortness of food and physical weakness of the worker because by all that this implies he is made the slave of our will, and he will not find in his own authorities either strength or energy to set against our will. Hunger creates the right of capital to rule the worker more surely than it was given to the aristocracy by the legal authority of kings.

By want and the envy and hatred which it engenders we shall move the mobs and with their hands we shall wipe out all those who hinder us on our way.

When the hour strikes for our Sovereign Lord of all the World to be crowned it is these same hands which will sweep away everything that might be a hindrance thereto.

The *goyim* have lost the habit of thinking unless prompted by the suggestions of our specialists. Therefore they do not see the urgent necessity of what we, when our kingdom comes, shall adopt at once, namely this, that *it is essential to teach in national schools one simple, true piece of knowledge, the basis of all knowledge — the knowledge of the structure of human life, of social existence, which requires division of labour, and, consequently, the division of men into classes and conditions.* It is essential for all to know that *owing to difference in the objects of human activity there cannot be any equality,* that he who by any act of his compromises a whole class cannot be equally responsible before the law with him who affects no one but only his own honour. The true knowledge of the structure of society, into the secrets of which we do not admit the *goyim,* would demonstrate to all men that the positions and work must be kept within a certain circle, that they may not become a source of human suffering, arising from an education which does not correspond with the work which individuals are called upon to do. After a thorough study of this knowledge the peoples will voluntarily submit to authority and accept such position as is appointed them in the State. In the present state of knowledge and the direction we have given to its development the people, blindly believing things in print — cherishes — thanks to promptings intended to mislead and to its own ignorance —a blind hatred towards all conditions which it considers above itself, for it has no understanding of the meaning of class and condition.

This hatred will be still further magnified by the effects of an *economic crisis,* which will stop dealings on the exchanges and bring industry to a standstill. We shall create by all the secret subterranean methods open to us and with the aid of gold, which is all in our hands, *a universal economic crisis whereby we shall throw upon the streets whole mobs of workers simultaneously in all the countries of Europe.* These mobs will *rush delightedly* to shed the blood of those whom, in the simplicity of their ignorance, they have envied from their cradles, and whose property they will then be able to loot.

"Ours" they will not touch, because the moment of attack will be known to us and we shall take measures to protect our own.

We have demonstrated that progress will bring all the *goyim* to the sovereignty of reason. Our despotism will be precisely that; for it will know how by wise severities to pacificate all unrest, to cauterise liberalism out of all institutons.

When the populace has seen that all sorts of concessions and indulgences are yielded it in the name of freedom it has imagined itself to be sovereign lord and has stormed its way to power, but, naturally, like every other blind man it has come upon a host of stumbling blocks, *it has rushed to find a guide, it has never had the sense to return to the former state* and it has laid down its plenipotentiary powers at *our* feet. Remember the French Revolution, to which it was we who gave the name of "Great": the secrets of its preparations are well known to us for it was wholly the work of our hands.

Ever since that time we have been leading the peoples from one disenchantment to another, so that in the end they should turn also from us in favour of that *King-*

Despot of the blood of Zion, whom we are preparing for the world.

At the present day we are, as an international force, invincible, because if attacked by some we are supported by other States. It is the bottomless rascality of the *goyim* peoples, who crawl on their bellies to force, but are merciless towards weakness ,unsparing to faults and indulgent to crimes, unwilling to bear the contradictions of a free social system but patient unto martyrdom under the violence of a bold despotism—it is those qualities which are aiding us to independence. From the premier-dictators of the present day the *goyim* peoples suffer patiently and bear such abuses as for the least of them they would have beheaded twenty kings.

What is the explanation of this phenomenon, this curious inconsequence of the masses of the peoples in their attitude towards what would appear to be events of the same order?

It is explained by the fact that these dictators whisper to the peoples through their agents that through these abuses they are inflicting injury on the States with the highest purpose — to secure the welfare of the peoples, the international brotherhood of them all, their solidarity and equality of rights. Naturally they do not tell the peoples that this unification must be accomplished only under our sovereign rule.

And thus the people condemn the upright and acquit the guilty, persuaded ever more and more that it can do whatsoever it wishes. Thanks to this state of things the people are destroying every kind of stability and creating disorders at every step.

The word "freedom" brings out the communities of men to fight against every kind of force, against every kind of authority, even against God and the laws of nature. For this reason we, when we come into our kingdom, shall have to erase this word from the lexicon of life as implying a principle of brute force which turns mobs into bloodthirsty beasts.

These beasts, it is true, fall asleep again every time when they have drunk their fill of blood, and at such times can easily be riveted into their chains. But if they be not given blood they will not sleep and continue the struggle.

PROTOCOL NO. 4

Stages of a Republic. Gentile Masonry. Freedom and Faith. International Industrial Competition. Role of Speculation. Cult of Gold.

Every republic passes through several stages. The first of these is comprised in the early days of mad raging by the blind mob, tossed hither and thither, right and left: the second is demogogy, from which is born anarchy, and that leads inevitably to despotism—not any longer legal and overt, and therefore responsible despotism, but to unseen and secretly hidden, yet nevertheless sensibly felt despotism in the hands of some secret organization or other, whose acts are the more unscrupulous inasmuch as it works behind a screen, behind the backs of all sorts of agents, the changing of whom not only does not injuriously affect but actually aids the secret force by saving it, thanks to continual changes, from the necessity of expending its resources on the rewarding of long services.

Who and what is in a position to overthrow an invisible force? And this is precisely what our force is. *Gentile* masonry blindly serves as a screen for us and our objects, but the plan of action of our force, even its very abiding-place, remains for the whole people an unknown mystery.

But even freedom might be harmless and have its place in the State economy without injury to the well-being of the peoples if it rested upon the foundation of faith in God, upon the brotherhood of humanity, unconnected with the conception of equality, which is negatived by the very laws of creation, for they have established subordination. With such a faith as this a people might be governed by a wardship of parishes, and would walk contentedly and humbly under the guiding hand of its spiritual pastor submitting to the dispositions of God upon earth. This is the reason why *it is indispensable for us to undermine all faith, to tear of minds out of the* GOYIM *the very principle of Godhead and the spirit, and to put in its place arithmetical calculations and material needs.*

In order to give the *goyim* no time to think and take note, their minds must be diverted towards industry and trade. Thus, all the nations will be swallowed up in the pursuit of gain and in the race for it will not take note of their common foe. But again, in order that freedom may once for all disintegrate and ruin the communities of the *goyim,* we must put industry on a speculative basis: the result of this will be that what is withdrawn from the land by industry will slip through the hands and pass into speculation, that is, to our classes.

The intensified struggle for superiority and shocks delivered to economic life will create, nay, have already created, disenchanted, cold and heartless communities. Such communities will foster a strong aversion towards the higher political and towards religion. Their only guide is gain, that is Gold, which they will erect into a veritable cult, for the sake of those material delights which it can give. Then will the hour strike when, not for the sake of attaining the good, not even to win wealth, but solely out of hatred towards the privileged, the lower classes of the *goyim* will follow our lead against our rivals for power, the intellectuals of the *goyim.*

PROTOCOL NO. 5

Creation of an intensified centralization of government. Methods of seizing power by masonry. Causes of the impossibility of agreement between States. The state of "predestination" of the Jews. Gold — the engine of the machinery of States. Significance of criticism. "Show" institutions. Weariness from word-spinning. How to take a grip of public opinion. Significance of personal initiative. The Super-Government.

What form of administrative rule can be given to communities in which corruption has penetrated everywhere, communities where riches are attained only by the clever surprise tactics of semi-swindling tricks; where looseness reigns: where morality is maintained by penal measures and harsh laws but not by voluntarily accepted principles: where the feelings toward faith and country are obliterated by cosmopolitan convictions? What form of rule is to be given to these commuinties if not that despotism which I shall describe to you later? We shall create an intensified centralization of government in order to grip in or hands all the forces of the community. We shall regulate mechanically all the actions of the political life of our subjects by new laws. These laws will withdraw one by one all the indulgences and liberties which have been permitted by the *goyim,* and our kingdom will be distinguished by a despotism of such magnificent proportions as to be at any moment and in every place in a position to wipe out any *goyim* who oppose us by deed or word.

We shall be told that such a despotism as I speak of is not consistent with the progress of these days, but I will prove to you that it is.

In the times when the peoples looked upon kings on their thrones as on a pure manifestation of the will of God, they submitted without a murmur to the despotic power of kings: but from the day when we insinuated into their minds the conception of their own rights they began to regard the occupants of thrones as mere ordinary mortals. The holy unction of the Lord's Anointed has fallen from the heads of kings in the eye of the people, and when we also robbed them of their faith in God the might of power was flung upon the streets into the place of public proprietorship and was seized by us.

Moreover, the art of directing masses and individuals by means of cleverly manipulated theory and verbiage, by regulations of life in common and all sorts of other quirks, in all which the *goyim* understand nothing, belongs likewise to the specialists of our administrative brain. Reared on analysis, observation, on delicacies of fine calculation, in this species of skill we have no rivals, any more than we have either in the drawing up of plans of political actions and solidarity. In this respect the Jesuits alone might have compared with us, but we have contrived to discredit them in the eyes of the unthinking mob as an overt organization, while we ourselves all the while have kept our secret organization in the shade. However, it is probably all the same to the world who is its sovereign lord, whether the head of Catholicism or our despot of the blood of Zion! But to us, the Chosen People, it is very far from being a matter of indifference.

For a time perhaps we might be successfully dealt with by a coalition of the GOYIM *of all the world*: but from this danger we are secured by the discord existing among them whose roots are so deeply seated that they can never now be plucked up. We have set one against another the personal and national reckonings of the *goyim,* religious and race hatreds, which we have fostered into a huge growth in the course of the past twenty centuries. This is the reason why there is not one State which would anywhere receive support if it were to raise its arm, for every one of them must bear in mind that any agreement against us would be unprofitable to itself. We are too strong — there is no evading our power. *The nations cannot come to even an inconsiderable private agreement without our secretly having a hand in it.*

"Per Me reges regnant". ("It is through me that Kings reign.") And it was said by the prophets that we were chosen by God Himself to rule over the whole earth. God has endowed us with genius that we may be equal to our task. Were genius in the opposite camp it would still struggle against us, but even so a newcomer is no match for the old-established settler; the struggle would be merciless between us, such a fight as the world has never yet seen. Aye, and the genius on their side would have arrived too late. All the wheels of the machinery of all States go by the force of the engine, which is in our hands, and that engine of the machinery of States is — Gold. The science of political economy invented by our learned elders has for long past been giving royal prestige to capital.

Capital, if it is to co-operate untrammelled, must be free to establish a monopoly of industry and trade: this is already being put in execution by an unseen hand in all quarters of the world. This freedom will give political force to those engaged in industry, and that will help to oppress the people. Nowadays it is more important to disarm the peoples than to lead them into war; more important to use for our advantage the passions which have burst into flames than to quench their fire; more important to catch up and interpret the ideas of others to suit ourselves than to eradicate them. *The principal object of our directorate consists in this: to debilitate the public mind by criticism; to lead it away from serious reflections calculated to arouse resistance; to distract the forces of the mind towards a sham fight of empty eloquence.*

In all ages the peoples of the world, equally with individuals, have accepted words for deeds, for *they are content with a show* and rarely pause to note, in the public arena, whether promises are followed by performance.

Therefore we shall establish show institutions which will give eloquent proof of their benefit to progress.

We shall assume to ourselves the liberal physiognomy of all parties, of all directions, and we shall give that physiognomy a voice *in orators who will speak so much that they will exhaust the patience of their hearers and produce an abhorrence of oratory.*

In order to put public opinion into our hands we must bring it into a state of bewilderment by giving expression from all sides to so many contradictory opinions and for such length of time as will suffice to make the GOYIM *lose their heads in the labyrinth and come to see that the best thing is to have no opinion of any kind in matters political,* which it is not given to the public to understand, because they are understood only by him who guides the public. This is the first secret.

The second secret reqiusite for the success of our government is comprised in the following: To multiply to such an extent national failings, habits, passions, conditions of civil life, that it will be impossible for anyone to know where he is in the resulting chaos, so that the people in consequence will fail to understand one another. This measure will also serve us in another way, namely, to sow discord in all parties, to dislocate all collective forces which are still unwilling to submit to us, and to discourage any kind of personal initiative which might in any degree hinder our affair. *There is nothing more dangerous than personal initiative;* if it has genius behind it, such initiative can do more than can be done by millions of people among whom we have sown discord. We must so direct the education of the *goyim* communities that whenever they come upon a matter requiring initiative they may drop their hands in despairing impotence. The strain which results from freedom of action saps the forces when it meets with the freedom of another. From this collision arise grave moral shocks, disenchantments, failures. *By all these means we shall so wear down the*

GOYIM *that they will be compelled to offer us international power of a nature that by its position will enable us without any violence gradually to absorb all the State forces of the world and to form a Super-Government.* In place of the rulers of to-day we shall set up a bogey which will be called the Super-Government Administration. Its hands will reach out in all directions like nippers and its organization will be of such colossal dimensions that it cannot fail to subdue all the nations of the world.

PROTOCOL NO. 6

Monopolies; upon them depend the fortunes of the *goyim*. Taking of the land out of the hands of the aristocracy. Trade, Industry and Speculation. Luxury. Rise of wages and increase of price in the articles of primary necessity. Anarchism and drunkeness. Secret meaning of the propaganda of economic theories.

We shall soon begin to establish huge monopolies, reservoirs of colossal riches, upon which even large fortunes of the *goyim* will depend to such an extent that they will go to the bottom together with the credit of the States on the day after the poilical smash....

You gentlemen here present who are economists, just strike an estimate of the significance of this combination!

In every possible way we must develop the significance of our Super-Government by representing it as the Protector and Benefactor of all those who voluntarily submit to us.

The aristocracy of the *goyim* as a political force, is dead — we need not take it into account; but as landed proprietors they can still be harmful to us from the fact that they are self-sufficing in the resources upon which they live. It is essential therefore for us at whatever cost to deprive them of their land. This object will be best attained by increasing the burdens upon landed property

— in loading lands with debt. These measures will check land-holding and keep it in a state of humble and unconditional submission.

The aristocrats of the *goyim,* being hereditarily incapable of contenting themselves with little, will rapidly burn up and fizzle out.

At the same time we must intensively patronize trade and industry, but, first and foremost, speculation, the part played by which is to provide a counterpoise to industry: the absence of speculative industry will multiply capital in private hands and will serve to restore agriculture by freeing the land from indebtedness to the land banks. What we want is that industry should drain off from the land both labour and capital and by means of speculation transfer into our hands all the money of the world, and thereby throw all the *goyim* into the ranks of the proletariat. Then the *goyim* will bow down before us, if for no other reason but to get the right to exist.

To complete the ruin of the industry of the *goyim* we shall bring to the assistance of speculation the luxury which we have developed among the *goyim,* that greedy demand for luxury which is swallowing up everything. *We shall raise the rate of wages which, however, will not bring any advantage to the workers, for at the same time, we shall produce a rise in prices of the first necessaries of life, alleging that it arises from the decline of agriculture and cattle-breeding: we shall further undermine artfully and deeply sources of production, by accustoming the workers to anarchy and to drunkenness and side by side therewith taking all measure to extirpate from the fact of the earth all the educated forces of the* GOYIM.

In order that the true meaning of things may not strike the GOYIM *before the proper time we shall mask it under an alleged ardent desire to serve the working classes and the great principles of political economy about which our economic theories are carrying on an energetic propaganda.*

PROTOCOL NO. 7

Object of the intensification of armaments. Ferments, discords and hostility all over the world. Checking the opposition of the *goyim* by wars and by a universal war. Secrecy means success in the political. The Press and public opinion. The guns of America, China and Japan.

The intensification of armaments, the increase of police forces — are all essential for the completion of the aforementioned plans. What we have to get at is that there should be in all the States of the world, besides ourselves, only the masses of the proletariat, a few millionaries devoted to our interests, police and soldiers.

Throughout all Europe, and by means of relations with Europe, in other continents also, we must create ferments, discords and hostility. Therein we gain a double advantage. In the first place we keep in check all countries, for they well know that we have the power whenever we like to create disorders or to restore order. All these countries are accustomed to see in us an indispensable force of coercion. In the second place, by our intrigues we shall tangle up all the threads which we have stretched into the cabinets of all States by means of the political, by economic treaties, or loan obligations. In order to succeed in this we must use great cunning and penetration during negotiations and agreements, but, as regards what is called the "official laguage," we shall keep to the opposite tactics and assume the mask of honesty and compliancy. In this way the peoples and governments of the *goyim,* whom we have taughts to look only at the outside whatever we present to their notice, will still continue to accept us as the benefactors and saviours of the human race.

We must be in a position to respond to every act of opposition by war with the neighbours of that country which dares to oppose us: but if these neighbours should also venture to stand collectively together against us, then we must offer resistance by a universal war.

The principal factor of success in the political is the secrecy of its undertakings: the word should not agree with the deeds of the diplomat.

We must compel the governments of the *goyim* to take action in the direction favoured by our widely-conceived plan, already approaching the desired consummation, by what we shall represent as public opinion, secretly prompted by us through the means of that so-called "Great Power" — *the Press, which, with a few exceptions that may be disregarded, is already entirely in our hands.*

In a word, to sum up our system of keeping the governments of the *goyim* in Europe in check, we shall show our strength to one of them by terrorist attempts and to all, if we allow the possibility of a general rising against us, we shall respond with the guns of America or China or Japan.

PROTOCOL NO. 8

Ambiguous employment of juridical rights. Assistants of the Masonic directorate. Special schools and super-educational training. Economists and millionaires. To whom to entrust responsible posts in the government.

We must arm ourselves with all the weapons which our opponents might employ against us. We must search out in the very finest shades of expression and the knotty points of the lexicon of law justification for those cases where we shall have to pronounce judgments that might appear abnormally audacious and unjust, for it is important that these resolutions should be set forth in expressions that shall seem to be the most exalted moral principles cast into legal form. Our directorate must surround itself with all these forces of civilization among which it will have to work. It will surround itself with publicists, practical jurists, administrators, diplomats and, finally, with persons prepared by a special super-educational training *in our special schools.* These persons will have cognisance of all the secrets of the social structure, they will know all the languages that can be made up by political alphabets and words; they will be made acquainted with the whole underside of human nature, with all its sensitive chords on which they will have to play. These chords are the cast of mind of the *goyim,* their tendencies, shortcomings, vices and qualities, the particularities of classes and conditions. Needless to say that the talented assistants of authority, of whom I speak, will be taken not from among the *goyim,* who are accustomed to perform their administrative work without giving themselves the trouble to think what its aim is, and never consider what it is needed for. The administrators of the *goyim* sign papers without reading them, and they serve either for mercenary reasons or from ambition.

We shall surround our government with a whole world of economists. That is the reason why economic sciences from the principal subject of the teaching given to the Jews. Around us again will be a whole constellation of bankers, industrialists, capitalists and — *the main thing — millionaires, because in substance everything will be settled by the question of figures.*

For a time, until there will no longer be any risk in entrusting responsible posts in our States to our brother-Jews, we shall put them in the hands of persons whose past and reputation are such that between them and the people lies an abyss, persons who, in case of disobedience to our instructions, must face criminal charges or disappear — this in order to make them defend our interests to their last gasp.

PROTOCOL NO. 9

Application of masonic principles in the matter of re-educating the peoples. Masonic watchword. Meaning of Anti-Semitism. Dictatorship of masonry. Terror. Who are the servants of masonry. Meaning of the "clear-sighted" and the "blind" forces of the *goyim* States. Communion between authority and mob. Licence of liberalism. Seizure of education and training. False theories. Interpretation of laws. The "undergrounds" (*metropolitains*).

In applying our principles let attention be paid to the character of the people in whose country you live and act; a general, identical application of them, until such time as the people shall have been re-educated to our pattern, cannot have success. But by approaching their application cautiously you will see that not a decade will pass before the most stubborn character will change and we shall add a new people to the ranks of those already subdued by us.

The words of the liberal, which are in effect the words of our masonic watchword, namely, "Liberty, Equality, Fraternity," will, when we come into our kingdom, be changed by us into words no longer of a watchword, but only an expression of idealism, namely, into: "The right of liberty, the duty of equality, the ideal of brotherhood." That is how we shall put it, — and so we shall catch the bull by the horns. . . . . . *De facto* we have already wiped out every kind of rule except our own, although *de jure* there still remain a good many of them. Nowadays, if any States raise a protest against us it is only *pro forma* at our discretion and by our direction, for *their anti-Semitism is indispensable to us for the management of our lesser brethren.* I will not enter into further explanations, for this matter has formed the subject of repeated discussions amongst us.

For us there are no checks to limit the range of our activity. Our Super-Government subsists in extra-legal conditions which are described in the accepted terminology by the energetic and forcible word — Dictatorship. I am in a position to tell you with a clear conscience that at the proper time we, the lawgivers, shall execute judgement and sentence, we shall slay and we shall spare, we, as head of all our troops, are mounted on the steed of the leader. We rule by force of will, because in our hands are the fragments of a once powerful party, now vanquished by us. *And the weapons in our hands are limitless ambitions, burning greediness, merciless vengeance, hatreds and malice.*

It is from us that the all-engulfing terror proceeds. We have in our service persons of all opinions, of all doctrines, restorating monarchists, demagogues, socialists, communists, and utopian dreamers of every kind. We have harnessed them all to the task: *each one of them on his own account is boring away at the last remnants of authority, is striving to overthrow all established form of order.* By these acts all States are in torture; they exhort to tranquillity, are ready to sacrifice everything for peace: *but we will not give them peace until they openly acknowledge our international Super-Government,* and with submissiveness.

The people have raised a howl about the necessity of settling the question of Socialism by way of an international agreement. *Division into fractional parties has given them into our hands, for, in order to carry on a contested struggle one must have money, and the money is all in our hands.*

We might have reason to apprehend a union between the "clear-sighted" force of the *goy* kings on their thrones and the *"blind"* force of the *goy* mobs, but we have taken all the needful measure against any such possibility: between the one and the other force we have erected a bulwark in the shape of a mutual terror between them. In this way the blind force of the people remains our support and we, and we only, shall provide them with a leader and, of course, direct them along the road that leads to our goal.

In order that the hand of the blind mob may not free itself from our guiding hand, we must every now and then enter into close communion with it, if not actually in person, at any rate through some of the most trusty of our brethren. When we are acknowledged as the only authority we shall discuss with the people personally on the market places, and we shall instruct them on questions of the political in such wise as may turn them in the direction that suits us.

Who is going to verify what is taught in the village schools? But what an envoy of the government or a king on his throne himself may say cannot but become immediately known to the whole State, for it will be spread abroad by the voice of the people.

In order not to annihilate the institutions of the *goyim* before it is time we have touched them with craft and delicacy, and have taken hold of the ends of the springs which move their mechanism. These springs lay in a strict but just sense of order; we have replaced them by the chaotic license of liberalism. We have got our hands into the administration of the law, into the conduct of elections, into the press, into liberty of the person, *but principally into education and training as being the corner-stones of a free existence.*

We have fooled, bemused and corrupted the youth of the goyim by rearing them in principles and theories which are known to us to be false although it is by us that they have been inculcated.

Above the existing laws without substantially altering them, and by merely twisting them into contradictions of interpertations, we have erected something grandiose in the way of results. These results found expression first in the fact that the *interpretations masked the laws*: afterwards they entirely hid them from the eyes of the governments owing to the impossibility of making anything out of the tangled web of legislation.

This is the origin of the theory of course of arbitration.

You may say that the *goyim* will rise upon us, arms in hand, if they guess what is going on before the time comes; but in the West we have against this a manoeuvre of such appalling terror that the very stoutest hearts quail — the undergrounds, metropolitains, those subterranean corridors which, before the time comes, will be driven under all the capitals and from whence those capitals will be blown into the air with all their organizations and archives.

PROTOCOL NO. 10

The outside appearances in the political. The "genius" of rascality. What is promised by a Masonic *coup d'état?* Universal suffrage. Self-importance. Leaders of Masonry. The genius who is guide of Masonry. Institutions and their functions. The poison of liberalism. Constitution — a school of party discords. Era of republics. Presidents — the puppets of Masonry. Responsibility of Presidents. "Panama" Part played by chamber of deputies and president. Masonry — the legislative force. New republican constitution. Transition to masonic "despotism." Moment for the proclamation of "The Lord of all the World." Inoculation of diseases and other wiles of Masonry.

To-day I begin with a repetition of what I said before, and *I beg you to bear in mind that governments and peoples are content in the political with outside appearances.* And how, indeed, are the *goyim* to perceive the underlying meaning of things when their representatives give the best of their energies to enjoying themselves? For

Our policy it is of the greatest importance to take cognisance of this detail; it will be of assistance to us when we come to consider the division of authority, freedom of speech, of the press, of religion (faith), of the law of association, of equality before the law, of the inviolability of property, of the dwelling, of taxation (the idea of concealed taxes), of the reflex force of the laws. All these questions are such as ought not to be touched upon directly and openly before the people. In cases where it is indispensable to touch upon them they must not be categorically named, it must merely be declared without detailed exposition that the principles of contemporary law are acknowledged by us. The reason of keeping silence in this respect is that by not naming a principle we leave ourselves freedom of action, to drop this or that out of it without attracting notice; if they were all categorically named they would all appear to have been already given.

The mob cherishes a special affection and respect for the geniuses of political power and accepts all their deeds of violence with the admiring response: "rascally, well, yes, it is rascally, but it's clever! . . . . a trick, if you like, but how craftily played, how magnificently done, what impudent audacity!" . . . .

We count upon attracting all nations to the task of erecting the new fundamental structure, the project for which has been drawn up by us. This is why, before everything, it is indispensable for us to arm ourselves and to store up in ourselves that absolutely reckless audacity and irresistible might of the spirit which in the person of our active workers will break down all hindrances on our way.

When we have accomplished our coup d'état we shall say then to the various peoples: "Everything has gone terribly badly, all have been worn out with sufferings. We are destroying the causes of your torment — nationalities, frontiers, differences of coinages. You are at liberty, of course, to pronounce sentence upon us, but can it pos-

sibly be a just one if it is confirmed by you before you make any trial of what we are offering you." . . . Then will the mob exalt us and bear us up in their hands in a unanimous triumph of hopes and expectations. Voting, which we have made the instrument will set us on the throne of the world by teaching even the very smallest units of members of the human race to vote by means of meetings and agreements by groups, will then have served its purposes and will play its part then for the last time by a unanimity of desire to make close acquaintance with us before condemning us.

To secure this we must have everybody vote without distinction of classes and qualifications, in order to establish an absolute majority, which cannot be got from the educated propertied classes. In this way, by inculcating in all a sense of self-importance, we shall destroy among the *goyim* the importance of the family and its educational value and remove the possibility of individual minds splitting off, for the mob, handled by us, will not let them come to the front nor even give them a hearing; it is accustomed to listen to us only who pay it for obedience and attention. In this way we shall create a blind, mighty force which will never be in a position to move in any direction without the guidance of our agents set at its head by us as leaders of the mob. The people will submit to this régime because it will know that upon these leaders will depend its earnings, gratifications and the receipt of all kinds of benefits.

A scheme of government should come ready made from one brain, because it will never be clinched firmly if it is allowed to be split into fractional parts in the minds of many. It is allowable, therefore, for us to have cognisance of the scheme of action but not to discuss it lest we disturb its artfulness, the interdependence of its component parts, the practical force of the secret meaning of each clause. To discuss and make alterations in a labor of this kind by means of numerous votings is to impress upon it the stamp of all ratiocinations and misunderstandings which have failed to penetrate the depth and nexus of its plottings. We want our schemes to be forcible and suitably concocted. Therefore WE OUGHT NOT TO FLING THE WORK OF GENIUS OF OUR GUIDE to the fangs of the mob or even of a select company.

These schemes will not turn existing institutions upside down just yet. They will only affect changes in their economy and consequently in the whole combined movement of their progress, which will thus be directed along the paths laid down in our schemes.

Under various names there exists in all countries approximately one and the same thing. Representation, Ministry, Senate, State Council, Legislative and Executive Corps. I need not explain to you the mechanism of the relation of these institutions to one another, because you are aware of all that; only take note of the fact that each of the above-named institutions corresponds to some important function of the State, and I would beg you to remark that the word "important" I apply not to the institution but to the function, consequently it is not the institutions which are important but their functions. These institutions have divided up among themselves all the functions of government — administrative, legislative, executive, wherefore they have come to operate as do the organs in the human body. If we injure one part in the machinery of State, the State falls sick, like a human body, and . . . . . . will die.

When we introduced into the State organism the poison of Liberalism its whole political complexion underwent a change. States have been seized with a mortal illness — blood-poisoning. All that remains is to await the end of their death agony.

Liberalism produced Constitutional States, which took the place of what was the only safeguard of the *goyim*, namely, Despotism; and a *constitution, as you well know, is nothing else but a school of discords,* misunderstandings, quarrels, disagreements, fruitless party agitations, party whims — in a word, a school of everything that serves to destroy the personality of State activity. *The tribune of the "talkeries" has, no less effectively than the Press, condemned the rulers to inactivity and impotence,* and thereby rendered them useless and superflous, for which reason indeed they have been in many countries deposed. *Then it was that the era of republics became possible of realization; and then it was that we replaced the ruler by a caricature of a government — by a president, taken from the mob, from the midst of our puppet creatures, our slaves.* This was the foundation of the mine which we have laid under the *goy* people, I should rather say, under the *goy* peoples.

In the near future we shall establish the responsibility of presidents.

By that time we shall be in a position to disregard forms in carrying through matters for which our impersonal puppet will be responsible. What do we care of the ranks of those striving for power should be thinned, if there should arise a deadlock from the impossibility of finding presidents, a deadlock which will finally disorganize the country? . . . .

In order that our scheme may produce this result we shall arrange elections in favour of such presidents as have in their past some dark, undiscovered stain, some "Panama" or other — then they will be trustworthy agents for the accomplishment of our plans out of fear of revelations and from the natural desire of everyone who has attained power, namely, the retention of the privileges, advantages and honour connected with the office of president. The chamber of deputies will provide cover for, will protect, will elect presidents, but we shall take from it the right to propose new, or make changes in existing laws, for this right will be given by us to the responsible president, a puppet in our hands. Naturally, the authority of the president will then become a target for every possible form of attack, but we shall provide him with a means of self-defense in the right of an appeal to the people, for the decision of the people over the heads of their representatives, that is to say, an appeal to that same blind slave of ours — the majority of the mob. Independently of this we shall invest the president with the right of declaring a state of war. We shall justify this last right on the ground that the president as chief of the whole army of the country must have it at his disposal, in case of need for the defense of the new republican constitution, the right to defend which will belong to him as the responsible representative of this constitution.

It is easy to understand that in these conditions the key of the shrine will lie in our hands, and no one outside ourselves will any longer direct the force of legislation.

Besides this we shall, with the introduction of the new republican constitution, take from the Chamber the right of interpellation on government measures, on the pretext of preserving political secrecy, and, further, we shall by the new constitution reduce the number of representatives to a minimum, thereby proportionately reducing political passions and the passion for politics. If, however, they should, which is hardly to be expected, burst into flame, even in this minimum, we shall nullify them by a stirring appeal and a reference to the majority of the whole people . . . . . Upon the president will depend the appointment of presidents and vice-presidents of the Chamber and the Senate. Instead of constant sessions of Parliaments we shall reduce their sittings to a few months. Moreover, the president, as chief of the executive power, will have the right to summon and dissolve Parliament, and, in the latter case, to prolong the time for the appointment of a new parliamentary assembly. But in order that the consequences of all these acts which in substance are illegal, should not, prematurely for our plans, fall upon the responsibility established by us of the president, *we shall instigate ministers and other officials of the higher administration about the president to evade his dispositions by taking measures of their own,* for doing which they will be made the scapegoats in his place. . . . This part we especially recommend to be given to be played by the Senate, the Council of State, or the Council of Ministers, but not to an individual official.

The president will, at our discretion, interpret the sense of such of the existing laws as admit of various interpretation; he will further annul them when we indicate to him the necessity to do so, besides this, he will have the right to propose temporary laws, and even new departures in the government constitutional working, the pretext both for the one and the other being the requirements for the supreme welfare of the State.

By such measures we shall obtain the power of destroying little by little, step by step, all that at the outset when we enter on our rights, we are compelled to introduce into the constitutions of States to prepare for the transition to an imperceptible abolition of every kind of constitution, and then the time is come to turn every form of government into *our despotism.*

The recognition of our despot may also come before the destruction of the constitution; the moment for this recognition will come when the peoples, utterly wearied by the irregularities and incompetence — a matter which we shall arrange for — of their rulers, will clamour: "Away with them and give us one king over all the earth who will unite us and annihilate the causes of discords — frontiers, nationalities, religions, State debts — who will give us peace and quiet, which we cannot find under our rulers and representatives."

But you yourselves perfectly well know that *to produce the possibility of the expression of such wishes by all the nations it is indispensable to trouble in all countries the people's relations with their governments so as to utterly exhaust humanity with dissension, hatred, struggle, envy and even by the use of torture, by starvation, BY THE INOCULATION OF DISEASES, by want, so that the* GOYIM *see no other issue than to take refuge in our complete sovereignty in money and in all else.*

But if we give the nations of the world a breathing space the moment we long for is hardly likely ever to arrive.

PROTOCOL NO. 11

Programme of the new constitution. Certain details of the proposed revolution. The *goyim* — a pack of sheep. Secret masonry and its "show" lodges.

The State Council has been, as it were, the emphatic expression of the authority of the ruler: it will be, as the "show" part of the Legislative Corps, what may be called the editorial committee of the laws and decrees of the ruler.

This, then, is the programme of the new constitution. We shall make Law, Right and Justice (1) in the guise of proposals to the Legislative Corps, (2) by decrees of the president under the guise of general regulations, of orders of the Senate and of resolutions of the State Council in the guise of ministerial orders, (3) and in case a suitable occasion should arise — in the form of a revolution in the State.

Having established approximately the *modus agendi* we will occupy ourselves with details of those combinations by which we have still to complete the revolution in the course of the machinery of State in the direction already indicated. By these combinations I mean the freedom of the Press, the right of association, freedom of conscience, the voting principle, and many another that must disappear for ever from the memory of man, or undergo a radical alteration the day after the promulgation of the new constitution. It is only at that moment that we shall be able at once to announce all our orders, for, afterwards, every noticable alteration will be dangerous, for the following reasons: if this alteration be brought in with harsh severity and in a sense of severity and limitations, it may lead to a feeling of despair caused by fear of new alterations in the same direction; if, on the other hand, it be brought in in a sense of further indulgences it will be said that we have recognized our own wrongdoing and this will destroy the prestige of the infallibility of our authority, or else it will be said that we have become alarmed and are compelled to show a yielding disposition, for which we shall get no thanks because it will be supposed to be compulsory . . . . Both the one and the other are injurious to the prestige of the new constitution. What we want is that from the first moment of its promulgation, while the peoples of the world are still stunned by the accomplished fact of the revolution, still in a condition of terror and uncertainty, they should recognize once for all that we are so strong, so inexpugnable, so superabundantly filled with power, that in no case shall we take any account of them, and so far from paying any attention to their opinions or wishes, we are ready and able to crush with irresistible power all expression or manifestation thereof at every moment and in every place, that we have seized at once everything we wanted and shall in no case divide our power with them . . . . Then in fear and trembling they will close their eyes to everything, and be content to await what will be the end of it all.

The *goyim* are a flock of sheep, and we are their wolves. And you know what happens when the wolves get hold of the flock? . . . .

There is another reason also why they will close their eyes: for we shall keep promising them to give back all the liberties we have taken away as soon as we have quelled the enemies of peace and tamed all parties . . . .

It is not worth while to say anything about how long

a time they will be kept waiting for this return of their liberties....

For what purpose then have we invented this whole policy and insinuated it into the minds of the goys without giving them any chance to examine its underlying meaning? For what, indeed, if not in order to obtain in a roundabout way what is for our scattered tribe unattainable by the direct road? It is this which has served as the basis for our organization of secret masonry which is not known to, and aims which are not even so much as suspected by, these *Goy* cattle, attracted by us into the "Show" army of Masonic Lodges in order to throw dust in the eyes of their fellows.

God has granted to us, His Chosen People, the gift of the dispersion, and in this which appears in all eyes to be our weakness, has come forth all our strength, which has now brought us to the threshold of sovereignty over all the world.

There now remains not much more for us to build up upon the foundation we have laid.

PROTOCOL NO. 12

Masonic interpretation of the word "freedom." Future of the press in the masonic kingdom. Control of the press. Correspondence agencies. What is progress as understood by masonry? More about the press. Masonic solidarity in the press of to-day. The arousing of "public" demands in the provinces. Infallibility of the new régime.

The word "freedom," which can be interpreted in various ways, is defined by us as follows:—

Freedom is the right to do that which the law allows. This interpretation of the word will at the proper time be of service to us, because all freedom will thus be in our hands, since the laws will abolish or create only that which is desirable for us according to the aforesaid programme.

We shall deal with the press in the following way: What is the part played by the press today? It serves to excite and inflame those passions which are needed for our purpose or else it serves selfish ends of parties. It is often vapid, unjust, mendacious, and the majority of the public have not the slightest idea what ends the press really serves. We shall saddle and bridle it with a tight curb: we shall do the same also with all productions of the printing press, for where would be the sense of getting rid of the attacks of the press if we remain targets for pamphlets and books? The produce of publicity, which nowadays is a source of heavy expense owing to the necessity of censoring it, will be turned by us into a very lucrative source of income to our State: we shall lay on it a special stamp tax and require deposits of caution-money before permitting the establishment of any organ of the press or of printing offices; these will then have to guarantee our government against any kind of attack on the part of the press. For any attempt to attack us, if such still be possible, we shall inflict fines without mercy. Such measures as stamp tax, deposits, of caution money and fines secured by these deposits, will bring in a huge income to the government. It is true that party organs might not spare money for the sake of publicity, but these we shall shut up at the second attack upon us. No one shall with impunity lay a finger on the aureole of our government infallibility. The pretext for stopping any publication will be the alleged plea that it is agitating the public mind without occasion or justification. *I beg you to note that among those making attacks upon us will also be organs established by us, but they will attack exclusively points that we have pre-determined to alter.*

Not a single announcement will reach the public without our control. Even now this is already attained by us inasmuch as all news items are received by a few agencies, in whose offices they are focused from all parts of the world. These agencies will then be already entirely ours and will give publicity only to what we dictate to them.

If already now we have contrived to possess ourselves of the minds of the *goy* communities to such an extent that they all come near looking upon the events of the world through the coloured glasses of those spectacles we are setting astride their noses: if already now there is not a single State where there exist for us any barriers to admittance into what *goy* stupidity calls State secrets: what will our position be then, when we shall be acknowledged supreme lords of the world in the person of our king of all the world. . . .

Let us turn again to the *future of the printing press*. Every one desirous of being a publisher, librarian, or printer, will be obliged to provide himself with the diploma instituted therefor, which, in case of any fault, will be immediately impounded. With such measures *the instrument of thought will become an educative means in the hands of our government, which will no longer allow the mass of the nation to be led astray in by-ways and fantasies about the blessings of progress.* Is there any one of us who does not know that these phantom blessings are the direct roads to foolish imaginings which give birth to anarchical relations of men among themselves and towards authority, because progress, or rather the idea of progress, has introduced the conception of every kind of emancipation, but has failed to establish its limits . . . All the so-called liberals are anarchists, if not in fact, at any rate in thought. Every one of them is hunting after phantoms of freedom, and falling exclusively into license, that is, into the anarchy of protest for the sake of protest.

We turn to the periodical press. We shall impose on it, as on all printed matter, stamp taxes per sheet and deposits of caution-money, and books of less than 30 sheets will pay double. We shall reckon them as pamphlets in order, on the one hand, to reduce the number of magazines, which are the worst form of printed poison, and, on the other, in order that this measure may force writers into such lenghty productions that they will be little read especially as they will be costly. At the same time what we shall publish ourselves to influence mental development in the direction laid down for our profit will be cheap and will be read voraciously. The tax will bring vapid literary ambitions within bounds and the liability to penalties will make literary men dependent upon us. And if there should be any found who are desirous of writing against us, they will not find any person eager to print their productions. Before accepting any production for publication in print the publisher or printer will have to apply to the authorities for permission to do so. Thus we shall know beforehand of all tricks preparing against us and shall nullify them by getting ahead with explanations on the subject treated of.

Literature and journalism are two of the most important educative forces, and therefore our government will become proprietor of the majority of the journals. This will neutralize the injurious influence of the privately-owned press and will put us in possession of the tremendous influence upon the public mind. . . . If we give permit for ten journals, we shall ourselves found thirty, and so on the same proportion. This, however, must in nowise be suspected by the public. For which reason all journals published by us will be of the most opposite, in appearance, tendencies and opinions, thereby creating confidence in us and bringing over to us our quite unsuspicious opponents, who will thus fall into our trap and be rendered harmless.

In the front rank will stand organs of an official character. They will always stand guard over our interests, and therefore their influence will comparatively insignificant.

In the second rank will be the semi-official organs, whose part it will be to attract the tepid and indifferent.

In the third rank we shall set up our own, to all appearance, opposition, which, in at least one of its organs, will present what looks like the very antipodes to us. Our real opponents at heart will accept this simulated opposition as their own and will show us their cards.

All our newspapers will be of all possible complexions — aristocratic, republican, revolutionary, even anarchical —for so long, of course, as the constitution exists . . . . . Like the Indian idol Vishnu they will have a hundred hands, and every one of them will have a finger on any one of the public opinions as required. When a pulse quickens these hands will lead opinion in the direction of our aims, for an excited patient loses all power of judgment and easily yields to suggestion. Those fools who will think they are repeating the opinion of a newspaper of their own camp will be repeating our opinion or any opinion that seems desirable for us. In the vain belief that they are following the organ of their party they will in fact follow the flag which we hang out for them.

In order to direct our newspaper militia in this sense we must take especial and minute care in organizing this matter. Under the title of central department of the press we shall institute literary gatherings at which our agents will without attracting attention issue the orders and watchwords of the day. By discussing and controverting, but always superficially, without touching the essence of the matter, our organs will carry on a sham fight fusillade with the official newspapers solely for the purpose of giving occasion for us to express ourselves more fully than could well be done from the outset in official announcements, whenever, of course, that is to our advantage.

These attacks upon us will also serve another purpose, namely, that our subjects will be convinced of the existence of full freedom of speech and so give our agents an occasion to affirm that all organs which oppose us are empty babblers, since they are incapable of finding any substantial objections to our orders.

Methods of organization like these, imperceptible to the public eye but absolutely sure, are the best calculated to succeed in bringing the attention and the confidence of the public to the side of our government. Thanks to such methods we shall be in a position as from time to time may be required, to excite or to tranquillise the public mind on political questions, to persuade or to confuse, printing now truth, now lies, facts or their contradictions, according as they may be well or ill received, always very cautiously feeling our ground before stepping upon it . . . *We shall have a sure triumph over our opponents since they will not have at their disposition organs of the press in which they can give full and final expression to their views* owing to the aforesaid methods of dealing with the press. We shall not even need to refute them except very superficially.

Trial shots like these, fired by us in the third rank of our press, in case of need, will be energetically refuted by us in our semi-official organs.

Even nowadays, already, to take only the French press, there are forms which reveal masonic solidarity in acting on the watchword: all organs of the press are bound together by professional secrecy; like the augurs of old, not one of their numbers will give away the secret of his sources of information unless it be resolved to make announcement of them. Not one journalist will venture to betray this secret, for not one of them is ever admitted to practise literature unless his whole past has some disgraceful sore or other. . . . These sores would be immediately revealed. So long as they remain the secret of a few the prestige of the journalist attracts the majority of the country — the mob follow after him with enthusiasm.

Our calculations are especially extended to the provinces. It is indispensable for us to inflame there those hopes and impulses with which we could at any moment fall upon the capital, and we shall represent to the capitals that these expressions are the independent hopes and impulses of the provinces. Naturally, the source of them will be always one and the same — ours. *What we need is that, until such time as we are in the plenitude of power, the capitals should find themselves stifled by the provincial opinion of the nation,* i.e., *of a majority arranged by our agentur.* What we need is that at the psychological moment the capitals should not be in a position to discuss an accomplished fact for the simple reason, if for no other, that it has been accepted by the public opinion of a majority in the provinces.

When we are in the period of the new régime transitional to that of our assumption of full sovereignty we must not admit any revelations by the press of any form of public dishonesty; it is necessary that the new régime should be thought to have so perfectly contented everybody that even criminality has disappeared . . . . Cases of the manifestation of criminality should remain known only to their victims and to chance witnesses — no more.

PROTOCOL NO. 13

The need for daily bread. Questions of the Political. Questions of industry. Amusements. People's Palaces. "Truth is One." The great problems.

The need for daily bread forces the *goyim* to keep silence and be our humble servants. Agents taken on to our press from among the goyim will at our orders discuss anything which it is inconvenient for us to issue directly in official documents, and we meanwhile, quietly amid the din of the discussion so raised, shall simply take and carry through such measures as we wish and then offer them to the public as an accomplished fact. No one will dare to demand the abrogation of a matter once settled, all the more so as it will be represented as an improvement. . . . . . And immediately the press will distract the current of thought towards new questions (have we not trained people always to be seeking something new?). Into the discussions of these new questions will throw themselves those of the brainless dispensers of fortunes who are not able even now to understand that they have not the remotest conception about the matters which they undertake to discuss. Questions of the political are unattainable for any save those who have guided it already for many ages, the creators.

From all this you will see that in securing the opinion of the mob we are only facilitating the working of our machinery, and you may remark that it is not for actions but for words issued by us on this or that question that we seem to seek approval. We are constantly making public declaration that we are guided in all our undertakings by the hope, joined to the conviction, that we are serving the common weal.

In order to distract people who may be too troublesome from discussions of questions of the political we are now putting forward what we allege to be new questions of the political, namely, questions of industry. In this sphere let them discuss themselves silly! The masses are agreed to remain inactive, to take a rest from what they suppose to be political activity (which we trained them to in order to use them as a means of combating the *goy* governments) only on condition of being found new employments, in which we are prescribing them something that looks like the same political object. In order that the masses themselves may not guess what they are about *we further distract them with amusements, games, pastimes, passions, people's palaces. . . Soon we shall begin through the press to propose competitions in art, in sport of all kinds*: these interests will finally distract their minds from question in which we should find ourselves compelled to oppose them. Growing more and more disaccustomed to reflect and form any opinions of their own, people will begin to talk in the same tone as we, because we alone shall be offering them new directions for thought . . . of course through such persons as will not be suspected of solidarity with us.

The part played by the liberals, utopian dreamers, will be finally played out when our government is acknowledged. Till such time they will continue to do us good service. Therefore we shall continue to direct their minds to all sorts of vain conceptions of fantastic theories, new and apparently progressive: for have we not with complete success turned the brainless heads of the *goyim* with progress, till there it not among the *goyim* one mind able to perceive that under this work lies a departure from truth in all cases where it is not a question of material inventions, for truth is one, and in it there is no place for progress. Progress, like a fallacious idea, serves to obscure truth so that none may know it except us, the Chosen of God, its guardians.

When we come into our kingdom our orators will expound great problems which have turned humanity upside down in order to bring it at the end under our beneficent rule.

Who will ever suspect then that *all these peoples were stage-managed by us according to political plan which no one has so much as guessed at in the course of many centuries?* . . . .

PROTOCOL NO. 14

The religion of the future. Future conditions of serfdom. Inaccessibility of knowledge regarding the religion of the future. Pornography and the printed matter of the future.

When we come into our kingdom it will be undesirable for us that there should exist any other religion than ours of the One God with whom our destiny is bound up by our position as the Chosen People and through whom our same destiny is united with the destinies of the world. We must therefore sweep away all other forms of belief. If this gives birth to the atheists whom we see to-day, it will not, being only a transitional stage, interfere with our views, but will serve as a warning for those generations which will hearken to our preaching of the religion of Moses, that, by its stable and thoroughly elaborated system has brought all the peoples of the world into subjection to us. Therein we shall emphasize its mystical right, on which, as we shall say, all its educative power is based. . . . Then at every possible opportunity we shall publish articles in which we shall make comparisons between our beneficent rule and those of past ages. The blessings of tranquillity, though it be a tranquillity forcibly brought about by centuries of agitation, will throw into higher relief the benefits to which we shall point. The errors of the *goyim* governments will be depicted by us in the most vivid hues. We shall implant such an abhorrence of them that the peoples will prefer tranquillity in a state of serfdom to those rights of vaunted freedom which have tortured humanity and exhausted the very sources of human existence, sources which have been exploited by a mob of rascally adventurers who know not what they do . . . . *Useless changes of forms of government to which we instigated the* GOYIM *when we were undermining their state structures, will have so wearied the peoples by that time that they will prefer to suffer anything under us rather than run the risk of enduring again all the agitations and miseries they have gone through.*

At the same time we shall not omit to emphasize the historical mistakes of the *goy* governments which have tormented humanity for so many centuries by their lack of understanding of everything that constitutes the true good of humanity in their chase after fantastic schemes of social blessings, and have never noticed that these schemes kept on producing a worse and never a better state of the universal relations which are the basis of human life. . . .

The whole force of our principles and methods will lie in the fact that we shall present them and expound them as a splendid contrast to the dead and decomposed old order of things in social life.

Our philsosophers will discuss all the shortcomings of the various beliefs of the GOYIM, *but no one will ever bring under discussion our faith from its true point of view since this will be fully learned by none save ours, who will never dare to betray its secrets.*

In countries known as progressive and enlightened we have created a senseless, filthy, abominable literature. For some time after our entrance to power we shall continue to encourage its existence in order to provide a telling relief by contrast to the speeches, party programme, which will be distributed from exalted quarters of ours. . . . Our wise men, trained to become leaders of the *goyim,* will compose speeches, projects, memoirs, articles, which will be used by us to influence the minds of the *goyim,* directing them towards such understanding and forms of knowledge as have been determined by us.

PROTOCOL NO. 15

One-day *coup d'état* (revolution) over all the world. Executions. Future lot of *goyim*-masons. Mysticism of authority. Multiplication of masonic lodges. Central governing board of masonic elders. The "Azev-tactics." Masonry as leader and guide of all secret societies. Significance of public applause. Collectivism. Victims. Executions of masons. Fall of the prestige of laws and authority. Our position as the Chosen people. Brevity and clarity of the laws of the kingdom of the future.

Obedience to orders. Measures against abuse of authority. Severity of penalties. Age-limit for judges. Liberalism of judges and authorities. The money of all the world. Absolutism of masonry. Right of appeal. Patriarchal "outside appearance" of the power of the future "ruler." Apotheosis of the ruler. The right of the strong as the one and only right. The King of Israel. Patriarch of all the world.

When we at last definitely come into our kingdom by the aid of *coups détat* prepared everywhere for one and the same day, after the worthlessness of all existing forms of government has been definitely acknowledged (and not a little time will pass before that comes about, perhaps even a whole century) we shall make it our task to see that against us such things as plots shall no longer exist. With this purpose we shall slay without mercy all who take arms (in hand) to oppose our coming into our kingdom. Every kind of new institution of anything like a secret society will also be punished with death; those of them which are now in existence, are known to us, serve us and have served us, we shall disband and send into exile to continents far removed from Europe. *In this way we shall proceed with those* GOY *masons who know too much;* such of these as we may for some reason spare will be kept in constant fear of exile. We shall promulgate a law making all former members of secret societies liable to exile from Europe as the centre of our rule.

Resolutions of our government will be final, without appeal.

In the *goy* societies, in which we have planted and deeply rooted discord and protestantism, the only possible way of restoring order is to employ merciless measures that prove the direct force of authority: no regard must be paid to the victims who fall, they suffer for the well-being of the future. The attainment of that well-being, even at the expense of sacrifices, is the duty of any kind of government that acknowledges as justification for its existence not only its privileges but its obligations. The principal guarantee of stability of rule is to confirm the aureole of power, and this aureole is attained only by such a majestic inflexibility of might as shall carry on its face the emblems of inviolability from mystical causes — from the choice of God. *Such was, until recent times, the Russian autocracy, the one and only serious foe we had in the world, without counting the Papacy.* Bear in mind the example when Italy, drenched with blood, never touched a hair of the head of Sulla who had poured forth that blood: Sulla enjoyed an apotheosis for his might in the eyes of the people, though they had been torn in pieces by him, but his intrepid return to Italy ringed him round with inviolability. The people do not lay a finger on him who hypnotizes them by his daring and strength of mind.

Meantime, however, until we come into our kingdom, we shall act in the contrary way: we shall create and multiply free masonic lodges in all the countries of the world, absorb into them all who may become or who are prominent in public activity, for in these lodges we shall find our principal intelligence office and means of influence. All these lodges we shall bring under one central administration, known to us alone and to all others absolutely unknown, which will be composed of our learned elders. The lodges will have their representatives who will serve to screen the above-mentioned administration of *masonry* and from whom will issue the watchword and programme. In these lodges we shall tie together the knot which binds together all revolutionary and liberal elements. Their composition will be made up of all strata of society. The most secret political plots will be known to us and will fall under our guiding hands on the very day of their conception. *Among the members of these lodges will be almost all the agents of international and national police* since their service is for us irreplaceable in the respect that the police is in a position not only to use its own particular measures with the insubordinate, but also to screen our activities and provide pretexts for discontents, *et cetera.*

The class of people who most willingly enter into secret societies are those who live by their wits, careerists, and in general people, mostly light-minded, with whom we shall have no difficulty in dealing and in using to wind up the mechanism of the machine devised by us. If this world grows agitated the meaning of that will be that we have had to stir it up in order to break up its too great solidarity. *But if there should arise in its midst a plot, then at the head of that plot will be no other than one of our most trusted servants.* It is natural that we and no other should lead *masonic* activities, for we know whither we are leading, we know the final goal of every form of activity whereas the *goyim* have knowledge of nothing, not even of the immediate effect of action; they put before themselves, usually, the momentary reckoning of the satisfaction of their self-opinion in the accomplishment of their thought without even remarking that the very conception never belonged to their initiative but to our instigation of their thought. . . .

The goyim enter the lodges out of curiosity or in the hope by their means to get a nibble at the public pie, and some of them in order to obtain a hearing before the public for their impracticable and groundless fantasies: they thirst for the emotion of success and applause, of which we are remarkably generous. And the reason why we give them this success is to make use of the high conceit of themselves to which it gives birth, for that insensibly disposes them to assimilate our suggestions without being on their guard against them in the fullness of their confidence that it is their own infallibility which is giving utterance to their own thoughts and that it is impossible for them to borrow those of others. . . . You cannot imagine to what extent the wisest of the *goyim* can be brought to a state of unconscious naiveté in the presence of this condition of high conceit of themselves, and at the same time how easy it is to take the heart out of them by the slightest ill-success, though it be nothing more than the stoppage of the applause they had, and to reduce them to a slavish submission for the sake of winning a renewal of success. . . . *By so much as ours disregard success if only they can carry through their plans, by so much the* GOYIM *are willing to sacrifice any plans only to have success.* This psychology of theirs materially facilitates for us the task of setting them in the required direction. These tigers in appearance have the souls of sheep and the wind blows freely through their heads. We have set them on the hobby-horse of an idea about the absorption of individuality by the symbolic unit of *collectivism.* They have never yet and they never will have the sense to reflect that this hobby-horse is a manifest violation of the most important law of nature, which has established from the very creation of the world one unit unlike another and precisely for the purpose of instituting individuality. . . . .

If we have been able to bring them to such a pitch of stupid blindness is it not a proof, and an amazingly clear proof, of the degree to which the mind of the *goyim* is undeveloped in comparison with our mind? This it is, mainly, which guarantees our success.

And how far-seeing were our learned elders in ancient times when they said that to attain a serious end it behooves not to stop at any means or to count the victims sacrificed for the sake of that end. . . We have not counted the victims of the seed of the goy cattle, though we have sacrificed many of our own, but for that we have now already given them such a position on the earth as they could not even have dreamed of. The comparatively small numbers of the victims from the number of ours have preserved our nationality from destruction.

Death is the inevitable end for all. It is better to bring that end nearer to those who hinder our affairs than to ourselves, to the founders of this affair. *We execute masons in such wise that none save the brotherhood can ever have a suspicion of it, not even the victims themselves of our death sentence, they all die when required as if from a normal kind of illness.* . . . Knowing this, even the brotherhood in its turn dare not protest. By such methods we have plucked out of the midst of *masonry* the very root of protest against our disposition. While preaching liberalism to the *goyim* we at the same time keep our own people and our agents in a state of unquestioning submission.

Under our influence the execution of the laws of the *goyim* has been reduced to a minimum. The prestige of the law has been exploded by the liberal interpretations introduced into this sphere. In the most important and fundamental affairs and questions judges decide as we dictate to them, see matters in the light wherewith we enfold them for the administration of the *goyim,* of course, through persons who are our tools though we do not appear to have anything in common with them — by newspaper opinion or by other means. . . . Even senators and the higher administration accept our counsels. The purely brute mind of the *goyim* is incapable of use for analysis and observation, and still more for the foreseeing whither a certain manner of setting a question may tend.

In this difference in capacity for thought between the *goyim* and ourselves may be clearly discerned the seal of our position on the Chosen People and of our higher quality of humanness, in contradistinction to the brute mind of the *goyim.* Their eyes are open, but see nothing before them and do not invent (unless, perhaps, material things). From this it is plain that nature herself has destined us to guide and rule the world.

When comes the time of our overt rule, the time to manifest its blessings, we shall remake all legislatures, all our laws will be brief, plain, stable, without any kind of interpretations, so that anyone will be in a position to know them perfectly. The main feature which will run right through them is submission to orders, and this principle will be carried to a grandiose height. Every abuse will then disappear in consequence of the responsibility of all down to the lowest unit before the higher authority of the representative of power. Abuses of power subordinate to this last instance will be so mercilessly punished that none will be found anxious to try experiments with their own powers. We shall follow up jealously every action of the administration on which depends the smooth running of the machinery of the State, for slackness in this produces slackness everywhere; not a single case of illegality or abuse of power will be left without exemplary punishment.

Concealment of guilt, connivance between those in the service of the administration — all this kind of evil will disappear after the very first examples of severe punishment. The aureole of our power demands suitable, that is, cruel, punishments for the slightest infringement, for the sake of gain, of its supreme prestige. The sufferer, though his punishment may exceed his fault, will count as a soldier falling on the administrative field of battle in the interest of authority, principle and law, which do not permit that any of those who hold the reins of the public coach should turn aside from the public highway to their own private paths. *For example: our judges will know that whenever they feel disposed to plume themselves on foolish clemency they are violating the law of justice which is instituted for the exemplary edification of men by penalties for lapses and not for display of the spiritual qualities of the judge....* Such qualities it is proper to show in private life, but not in a public square which is the educationary basis of human life.

Our legal staff will serve not beyond the age of 55, firstly because old men more obstinately hold to prejudiced opinions, and are less capable of submitting to new directions, and secondly because this will give us the possibility by this measure of securing elasticity in the changing of staff, which will thus the more easily bend under our pressure: he who wishes to keep his place will have to give blind obedience to deserve it. In general, our judges will be elected by us only from among those who thoroughly understand that the part they have to play is to punish and apply laws and not to dream about the manifestations of liberalism at the expense of the educationary scheme of the State, as the *goyim* in these days imagine it to be. . . . . This method of shuffling the staff will serve also to explode any collective solidarity of those in the same service and will bind all to the interests of the government upon which their fate will depend. The young generation of judges will be trained in certain views regarding the inadmissibility of any abuses that might disturb the established order of our subjects among themselves.

In these days the judges of the *goyim* create indulgences to every kind of crimes, not having a just understanding of their office, because the rulers of the present age in appointing judges to office take no care to inculcate in them a sense of duty and consciousness of the matetr which is demanded of them. As a brute beast lets out its young in search of prey, so do the *goyim* give their subjects places of profit without thinking to make clear to them for what purpose such place was created. This is the reason why their governments are being ruined by their own forces through the acts of their own administration.

Let us borrow from the example of the results of these actions yet another lesson for our government.

We shall root out liberalism from all the important strategic posts of our government on which depends the training of subordinates for our State structure. Such posts will fall exclusively to those who have been trained by us for administrative rule. To the possible objection that the retirement of old servants will cost the Treasury heavily, I reply, firstly, they will be provided with some private service in place of what they lose, and, secondly, I have to remark that all the money in the world will be concentrated in our hands, consequently it is not our government that has to fear expense.

Our absolutism will in all things be logically consecutive and therefore in each one of its decrees our supreme will will be respected and unquestionably fulfilled: it will ignore all murmurs, all discontents of every kind and will destroy to the root every kind of manifestation of them in act by punishment of an exemplary character.

We shall abolish the right of cassation, which will be transferred exclusively to our dispotal—to the cognisanze of him who rules, for we must not allow the conception among the people of a thought that there could be such a thing as a decision that is not right of judges set up by us. If, however, anything like this should occur, we shall ourselves cassate the decision, but inflict therewith such exemplary punishment on the judge for lack of understanding of his duty and the purpose of his appointment as will prevent a repetition of such cases. . . . I repeat that it must be borne in mind that we shall know every step of our administration which only needs to be closely watched for the people to be content with us, for it has the right to demand from a good government a good official.

Our government will have the appearance of a patriarchial paternal guardianship on the part of our ruler. Our own nation and our subjects will discern in his person a father caring for their every need, their every act, their every inter-relation as subjects one with another, as well as their relations to the ruler. They will then be so thoroughly imbued with the thought that it is impossible for them to dispense with this wardship and guidance, if the wish to live in piece and quiet, *that they will acknowledge the autocracy of our ruler with a devotion bordering on APOTHEOSIS,* especially when they are convinced that those whom we set up do not put their own in place of his authority, but only blindly execute his dictates. They will be rejoiced that we have regulated everything in their lives as is done by wise parents who desire to train their children in the cause of duty and submission. For the peoples of the world in regard to the secrets of our polity are ever through the ages only children under age, precisely as are also their governments.

As you see, I found our despotism on right and duty: the right to compel the execution of duty is the direct obligation of a government which is a father for its subjects. It has the right of the strong that it may use it for the benefit of directing humanity towards that order which is defined by nature, namely, submission. Everything in the world is in a state of submission, if not to man, then to circumstances or its own inner character, in all cases, to what is stronger. And so shall we be this something stronger for the sake of good.

We are obliged without hestitation to sacrifice individuals, who commit a breach of established order, for in the exemplary punishment of evil lies a great educational problem.

When the King of Israel sets upon his sacred head the crown offered him by Europe he will become patriarch of the world. The indispensable victims offered by him in consequence of their suitability will never reach the number of victims offered in the course of conturies by the mania of magnificence, the emulation between the *goy* governments. . .

Our King will be in constant communion with the peoples, making to them from the tribune speeches which fame will in that same hour distribute over all the world.

PROTOCOL NO. 16

Emasculation of the universities. Substitute for classicism. Training and calling. Advertisement of the authority of "the ruler" in the schools. Abolition of freedom of instruction. New Theories. Independence of thought. Teaching by object lessons.

In order to effect the destruction of all collective forces except ours we shall emasculate the first stage of collectivism — the *universities*, by re-educating them in a new direction. *Their officials and professors will be prepared for their business by detailed secret programmes of action from which they will not with immunity diverge, not by one iota. They will be appointed with especial precaution, and will be so placed as to be wholly dependent upon the Government.*

We shall exclude from the course of instruction State Law as also all that concerns the political question. These subjects will be taught to a few dozens of persons chosen for their pre-eminent capacities from among the number of the initiated. *The universities must no longer send out from their halls milksops concocting plans for a constitution, like a comedy or a tragedy, busying themselves with questions of policy in which even their own fathers never had any power of thought.*

The ill-guided acquaintance of a large number of persons with questions of polity creates utopian dreamers and bad subjects, as you can see for yourselves from the example of the universal education in this direction of the *goyim*. We must introduce into their education all those principles which have so brillantly broken up their order. But when we are in power we shall remove every kind of disturbing subject from the course of education and shall make out of the youth obedient children of authority, loving him who rules as the support and hope of peace and quiet.

Classicism, as also any form of study of ancient history, in which there are more bad than good examples, we shall replace with the study of the programme of the future. We shall erase from the memory of men all facts of previous centuries which are undesirable to us, and leave only those which depict all the errors of the governments of the *goyim*. The study of practical life, of the obligations of order, of the relations of people one to another, of avoiding bad and selfish examples which spread the infection of evil, and similar questions of an educative nature, will stand in the forefront of the teaching programme, which will be drawn up on a separate plan for each calling or state of life, in no wise generalising the teaching. This treatment of the question has special importance.

Each state of life must be trained within strict limits corresponding to its destination and work in life. The *occasional genius has always managed and always will manage to slip through into other states of life, but it is the most perfect folly for the sake of this rare occasional genius to let through into ranks foreign to them the untalented who thus rob of their places those who belong to those ranks by birth or employment. You know yourselves in what all this has ended for the goyim who allowed this crying absurdity.*

In order that he who rules may be seated firmly in the hearts and minds of his subjects it is necessary for the time of his activity to instruct the whole nation in the schools and on the market places about his meaning and his acts and all his beneficent initiatives.

We shall abolish every kind of freedom of instruction. Learners of all ages will have the right to assemble together with their parents in the educational establishments as it were in a club: during these assemblies, on holydays, teachers will read what will pass as free lectures on questions of human relations, of the laws of examples, of the limitations which are born of unconscious relations, and, finally, of the philosophy of new theories not yet declared to the world. These theories will be raised by us to the stage of a dogma of faith as a transitional stage towards our faith. On the completion of this exposition of our programme of action in the present and the future I will read you the principles of these theories.

In a word, knowing by the experience of many centuries that people live and are guided by ideas, that these ideas are imbibed by people only by the aid of education provided with equal success for all ages of growth, but of course by varying methods, we shall swallow up and confiscate to our own use the last scintilla of independence of thought, which we have for long past been directing towards subjects and ideas useful for us. The system of bridling thought is already at work in the so-called system of teaching by *object lessons,* the purpose of which is to turn the *goyim* into unthinking submissive brutes waiting for things to be presented before their eyes in order to form an idea of them. . . In France, one of four best agents, Bourgeois, has already made public a new programme of teaching by object lessons.

PROTOCOL NO. 17

Advocacy. Influence of the priesthood of the *goyim.* Freedom of conscience. Papal Court. King of the Jews as Patriarch-Pope. How to fight the existing Church. Function of contemporary press. Organization of police. Volunteer police. Espionage on the pattern of the *kabal* espionage. Abuses of authority.

The practice of advocacy produces men cold, cruel, persistent, unprincipled, who in all cases take up an impersonal purely legal standpoint. They have the inveterate habit to refer everything to its value for the defence, not to the public welfare of its results. They do not usually decline to undertake any defence whatever, they strive for an acquittal at all costs, cavilling over every petty crux of jurisprudence and thereby they demoralize justice. For this reason we shall set this profession into narrow frames which will keep it inside this sphere of executive public service. Advocates, equally with judges, will be deprived of the right of communication with litigants; they will receive business only from the court and will study it by notes off report and documents, defending their clients after they have been interrogated in court on facts that have appeared. They will receive an honorarium without regard to the quality of the defence. This will render them mere reporters on law-business in the interests of justice and as counterpoise to the proctor who will be the reporter in the interests of prosecution; this will shorten business before the courts. In this way will be established a practice of honest unprejudiced defence conducted not from personal interest but by conviction. This will also, by the way, remove the present practice of corrupt bargain between advocates to agree only to let that side win which pays most. . . .

We have long past taken care to discredit the priesthood of the goyim, and thereby to ruin their mission on earth which in these days might still be a great hindrance to us. Day by day its influence on the peoples of the world is falling lower. *Freedom of conscience* has been declared everywhere, so *that now only years divide us from the moment of the complete wrecking of that Christian religion,* as to other religions we shall have still less difficulty in dealing with them, but it would be premature to speak of this now. We shall set clericalism and clericals into such narrow frames as to make their influence move in retrogressive proportion to its former progress.

When the time comes finally to destroy the papal court the finger of an invisible hand will point the nations towards this court. When, however, the nations fling themselves upon it, we shall come forward in the guise of its defenders as if to save excessive bloodshed. By this diversion we shall penetrate to its very bowels and be sure we shall never come out again until we have gnawed through the entire strength of this place.

The King of the Jews will be the real Pope of the Universe, the patriarch of an international Church.

But, *in the meantime,* while we are re-educating youth in new traditional religions and afterwards in ours, *we shall not overtly lay a finger on existing churches, but we shall fight against them by criticism calculated to produce schism.* . . . .

In general, then, our contemporary press will continue to *convict* State affairs, religions, incapacities of the *goyim,* always using the most unprincipled expressions in order by every means to lower their prestige in the manner which can only be practiced by the genius of our gifted tribe. . . . .

Our kingdom will be an apologia of the divinity Vishnu, in whom is found its personification — in our hundred hands will be, one in each, the springs of the machinery of social life. We shall see everything without the aid of official police which, in that scope of its rights which we elaborated for the use of the *goyim,* hinders governments from seeing. In our programme *one-third of our subjects will keep the rest under observation* from a sense of duty, on the principle of volunteer service to the State. It will then be no disgrace to be a spy and informer, but a merit: unfounded denunciations, however, will be cruelly punished that there may be no development of abuses of this right.

Our agents will be taken from the higher as well as the lower ranks of society, from among the administrative class who spend their time in amusements, editors, printers and publishers, booksellers, clerks, and salesmen, workmen, coachmen, lackeys, etcetera. This body, having no rights and not being empowered to take any action on their own account, and consequently a police without any power, will only witness and report: verification of their reports and arrests will depend upon a responsible group of controllers of police affairs, while the actual act of arrest will be performed by the gendarmerie and the municipal police. Any person not denouncing anything seen or heard concerning questions of polity will also be charged with and made responsible for concealment, if it be proved that he is guilty of this crime.

Just as nowadays our brethren are obliged at their own risk to denounce to the kabal apostates of their own family or members who have been noticed doing anything in opposition to the *kabal, so in our kingdom over all the world it will be obligatory for all our subjects to observe the duty of service to the State in this direction.*

Such an organization will extirpate abuses of authority, of force, of bribery, everything in fact which we by our counsels, by our theories of the superhuman rights of man, have introduced into the customs of the *goyim*. . . . But how else were we to procure that increase of causes predisposing to disorders in the midst of their administration? . . . Among the number of those methods one of the most important is — agents for the restoration of order, so placed as to have the opportunity in their disintegrating activity of developing and displaying their evil enclinations — obstinate self-conceit, irresponsible exercise of authority, and, first and foremost, venality.

PROTOCOL NO. 18

Measures of secret defense. Observation of conspiracies from the inside. Overt secret defense — the ruin of authority. Secret defense of the King of the Jews. Mystical prestige of authority. Arrest on the first suspicion.

When it becomes necessary for us to strengthen the strict measures of secret defense (the most fatal poison for the prestige of authority) we shall arrange a simulation of disorders or some manifestation of discontents finding expression through the co-operation of good speakers. Round these speakers will assemble all who are sympathetic to his utterances. This will give us the pretext for domiciliary perquisitions and surveillance on the part of our servants from among the number of the *goyim police*. . . . . .

As the majority of conspirators act out of love for the game, for the sake of talking, so, until they commit some overt act we shall not lay a finger on them but only introduce into their midst observation elements. . . . . It must be remembered that the prestige of authority is lessened if it frequently discovers conspiracies against itself: this implies a presumption of consciousness of weakness, or, what is still worse, of injustice. You are aware that we have broken the prestige of the *goy* kings by frequent attempts upon their lives through our agents, blind sheep of our flock, who are easily moved by a few liberal phrases to crimes provided only they be painted in political colours. *We have compelled the rulers to acknowledge their weakness in advertising overt measures of secret defence and thereby we shall bring the promise of authority to destruction.*

Our ruler will be secretly protected only by the most insignificant guard, because we shall not admit so much as a thought that there could exist against him any sedition with which he is not strong enough to contend and is compelled to hide from it.

If we should admit this thought, as the *goyim* have done and are doing, we should *ipso facto* be signing a death sentence, if not for our ruler, at any rate for his dynasty, at no distant date.

According to strictly enforced outward appearances our ruler will employ his power only for the advantage of the nation and in no wise for his own or dynastic profits. Therefore, with the observance of this decorum, his authority will be respected and guarded by the subjects themselves, it will receive an apotheosis in the admission that with it is bound up the well-being of every citizen of the State, for upon it will depend all order in the common life of the pack. . . . .

Overt defense of the kind argues weakness in the organization of his strength.

Our ruler will always among the people be surrounded by a mob of apparently curious men and women, who will occupy the front ranks about him, to all appearance by chance, and will restrain the ranks the rest out of respect as it will appear for good order. This will sow an example of restraint also in others. If a petitioner appears among the people trying to hand a petition and forcing his way through the ranks, the first ranks must receive the petition and before the eyes of the petitioner pass it to the ruler, so that all may know that what is handed in reaches its destination, that, consequently, there exists a control of the ruler himself. The aureole of power requires for its existence that the people may be able to say: "If the king knew of this," or: "the king will hear of it."

With the establishment of official secret defense the mystical prestige of authority disappears: given a certain audacity, and everyone counts himself master of it, the sedition-monger is conscious of his strength, and when occasion serves watches for the moment to make an attempt upon authority. . . . . For the *goyim* we have been preaching something else, but by that very fact we are enabled to see what measures of overt defense have brought them to. . . . .

Criminals with us will be arrested at the first more or less well-grounded *suspicion;* it cannot be allowed that out of fear of a possible mistake an opportunity should be given of escape to persons suspected of a political lapse or crime, for in these matters we shall be literally merciless. If it is still possible, by stretching a point, to admit a reconsideration of the motive causes in simple crimes, there is no possibility of excuse for persons occupying themselves with questions in which nobody except the government can understand anything. . . . . And it is not all goverments that understand true policy.

PROTOCOL NO. 19

The right of presenting petitions and projects. Sedition. Indictment of political crimés. Advertisement of political crimes.

If we do not permit any independent dabbling in the political we shall on the other hand encourage every kind of report or petition with proposals for the government to examine into all kinds of projects for the amelioration of the condition of the people; this will reveal to us the defects or else the fantasies of our subjects, to which we shall respond either by accomplishing them or by a wise rebutment to prove the short-sightedness of one who judges wrongly.

Sedition-mongering is nothing more than the yapping of a lap-dog at an elephant. For a government well organized, not from the police but from the public point of view, the lap-dog yaps at the elephant in entire unconsciousness of its strength and importance. It needs no more than to take a good example to show the relative importance of both and the lap-dogs will cease to yap and will wag their tails the moment they set eyes on an elephant.

In order to destroy the prestige of heroism for political crime we shall send it for trial in the category of thieving, murder, and every kind of abominable and filthy crime. Public opinion will then confuse in its conception this category of crime with the disgrace attaching to every other and will brand it with the same contempt.

We have done our best, and I hope we have succeeded. to obtain that the *goyim* should not arrive at this means of contending with sedition. It was for this reason that through the Press and in speeches, indirectly — in cleverly compiled schoolbooks on history, we have advertised the martyrdom alleged to have been accepted by sedition-mongers for the idea of the commonweal. This advertisement has increased the contingent of liberals and has brought thousands of *goyim* into the ranks of our livestock cattle.

PROTOCOL NO. 20

FINANCIAL PROGRAMME. Progressive tax. Stamp progressive taxation. Exchequer, interest-bearing papers and stagnation of currency. Method of accounting. Abolition of ceremonial displays. Stagnation of capital. Currency issue. Gold standard. Standard of cost of working man power. Budget. State loans. One per cent. interest series. Industrial shares. Rulers of the *goyim*: courtiers and favouritism, masonic agents.

To-day we shall touch upon the financial programme, which I put off to the end of my report as being the most difficult, the crowning and the decisive point of our plans. Before entering upon it I will remind you that I have already spoken before by way of a hint when I said that the sum total of our actions is settled by the question of figures.

When we come into our kingdom our autocratic government will avoid, from a principle of self-preservation, sensibly burdening the masses of the people with taxes, remembering that it plays the part of father and protector. But as State organization costs dear it is necessary nevertheless to obtain the funds required for it. It will, therefore, elaborate with particular precaution the question of equilibrium in this matter.

Our rule, in which the king will enjoy the legal fiction that everything in his State belongs to him (which may easily be translated into fact), will be enabled to resort to the lawful confiscation of all sums of every kind for the regulation of their circulation in the State. From this follows that taxation will best be covered by a progressive tax on property. In this manner the dues will be paid without straitening or ruining anybody in the form of a percentage of the amount of property. The rich must be aware that it is their duty to place a part of their superfluities at the disposal of the State since the State guarantees them security of possession of the rest of their property and the right of honest gains, I say honest, for the control over property will do away with robbery on a legal basis.

This social reform must come from above, for the time is ripe for it — it is indispensable as a pledge of peace.

The tax upon the poor man is a seed of revolution and works to the detriment of the state which in hunting after the trifling is missing the big. Quite apart from this, a tax on capitalists diminishes the growth of wealth in private hands in which we have in these days concentrated it as a counterpoise to the government strength of the *goyim* — their State finances.

A tax increasing in a percentage ratio to capital will give a much larger venue than the present individual or property tax, which is useful to us now for the sole reason that it excites trouble and discontent among the *goyim*.

The force upon which our king will rest consist in the equilibrium and the guarantee of peace, for the sake of which things it is indispensable that the capitalists should yield up a portion of their incomes for the sake of the secure working of the machinery of the State. State needs must be paid by those who will not feel the burden and have enough to take from.

Such a measure will destroy the hatred of the poor man for the rich, in whom he will see a necessary financial support for the State, will see in him the organizer of peace and well-being since he will see that it is the rich man who is paying the necessary means to attain these things.

In order that payers of the educated classes should not too much distress themselves over the new payments they will have full accounts given them of the destination of those payments, with the exception of such sums as well be appropriated for the needs of the throne and the administrative institutions.

He who reigns will not have any properties of his own once all in the State represents his patrimony, or else the one would be in contradiction to the other; the fact of holding private means would destroy the right of property in the common possessions of all.

Relatives of him who reigns, his heirs excepted, who will be maintained by the resources of the State, must enter the ranks of servants of the State or must work to obtain the right to property; the privilege of royal blood must not serve for the spoiling of the treasury.

Purchase, receipt of money or inheritance will be subject to the payment of a stamp progressive tax. Any transfer of property, whether money or other, without evidence of payment of this tax which will be strictly registered by names, will render the former holder liable to pay interest on the tax from the moment of transfer of these sums up to the discovery of his evasion of declaration of the transfer. Transfer documents must be presented weekly at the local treasury office with notifications of the name, surname and permanent place of residence of the former and the new holder of the property. This transfer with register of names must begin from a definite sum which exceeds the ordinary expenses of buying and selling of necessaries, and these will be subject to payment only by a stamp impost of a definite percentage of the unit.

Just strike an estimate of how many times such taxes as these will cover the revenue of the *goyim States*.

The State exchequer will have to maintain a definite complement of reserve sums, and all that is collected above that complement must be returned into circulation. On these sums will be organized public works. The initiative in works of this kind, proceeding from State sources, will bind the working class firmly to the interests of the State and to those who reign. From these same sums also a part will be set aside as rewards of inventiveness and productiveness.

On no account should so much as a single unit above the definite and freely estimated sums be retained in the State treasuries, for money exists to be circulated and any kind of stagnation of money acts ruinously on the running of the State machinery, for which it is the lubricant; a stagnation of the lubricant may stop the regular working of the mechanism.

The substitution of interest-bearing paper for a part of the token of exchange has produced exactly this stagnation. The consequences of this circumstance are already sufficiently noticeable.

A court of account will also be instituted by us and in it the ruler will find at any moment a full accounting for State income and expenditure, with the exception of the curret monthly account, not yet made up, and that of the preceding month, which will not yet have been delivered.

The one and only person who will have no interest in robbing the State is its owner, the ruler. This is why his personal control will remove the possibility of leakages of extravagances.

The representative function of the ruler at receptions for the sake of etiquette, which absorbs so much invaluable time, will be abolished in order that the ruler may have time for control and consideration. His power will not then be split up into fractional parts among time-serving favourites who surround the throne for its pomp and splendour, and are interested only in their own and not in the common interests of the State.

Economic crises have been produced by us from the *goyim* by no other means than the withdrawal of money from circulation. Huge capitals have stagnated, withdrawing money from States, which were constantly obliged to apply to those same stagnant capitals for loans. These loans burdened the finances of the State with the payment of interest and made them the bond slaves of these capitals. . . . . The concentration of industry in the hands of capitalists out of the hands of small masters has drained away all the juices of the peoples and with them also of the States. . . . .

The present issue of money in general does not correspond with the requirements per head, and cannot therefore satisfy all the needs of the workers. The issue of money ought to correspond with the growth of population and thereby children also must absolutely be reckoned as consumers of currency from the day of their birth. The revision of issue is a material question for the whole world.

You are aware that the gold standard has been the ruin of the States which adopted it, for it has not been able to satisfy the demands for money, the more so that we have removed gold from circulation as far as possible.

With us the standard that must be introduced is the cost of working-man power, whether it be reckoned in paper or in wood. We shall make the issue of money in accordance with the normal requirements of each subject, adding to the quantity with every birth and substracting with every death.

The accounts will be managed by each department (the French administrative division), each circle.

In order that there may be no delays in paying out of money for State needs the sums and terms of such payments will be fixed by decree of the ruler; this will do away with the protection by a ministry of one institution to the detriment of others.

The budgets of income and expenditure will be carried out side by side that they may not be obscured by distance one to another.

The reforms projected by us in the financial institutions and principles of the *goyim* will be clothed by us in such forms as will alarm nobody. We shall point out the necessity of reforms in consequence of the disorderly darkness into which the *goyim* by their irregularities have plunged the finances. The first irregularity, as we shall point out, consists in their beginning with drawing up a single budget which year after year grows owing to the following cause: this budget is dragged out to half the year, then they demand a budget to put things right, and this they expend in three months, after which they ask for a supplementary budget, and all this ends with a liquidation budget. But, as the budget of the following year is drawn up in accordance with the sum of the total addition, the annual departure from the normal reaches as much as 50 percent in a year, and so the annual budget is trebled in ten years. Thanks to such methods, allowed by the carelessness of the *goy* States, their treasuries are empty. The period of loans supervenes, and that has swallowed up remainders and brought all the *goy* States to bankruptcy.

You understand perfectly that economic arrangements of this kind, which have been suggested to the *goyim* by us, cannot be carried on by us.

Every kind of loan proves infirmity in the State and a want of understanding of the rights of the State. Loans hang like a sword of Damocles over the heads of rulers, who, instead of taking from their subjects by a temporary tax, come begging with oustretched palm of our bankers. Foreign loans are leeches which there is no possibility of removing from the body of the State until they fall off of themselves or the State flings them off. But the *goy* States do not tear them off; they go on in persisting in putting more on to themselves so that they must inevitably perish, drained by voluntary blood-letting.

What also indeed is, in substance, a loan, especially a foreign loan? A loan is — an issue of government bills of exchange containing a percentage obligation commensurate to the sum of the loan capital. If the loan bears a charge of 5 per cent., then in twenty years the State vainly pays away in interest a sum equal to the loan borrowed, in forty years it is paying a double sum, in sixty—treble, and all the while the debt remains an unpaid debt.

From this calculation it is obvious that with any form of taxation per head the State is baling out the last coppers of the poor taxpayers in order to settle accounts with wealthy foreigners, from whom it has borrowed money instead of collecting these coppers for its own needs without the additional interest.

So long as loans were internal the *goyim* only shuffled money from the pockets of the poor to those of the rich, but when we bought up the necessary person in order to transfer loans into the external sphere all the wealth of States flowed into our cash-boxes and all the *goyim* began to pay us the tribute of subjects.

If the superficiality of *goy* kings on their thrones in regard to State affairs and the venality of ministers or the want of understanding of financial matters on the part of other ruling persons have made their countries debtors to our treasuries to amounts quite impossible to pay it has not been accomplished without on our part heavy expenditure of trouble and money.

Stagnation of money will not be allowed by us and therefore there will be no State-interest bearing paper, except a one-per-cent. series, so that there will be no payment of interest to leeches that suck all the strength out of the State. The right to issue interest-bearing paper will be given exclusively to industrial companies who will find no difficulty in paying interest out of profits, whereas the

State does not make interest on borrowed money like these companies, for the State borrows to spend and not to use in operations.

Industrial papers will be bought also by the government which from being as now a payer of tribute by loan operations will be transformed into a lender of money at a profit. This measure will stop the stagnation of money, parasitic profits and idleness, all of which were useful for us among the *goyim* so long as they were independent but are not desirable under our rule.

How clear is the undeveloped power of thought of the purely brute brains of the *goyim*, as expressed in the fact that they have been borrowing from us with payment of interest without ever thinking that all the same these very moneys plus an addition for payment of interest must be got by them from their own State pockets in order to settle up with us. What could have been simpler than to take the money they wanted from their own people?

But it is a proof of the genius of our chosen mind that we have contrived to present the matter of loans to them in such a light that they have even seen in them an advantage for themselves.

Our accounts, which we shall present when the time comes, in the light of centuries of experience gained by experiments made by us on the *goy* States, will be distinguished by clearness and definiteness and will show at a glance to all men the advantage of our innovations. They will put an end to those abuses to which we owe our mastery over the *goyim*, but which cannot be allowed in our kingdom.

We shall so hedge about our system of accounting that neither the ruler nor the most insignificant public servant will be in a position to divert even the smallest sum from its destination without detection or to direct it in another direction except that which will be once fixed in a definite plan of action.

And without a definite plan it is impossible to rule. Marching along an undetermined road and with undetermined resources brings to ruin by the way heroes and demi-gods.

The *goy* rulers, whom we once upon a time advised should be distracted from State occupations by representatives receptions, observances of etiquette, entertainments, were only screens for our rule. The accounts of favourite courtiers who replaced them in the sphere of affairs were drawn up for them by our agents, and every time gave satisfaction to short-sighted minds by promises that in the future economies and improvements were foreseen. . . . . Economies from what? From new taxes? — were questions that might have been but were not asked by those who read our accounts and projects. . . . .

You know to what they have been brought by this carelessness, to what a pitch of financial disorder they have arrived, notwithstanding the astonishing industry of their peoples. . . . .

PROTOCOL NO. 21

Internal loans. Debit and taxes. Conversions. Bankruptcy. Savings banks and rentes. Abolition of money markets. Regulation of industrial values.

To what I reported to you at the last meeting I shall now add a detailed explanation of internal loans. Of foreign loans I shall say nothing more, because they have fed us with the national moneys of the *goyim*, but for our State there will be no foreigners, that is, nothing external.

We have taken advantage of the venality of administrators and the slackness of rulers to get our moneys twice, thrice and more times over, by lending to the *goy* governments moneys which were not at all needed by the States. Could anyone do the like in regard to us? . . . . Therefore, I shall only deal with the details of internal loans.

States announce that such a loan is to be concluded and

open subscriptions for their own bills of exchange, that is, for their interest-bearing paper. That they may be within the reach of all the price is determined at from a hundred to a thousand; and a discount is made for the earliest subscribers. Next day by artificial means the price of them goes up, the alleged reason being that everyone is rushing to buy them. In a few days the treasury safes are as they say overflowing and there's more money than they can do with (why then take it?). The subscription, it is alleged, covers many times over the issue total of the loan: in this lies the whole stage effect — look you, they say, what confidence is shown in the government's bills of exchange.

But when the comedy is played out there emerges the fact that a debit and an exceedingly burdensome debit has been created. For the payment of interest it becomes necessary to have resource to new loans, which do not swallow up but only add to the capital debt. And when this credit is exhausted it becomes necessary by new taxes to cover, not the loan, but only the interest on it. These taxes are a debit employed to cover a debit. . . .

Later comes the time for conversions, but they deminish the payment of interest without covering the debt, and besides they cannot be made without the consent of the lenders; on announcing a conversion a proposal is made to return the money to those who are not willing to convert their paper. If everybody expressed his unwillingness and demanded his money back, the government would be hooked on their own flies and would be found insolvent and unable to pay the proposed sums. By good luck the subjects of the *goy* governments, knowing nothing about financial affairs, have always preferred losses on exchange and diminution of interest to the risk of new investments of their moneys, and have thereby many a time enabled these governments to throw off their shoulders a debit of several millions.

Nowadays, with external loans, these tricks cannot be

played by the *goyim* for they know that we shall demand all our moneys back.

In this way an acknowledged bankruptcy will best prove to the various countries the absence of any means between the interests of the peoples and of those who rule them.

I beg you to concentrate your particular attention upon this point, and upon the following: nowadays all internal loans are consolidated by so-called flying loans, that is, such as have terms of payment more or less near. These debts consist of moneys paid into the savings banks and reserve funds. It left for long at the disposition of a government these funds evaporate in the payment of interest on foreign loans, and are replaced by the deposit of equivalent amount of *rentes*.

And these last it is which patch up all the leaks in the State treasuries of the *goyim*.

When we ascend the throne of the world all these financial and similar shifts, as being not in accord with our interests, will be swept away so as not to leave a trace, as also will be destroyed all money markets, since we shall not allow the prestige of our power to be shaken by fluctuations of prices set upon our values, which we shall announce by law at the price which represents their full worth without any possibility of lowering or raising. (Raising gives the pretext for lowering, which indeed was where we made a beginning in relation to the values of the *goyim*.)

We shall replace the money markets by grandiose government credit institutions, the object of which will be to fix the price of industrial values in accordance with government views. These institutions will be in a position to fling upon the market five hundred millions of industrial paper in one day, or to buy up for the same amount. In this way all industrial undertakings will come into dependence upon us. You may imagine for yourselves what immense power we shall thereby secure for ourselves. . . . .

PROTOCOL NO. 22

The secret of what is coming. The evil of many centuries as the foundation of future well-being. The aureole of power and its mystical worship.

In all that has so far been reported by me to you, I have endeavoured to depict with care the secret of what is coming, of what is past, and of what is going on now, rushing into the flood of the great events coming already in the near future, the secret of our relations to the *goyim* and of financial operations. On this subject there remains still a little for me to add.

In our hands is the greatest power of our day — gold: in two days we can procure from our storehouses any quantity we may please.

Surely there is no need to seek further proof that our rule is predestined by God? Surely we shall not fail with such wealth to prove that all that evil which for so many centuries we have had to commit has served at the end of ends the cause of true well-being—the bringing of everything into order? Though it be even by the exercise of some violence, yet all the same it will be established. We shall contrive to prove that we are benefactors who have restored to the rend and mangled earth the true good and also freedom of the person, and therewith we shall enable it to be enjoyed in peace and quiet, with proper dignity of relations, on the condition, of course, of strict observance of the laws established by us. We shall make plain therewith that freedom does not consist in dissipation and in the right of unbridled licence any more than the dignity and force of a man do not consist in the right for everyone to promulgate destructive principles in the nature of freedom of conscience, equality and the like, that freedom of the person in no wise consists in the right to agitate oneself and others by abominable speeches before disorderly mobs, and that true freedom consists in the inviolability of the person who honourably and strictly observes all the laws of life in common, that human dignity is wrapped up in consciousness of the rights and also of the absence of rights of each, and not wholly and solely in fantastic imaginings about the subject of one's *ego*.

Our authority will be glorious because it will be all-powerful, will rule and guide, and not muddle along after leaders and orators shrieking themselves hoarse with senseless words which they call great principles and which are nothing else, to speak honestly, but utopian. . . . Our authority will be the crown of order, and in that is included the whole happiness of man. The aureole of this authority will inspire a mystical bowing of the knee before it and a reverent fear before it of all the peoples. True force makes no terms with any right, not even with that of God: none dare come near to it so as to take so much as a span from it away.

PROTOCOL NO. 23

Reduction of the manufacture of articles of luxury. Small master production. Unemployment. Prohibition of drunkenness. Killing out of the old society and its resurrection in a new form. The chosen one of God.

That the peoples may become accustomed to obedience it is necessary to inculcate lessons of humility and therefore to reduce the production of articles of luxury. By this we shall improve morals which have been debased by emulation in the sphere of luxury. We shall re-establish small master production which will mean laying a mine under the private capital of manufacturers. This is indispensable also for the reason that manufacturers on the grand scale often move, though not always consciously, the thoughts of the masses in directions against the government. A people of small masters knows nothing of unemployment and this binds him closely with existing order, and consequently with the firmness of authority. Unemployment is a most perilous thing for a government. For us its part will have been played out the moment authority is transferred into our hands. Drunkenness also will be prohibited by law and punishable as a crime against the humanness of man who is turned into a brute under the influence of alcohol.

Subjects, I repeat once more, give blind obedience only to the strong hand which is absolutely independent of them, for in it they feel the sword for defense and support against social scourges. . . . What do they want with an angelic spirit in a king? What they have to see in him is the personification of force and power.

The supreme lord who will replace all now existing rulers, dragging on their existence among societies demoralized by us, societies that have denied even the authority of God, from whose midst breaks out on all sides the fire of anarchy, must first of all proceed to quench this all-devouring flame. Therefore he will be obliged to kill off those existing societies, though he should drench them with his own blood, that he may resurrect them again in the form of regularly organized troops fighting consciously with every kind of infection that may cover the body of the State with sores.

This Chosen One of God is chosen from above to demolish the senseless forces moved by instinct and not reason, by brutishness and not humanness. These forces now triumph in manifestations of robbery and every kind of violence under the mask of principles of freedom and rights. They have overthrown all forms of social order to erect on the ruins the throne of the King of the Jews; but their part will be played out the moment he enters into his kingdom. Then it will be necessary to sweep them away from his path, on which must be left no knot, no splinter.

Then will it be possible for us to say to the peoples of the world: "Give thanks to God and bow the knee before him who bears on his front the seal of the predestination of man, to which God himself has led his star that none other but Him might free us from all the before-mentioned forces and evils."

PROTOCOL NO. 24

Confirming the roots of King David (?). Training of the king. Setting aside of direct heirs. The king and three of his sponsors. The king is fate. Irreproachability of exterior morality of the King of the Jews.

I pass now to the method of confirming the dynastic roots of King David to the last strata of the earth.

This confirmation will first and foremost be included in that in which to this day has rested the force of conservatism by our learned elders of the conduct of all the affairs of the world, in the directing of the education of thought of all humanity.

Certain members of the seed of David will prepare the kings and their heirs, selecting not by right of heritage but by eminent capacities, inducting them into the most secret mysteries of the political, into schemes of government, but providing always that none may come to knowledge of the secrets. The object of this mode of action is that all may know that government cannot be entrusted to those who have not been inducted into the secret places of its art. . . . .

To these persons only will be taught the practical application of the aforenamed plans by comparison of the experiences of many centuries, all the observations on the politico-economic moves and social sciences — in a word, all the spirit of laws which have been unshakably established by nature herself for the regulation of the relations of humanity.

Direct heirs will often be set aside from ascending the throne if in their time of training they exhibit frivolity, softness and other qualities that are the ruin of authority, which render them incapable of governing and in themselves dangerous for kingly office.

Only those who are unconditionally capable for firm, even if it be to cruelty, direct rule will receive the reins of rule from our learned elders.

In case of falling sick with weakness of will or other form of incapacity, kings must by law hand over the reins of rule to new and capable hands.

The king's plans of action for the current moment, and all the more so for the future, will be unknown, even to those who are called his closest counsellors.

Only the king and the three who stood sponsor for him will know what is coming.

In the person of the king who with unbending will is master of himself and of humanity all wiss discern as it were fate with its mysterious ways. None will know what the king wishes to attain by his dispositions, and therefore none will dare to stand across an unknown path.

It is understood that the brain reservoir of the king must correspond in capacity to the plan of government it has to contain. It is for this reason that he will ascend the throne not otherwise than after examination of his mind by the aforesaid learned elders.

That the people may know and love their king it is indispensable for him to converse in the market-places with his people. This ensures the necessary clinching of the two forces which are now divided one from another by us by the terror.

This terror was indispensable for us till the time comes for both these forces separately to fall under our influence.

The King of the Jews must not be at the mercy of his passions, and especially of sensuality: on no side of his character must he give brute instinct power over his mind, Sensuality worse than all else disorganizes the capacities of the mind and clearness of views, distracting the thoughts to the worst and most brutal side of human activity.

The prop of humanity in the person of the supreme lord of all the world of the holy seed of David must sacrifice to his people all personal inclinations.

Our supreme lord must be of an exemplary irreproachability.

CONCLUDING PASSAGE FROM THE EPILOGUE OF NILUS

(*Edition of* 1905)

According to the testament of Montefiore, Zion is not sparing, either of money or of any other means, to achieve its ends. In our day, all the governments of the entire world are consciously or unconsciously submissive to the commands of this great Supergovernment of Zion, because all the bonds and securities are in its hands; for all countries are indebted to the Jews for sums which they will never be able to pay. All affairs — industry, commerce, and diplomacy — are in the hands of Zion. It is by means of its capital loans that it has enslaved all nations. By keeping education on purely materialistic lines, the Jews have loaded the Gentiles with heavy chains with which they have harnessed them to their "Supergovernment".

The end of national liberty is near, therefore personal freedom is approaching its close; for true liberty cannot exist where Zion uses the lever of its gold to rule the masses and dominate the most respectable and enlightened class of society.

"He that hath ears to hear, let him hear".

It is nearly four years since the *Protocols of the Elders of Zion* came into my possession. Only God knows what efforts I have made to bring them to general notice — in vain — and even to warn those in power, by disclosing the causes of the storm about to break on apathetic Russia who seems, in her misfortune, to have lost all notion of what is going on around her.

And it is only now when I fear it may be too late, that I have succeeded in publishing my work, hoping to put on their guard those who still have ears to hear and eyes to see.

One can no longer doubt it, the triumphant reign of the King of Israel rises over our degenerate world as that of Satan, with his power and his terrors; the King born of the blood of Zion — the Antichrist — is about to mount the throne of universal empire.

Events are precipitated in the world at a terrifying speed: quarrels, wars, rumours, famines, epidemics, earthquakes — everything which even yesterday was impossible, today is an accomplished fact. One would think that the days pass so rapidly to advance the cause of the chosen people. Space does not allow us to enter into the details of world history with regard to the disclosed "mysteries of iniquity", to prove from history the influence which the "Wise Men of Zion" have exercised through universal misfortunes by foretelling the certain and already near future of humanity, or by raising the curtain for the last act of the world's tragedy.

Only the light of Christ and of his Holy Church Universal can fathom the abyss of Satan and disclose the extent of its wickedness.

I feel in my heart that the hour has already struck when there should urgently be convoked an Eighth Oecumenical Council which would unite the pastor and representatives of all Christendom. Secular quarrels and schisms would all be forgotten in the imminent need of preparing against the coming of the Antichrist. [1]

---

1. This forecast of Sergius Nilus is all the more remarkable, when one considers that it appeared in the Epilogue to his edition of the Protocols of 1905.

CHAPTER V

A FEW ILLUSTRATIVE FACTS

I

Jacob Braftmann and His Work

About the middle of the last century, Jacob Brafmann, a Jewish rabbi in Russia, became a convert to Christianity and spent the rest of his life endeavoring to throw light on the Jewish question in general, and on the situation in Russia in particular, both in the interest of gentiles and of the Jews themselves. His two works, *The Book of the Kahal,* [1] and *The Jewish Brotherhoods,* [2] were first published at government expense some sixty years ago and are still the best sourc e of information on many points. Brafmann's story, given in his own words in the preface to *the Book of the Kahal,* is reprinted here [3]

"During his majesty's (Alexander II) stay at Minsk in 1858, I submitted to him a report on the social status and organization of the Jews in Russia. Some time after, by order of the Holy Synod (April 29, 1859), I was called to St. Petersburg in connection with the report, and

---

1. First edition (Vilna, 1869), excellent German translation by Siegfried Passarge, "Das Buch vom Kahal" (Hammer Verlag, Leipzig, 1928), 2 vol. French translation by Mgr. Jouin, "Les Sources de l'imperialisme juif": Le Qahal (Paris, 1925).

2. (Vilna, 1868).

3. Our translation, somewhat abbreviated.

was subsequently (May 13, 1860) appointed professor of Hebrew at the Minsk seminary. I was also charged with finding a means for overcoming the obstacles to conversion to Christianity set up by the Jews. Thoroughly familiar with the Jewish question, (as I had professed Judaism till the age of thirty-four) I knew where to draw the materials necessary for the work, and the archbishop of Minsk furnished me with the means. My task was faciliated by the cooperation of several enlightened Jews. [4] I thus obtained valuable material which served not only for the work in hand, but also to throw light on the Jewish question in general, as well as their social and religious organization in Russia.

This material included over a thousand acts of the Jewish *Kahal* (civil administration), and of the Beth-Dins (Talmudic law courts), showing the power and extent of their secret government. The *Kahal* goes so far as to decree what individuals may be invited to, and what dishes served at, a Jewish family feast.

On the important question, whether the law of the land is binding on the Jews, the comments in the Talmud are evasive, but the documents here listed (under Nos. 5, 16, 166) show that the Jews must abide by the instructions of the *Kahal* and the Beth-Din, in contradistinction to the law of the land and their own conscience.

Similarly, on the question of the real estate and appurtenances belonging to non-Jews, the Talmud is obscure; but the thirty-seven acts cited in our fifth article prove conclusively that the *Kahal* may sell to Jews the right (*Hasaka* and *Meropie*) to the real estate and appurtenances of any gentile. The documents also prove that the *Kahal* and the Beth-Din are not bound to judge according to Jewish law, but may hand down personal decisions as

---

4. See Vilna Gazette (1866), 169: "Views of an individual Jew".

The Cabbalistic Inscription found on the wall of the Room in which Imperial Russian Family was murdered.

they please.....

Thus, by secret acts, the Jews circumvent their Christian competitors and acquire a controlling share of the capital and real estate of the country.

I submitted these documents together with my recommendations to Gov. Gen. von Kaufmann, who appointed a commission to examine them, with the result that the official Jewish *Kahal* was suppressed by the circular of August 34, 1867.

The authenticity of all the documents is thoroughly established: the 290 documents published herewith cover the period from 1794 to 1803. To facilitate their study, they have been arranged in seventeen categories, each preceded by a short explanation on the laws and customs referred to, and indicating their real aim and influence on the Jews and on the gentiles".

As the subject of Brafmann's other work. *The Jewish Brotherhoods*, has been treated rather fully in chapter II, it is hardly necessary to give an analysis of the book here.

2

The Writing on the Wall

The Cabbalistic Significance of the Mysterious inscription found on the wall of the room in which the imperial Russian Family was murdered.

The three letters ʃ ʅ ʎ of the inscription are the letter "L" repeated three times in three different languages.[1] The first letter on the right is a ל (*lamed*) in the cursive handwriting of the ancient Hebrew alphabet. It is the twelfth letter of that alphabet with the numerical

1. The student may be confused by the fact that, in the photograph which is reproduced on the opposite page, the characters appear as though reversed, and written from right

value of 30 (cabbalistically reduced to the fundamental number: - 3 + 0 - 3, which explain why the letter "L" is thrice repeated in the inscription). [2] The second letter is also the letter *lamed* but in the Samaritan script. [3]

The third letter ϒ is the Greek letter *lambda,* corresponding to the same letter *lamed.*

In ancient sacred Hebrew, based on the ancient sacred language of the Egyptian temples, each letter, apart from its vernacular value as sound and number, has, moreover, secret meanings known only to adepts. Fabre d'Olivet thus characterizes the accumulation of the different meanings contained in the ancient Hebrew alphabet:—

"Moses, in his teaching, followed the method of the Egyptian priests who made use of three methods to express their thoughts: the first was the common use; the second was symbolical or figurative; the third was sacred or hieroglyphic. Such was the character of that language. According to their will, the same word had the ordinary, figurative or the allegorical meaning. Heraclitus has expressed this difference in three terms: namely, the spoken word, the symbol, and the hidden meaning". [4]

Moreover, each letter stood for one of the names of God, and or one of the mysterious keys of the *Tarot,* the sacred book wherein, under different images, is concentrated all the ancient practice of magical science. [5]

---

to left. But this is not the case, and is explained by the position assumed by the writer, who stood with his back to the wall, with his right arm stretched down, and formed the letters from right to left, in the Hebrew manner.

2. The cabbalistic interpretation of letters and words is found in the following books: Kircher, "Oedipus Aegyptiacus"; Lenain, "La Science Cabbalistique"; Dée, "Monas Hieroglyphcia"; H. Krumrath, "Amphithéatre de l'éternel sapience;" Franck, "La Cabbale."

3. Fabre d'Olivet, "La Langue hébraique restituée.

4. Fabre d'Olivet, op. cit.

5. Eliphas Lévy, "Dogme et Rituel de la haute magie".

The name of God, corresponding to the letter *lamed*, is *Shadaï*, composed of three letters, represented by Δ (the Greek capital letter D) and it governs the sphere of Saturn. The number of Saturn is also 3. This explains once again why the letter *lamed* is thrice repeated. [6]

On the other hand, following cabbalistic teaching, the letter *lamed* stands for the heart, the king of the body, wherein dwells the soul — *Ruach*, Cabbalists affirm that man is formed of three main invisible parts: namely, *Nesham*, the mind, *Ruach*, the soul, and *Nefesh*, the lower soul or subconscience which governs directly the material body. *Nesham* has its seat in the brain; *Nefesh*, in the liver, and *Ruach*, in the centre, between liver and brain, namely, in the heart. According to the ancients, the heart is king of the body (*Melek - king*), and, we repeat again, was situated in the body between brain and liver, that is, in the centre. [7] This is clearly shown by the cabbalistic analysis of the word *Melek* - king.

Three words are fused in one: "brain", represented by the first letter of the word *mem*; "heart" by the first letter of the word *lamed*; and "liver", by the first letter of the word *kaph*, which is the same letter as כ, but in the form used at the end of a word. It is clear, therefore, that the letter ל (*lamed*), symbolising the "heart", which is found in the centre between "liver" and "brain", is placed in the word *Melek* between letters representing these two organs. [8]

---

6. Cornelius Agrippa, "Philosophie Occulte".

7. Cf. The report made by Leinigen to the Munich Psychological Society, March 3, 1887.

8. The cipher the real meaning, cabbalists frequently resort to a special kind of hieroglyphics, one form of which is synthetic, whereby a word is concealed by several others. For intance, the first letters of several words are taken and assembled in one word, as in the present case in the world "Melek". See Molitor, "Philosophie de la Tradition".

Therefore, according to the ancients, the heart (*lamed*) is the king (*Melek*) of the organism and the seat of life. The destruction of the heart causes the death of the organism and the seat of life. The destruction of the heart causes the death of the organism and, in symbolical language, it also means that the destruction of the king brings about the downfall of the kingdom.

Furthermore, in studying the hidden meaning of the roots, one discovers that the root לל (double *lamed*), still found in Arabic, means the agony of a man being torn to pieces. [9] The addition of a third only strengthens this meaning and indicates the agony of a desperate situation.

Interpreting the inscription on the wall with the help of the Tarot, [10] one finds that the letter כ corresponds to the twelfth card of the *Geat Arcana,* [1] and also to the letter *Luzain,* of the sacred language of the Egyptian Magi. This arcanum represents a man hanging by one foot from a pole whose two ends rest on two trees from each of which six branches have been cut. The man's arms are tied behind his back and folded so as to form the base of a triangle pointing downwards; the apex is formed by the head of the man. It is the sign of *violent death,* but it can also mean *sacrifice.* [12]

---

9. Fabre d'Olivet, op. cit.

10. Eliphas Lévy, op. cit. Papus, "Tarot des Bohêmiens".

11. The Arcana (arcana - mysterious) are the cards of the Tarot: the Great Arcana, of which there are twenty-two, correspond to the letters of the sacred alphabet which was first of all Egyptian and afterwards became Jewish. Their invention is attributed to the founder of the Egyptia secret science, Hermes Tot or Trismegistos. Our playing cards today originally came from the Lesser Arcana.

12. P. Christian, "Histoire de la Magie".

Therefore, reading the cabbalistic meaning of the three letters, one gets: —

Here the King was struck to the heart in punishment of his crimes,
or, *Here the King was sacrificed to bring about the Destruction of his Kingdom.*

Finally, the line drawn beneath these three letters (in Magical Science the horizontal line is the symbol of the passive principle) indicates that those who killed the king did not do so of their own will, but in obedience to superior command.

Whoever wrote this inspription was a man well versed in the secrets of the ancient Jewish cabbalism, as contained in the *Cabbala* and the *Talmud*. In accomplishing the deed in obedience to superior order, this man performed a rite of Black Magic. It is for this reason that he commemorated his act by a cabbalistic inscription in cipher, which belonged to the rite.

The inscription therefore proves: —

1. That the Tsar was killed.
2. That the murder of the Tsar was committed by men under the command of occult forces; and by an organization which, in its struggle against existing power resorted to the ancient cabbalism in which it was well versed.

3.

The Kellogg Palestine Pact

Extract from *League of Nations* — *Treaty Series*, vol. XLIII-1926, No. 1046, pages 41-59.

Convention respecting the Rights of the Governments of the two Countries and their respective Nationals in Palestine, signed at London, December 3, 1924.

English official text communicated by His Britannic

Majesty's Foreign Office. The registration of this Convention took place January 6, 1926. This Convention was also transmitted to the Secretariat by the Department of State of the Government of the United States of America, February 17, 1926.

(Preamble followed by the text of the mandate as it was approved by the Council of the League of Nations, 28 articles, signed at London, July 3, 1922.)

Whereas the mandate in the above terms came into force on September 29, 1923; and

Whereas the United States of America, by participating in the war against Germany, contributed to her defeat and the defeat of her Allies; and to the renunciation of the rights and titles of her Allies in the territory transferred by them, but has not ratified the Covenant of the League of the Nations embodied in the Treaty of Versailles; and

Whereas the Government of the United States and the Government of His Britannic Majesty desire to reach a definite agreement independently with respect to the rights of the two Governments and their respective Nationals in Palestine;

His Britannic Majesty and the President of the United States of America have decided to conclude a convention to this effect, and have named as plenipotentiaries:

His Majesty (titles):

The Right Honourable Joseph Austen Chamberlain (titles);

The President of the United States of America:

His Excellency the Honourable Frank B. Kellogg (titles);

Who..... have agreed as follows:

ARTICLE 1.

Subject to the provisions of the present Convention the United States consents to the dominion of Palestine by

His Britannic Majesty, pursuant to the mandate recited above.

ARTICLE 2.

The United States and its nationals shall have and enjoy all the rights and benefits secured under the terms of the mandate to Members of the League of Nations and their nationals, notwithstanding the fact that the United States is not a Member of the League of Nations.

ARTICLE 3.

Vested American property rights in the mandated territory shall be respected and in no way impaired.

ARTICLE 4.

A duplicate of the annual report to be made by the Mandatory under Art. 24 of the mandate shall be furnished to the United States.

ARTICLE 5.

Subject to the provisions of any local laws for the maintenance of public order and public morals, the nationals of the United States will be permitted freely to establish and maintain educational, philanthropic, and religious institutions in the mandated territory, and to receive voluntary applicants and to teach in the English language.

ARTICLE 6

The extradition treaties and conventions which are or may be in force between the United States and Great Britain, and the provisions of any treaties which are or may be in force between the two countries which relate to extradition or consular rights shall apply to the mandated territory.

ARTICLE 7.

Nothing contained in the present Convention shall be affected by any modification which may be made in the terms of the mandate, as recited above, unless such modification shall have been assented to by the United States.

ARTICLE 8.

The present Convention shall be ratified in accordance with etc. Done in duplicate at London this 3rd day of December, 1924.

(L.S.) Austen Chamberlain.
(L.S.) Frank B. Kellogg.

4.

Note on the Kellogg-Briand Pact

This part was not written by Secretary of State Frank B. Kellogg, but was entirely the work of a Jewish Chicago lawyer, Solomon O. Levinsohn. He first presented it to the late M. Briand and later to Mr. Kellog, who sponsored it.

It became known as the Kellogg-Briand Pact and was signed in Paris on August 27, 1928. (Cf. The story of this Pact in the *Revue Internationale des Sociétés Secreetes*, Paris, 1930).

INDEPENDENT ORDER OF B'NAI B'RITH
I. O. B. B.

(Jewish Masonry)

(Founded 1843)

B'nai B'rith means "Sons of Covenent", the Covenent being that of circumcision practiced according to the Mosaic law. Hence the Independent Order of the B'nai B'rith admits only Jews as members.

This rite "was founded in New York in 1843 by a number of German Jews, headed by Henry Jones." [1]

Its constitution, District Lodges, Grand Lodges, stamp it as a Jewish Masonic Society.

Like most societies, it covers its political activities under the cloak of "benevolence and philanthropy."

From its inception until the present time, its main contact has been with Germany and its chief aim the establishment of the supremacy of the German Jews in all world affair through the channel of "Internationalism."

In 1882, the strength of the I. O. B. B. in the United States warranted the opening of Lodges in Germany by Moritz Ettinger, and the growth of the order was so rapid there that in 1885, Julius Bien, President of the Order in New York, went over and inaugurated the first German Grand Lodge of the I. O. B. B.

The political activities of the leaders of the order in Rumania, Austria and Hungary are a matter of record,

---

1. **Jewish Encyclopaedia,** Art. B'nai Brith. Italics.

although the chief centre of their power is in the United States where they have lately attained supremacy in the Jewish World by absorbing "national" Zionism and submitting it wholly to their own "international" policy when the Jewish World Agency was created in October, 1928.

It will be well for the reader to bear in mind that, however united a front the Jews may present to the Gentiles, yet among themselves they are divided, and the fight for supremacy and the attainment of world power is not less bitter between their various camps than it is among the different sects of Freemasonry.

Rabbi Dr. Leo Bach was the president of the B'Nai B'rith of Germany in 1928.

Grand Master for Russia, of the International Order of B'nai B'rith at the time of the Russian Revolution of 1917 was Sliozberg. He was one of the inspirers of Kerensky, the leader of the first revolution of 1917 [2], Alexander Kerensky, real name Aron Kirbiz, Kerensky having been the name of his Step-father.

---

2. Le Cahiers de l'Ordre, November 1927.

CHAPTEL LXXXIV

L'ALLIANCE ISRAELITE UNIVERSELLE

(A Branch of Jewish Masonry)

(Founded 1860)

If, as it has been appropriately defined, Judaism is a sect, the creation of the Alliance Israelite Universelle which took place in 1860 can be regarded as that of its exoteric centre.

It was founded in 1860 by Aristide Astruc, Isidor Cahen, Jules Carvalho, Narcisse Leven, Eugene Manuel and Charles Netter. Its first president was Konigswarter, Adolph Cremieux was president from 1863-1867 and again from 1868-1880.

In 1840, the world had been startled by the news of the fearful murder of Pere Thomas at Damascus. Serious investigations had resulted in the conviction of three Jews who had confessed to the commission of the abominable crime for Jewish ritual purposes of procuring human blood.

The indignation of the whole world rising against Jewry made its prominent members realize the danger threatening their newly acquired emancipation in most countries, and they made a concerted effort to disprove Jewish guilt in the Damascus affair. Foremost among them had been Moses Montefiore, Adolphe Cremieux and Solomon Munk. Yet, the real inspirer of the Alliance Israelite Universelle was Hirsch Kalisher, Rabbi of Thorn (Russia) and its enthusiastic exponent, Moses Hess.

The chief aim of the Alliance Israelite Universelle was political, and was clearly expressed in the report circulated after its foundation in which was stated: All important faiths are represented in the world by nations, that is to say, they are incarnated in governments especially interested in them and officially authorized to represent them and speak for them only. Our faith alone is without this important advantage; it is represented neither by a state nor by a society, nor does it occupy a clearly defined territory.

The Alliance Israelite Universelle therefore was destined to be the governmental representative of all Jews from whatever country they lived in under the authority of their secret Kahal or community rule.

The first political manifestation of the Alliance Israelite Uinverselle took place at the Berlin Congress in 1878 where it was represented by three of its delegates: Kann, Netter and Veneziani.

The link between the Alliance Israelite Universelle and Freemasonry was for many years Adolphe Cremieux and Masonic writers have asserted that the 18th degree, conferred by the Grand Orient, makes the initiate, if not a member, at any rate a supporter of the Alliance.

The Alliance Israelite Universelle saw its dream of international Jewish Government shattered when Zionism emerged and came to the fore in 1897. It is noteworthy that the "Prophet" of Zionism: Ahad Ha'am (Asher Ginsberg) was a member of the Alliance Israelite Universelle and a disciple of Charles Netter. The avowed aims of the A. I. U., namely a super-government of the world and a universal religion, both to be Judaic, are being steadily pursued by the "Jewish World Agency" functioning today.

PART IV

THE SOVIETIZATION OF THE BRITISH EMPIRE AND THE UNITED STATES

CHAPTER I

FABIANISM

The preceding chapters have been devoted to a study of the Jewish world organization, its historical background, its branches, its aims and the methods whereby they are obtained. If the reader has followed the thread thus far patiently and objectively, his mind has doubtless grasped, not only the historical facts and specific Jewish plans for the immediate future, but also something of Jewish character and psychology in general. A full knowledge of the latter — which can be gained only through personal experience — is the greatest safeguard against Jewish snares and pitfalls of everyday life.

In the following pages will be found the names of men and women prominent in political, economic and social circles who, lured by the tempting bait, have become enmeshed in Jewish intrigue. To all the world they appear to play an independent role; but in reality they are merely puppets whose every move is worked by strings from behind the scene. [1]

The close observer will discover, slavishly serving the Jewish cause under the mask of benevolence, democracy

---

1. "Who will ever suspect that all these peoples were stage-managed by us according to a political plan which no one has so much as guessed at in the course of many centuries?" Protocol No. 13. See also quotation from Coningsby.

or liberalism, bishops, archbishops, prime ministers and national presidents, government officials of every rank and leading representatives of all other professions (lawyers, economists, scientists and the rest). He will recognize them at once as traitors who have sold themselves and their country for their own personal advantage.

"Every man aims at power, everyone would like to become a dictator if only he could, and rare indeed are the men who would not be willing to sacrifice the welfare of all for the sake of securing their own welfare." [2] But these traitors, when the great day comes, like their counterparts in the French and in the recent Russian revolutions, will pay the price of treason with their heads. [3]

Not less useful to the Jewish cause than those holding official positions, are the rich scions of socially prominent families: their wealth and their prestige are the "force and make-believe" of the Jewish countersign. [4] A rich young Bostonian, Garland, gave millions of dollars to the foundation which bears his name, and appointed as one of its trustees the notorious "red", William Zebulon Foster.

"Foster told them that the Garland Foundation could be depended upon whenever anyone get into trouble because of radical political opinions. Several of the organizers of the Communist party and of its 'legal' political branch, the Workers' party, were promised regular monthly salaries by Foster, to be paid from the Garland Foundation". [5]

---

2. Protocol No. 1. It must be borne in mind that many of these men have, at one time or another in their lives, been involved in some crooked business or scandal and dread its disclosure.

3. The aristocracy who served the Jewish cause in bringing about these revolutions were not even rewarded with life, but perished with the innocent under the edifice they had so efficiently undermined.

4. Protocoll No. 1.

5. Whitney, "Reds in America". (Beckwith Press, New York, 1924), pp. 80-81.

Another example is the Philadelphian, William Curtis Bok, who, on the death of his grandfather, Cyrus H. K. Curtis, in 1933, inherited [6] a major interest in the huge Curtis Publishing Company, comprising *The Ladies Home Journal, Good Housekeeping, The Philadelphia Public Ledge, The New York Evening Post* and other journals [7]. Bok, now 35, on his return from Soviet Russia, founded a new group to facilitate Bolshevik propaganda in America: "There came into being in Philadelphia last week (July 1933) a new investigating agency sponsored by the American Foundation. It was called the Committee on Russian-American Relations and its membership included such potent figures as the Morgan partner, Thomas W. Lamont, whose son Corliss is a near Communist; the Harvard economist Frank W. Taussig; [8] the lawyer Paul D. Cravath, [9] a Russian recognitionist; James D. Mooney, President of General Motors Export Co.; Dean Roscoe Pound, [10] of Harvard Law School, a Liberal of the first water; Hugh L. Cooper, the engineer who built the Dnieprostry Dam for the U. S. S. R. Modestly buried away in the middle of the committee list was the name of its Chairman and sponsor — Curtis Bok." [11] Many more examples of rich people of good families, such as Mrs. Elmhurst (née Dorothy Whitney), [12] Lady Astor,

---

6. Together with his mother and younger brother.

7. Curtis's gross receipts from advertising for 1929 amounted to 73 million dollars; and for 1930, to 67 millions.

8. See infra, p. 217.

9. Notorious radical and shadow of Otto H. Kahn. In 1924 Cravath tried to secure the nomination of Otto Kahn as President of the English Speaking Union; and the manoeuvre was defeated only by the timely exposure of Kahn's bolshevist activities. It was proved that Kahn's house was a meeting place for Soviet agents, such as Nina Somorodin, Claire Sheridan, Louise Bryant and Margaret Harrison.

10. Notorious radical, see infra, p. 217.

11. See "Time" (Chicago Weekly) for July 17, 1933.

12. See infra, pp. 218, 230.

the Dowager Countess of Warwick, come to mind, but space does not allow mention of all here, nor of a discussion of how and why each was inveigled into the Jewish net and into the base role of patron and purveyor to criminals.

Suffice it so that that, in general, these people "thirst for the emotion of success and applause, of which we (the Jews) are remarkably generous. And the reason why we give them this success is to make use of their high conceit of themselves, to which it gives birth. For that insensibly dispose them to assimilate our suggestions without being on their guard against them, in the fullness of their confidence that it is their own infallibility which is giving utterance to their own thoughts, and that it is impossible for them to borrow those of others. . . You cannot imagine to what extent the wisest of the *goyim* can be brought to a state of unconscious naïveté in the presence of this high conceit of themselves; and at the same time how easy it is to take the heart out of them by the slightest ill-success, though it be nothing more than the stoppage of the applause they had, and to reduce them to a slavish submission for the sake of winning a renewal of success." [13]

Much has already been written about Bolshevism being led by Jews; the same applies to it in Mexico, China and Spain, where the systematic violence and terrorism, oft alluded to in the Protocols as Jewish means of exercising power, have had full play. War is now waged against civilization in Europe and the United States, but it assumes another aspect. The ascent of the Jew to power in those countries is made on the ladder of Fabianism, of which Socialism, Marxism, Communism, Bolshevism and Internationalism are the chief rungs.

---

13. Protocol No. 15.

The definition and aims of Fabianism are given by the Fabians themselves as follows:—

Basis of the Fabian Society

The Fabian Society consists of Socialists.

It therefore aims at the reorganization of Society by the emancipation of Land and Industrial Capital from individual ownership and the vesting of them in the community for the general benefit. In this way only can the natural and acquired advantages of the country be equitably shared by the whole people.

The Society accordingly works for the extinction of private property in land, *with equitable consideration of established expectations, and due provision as to the tenure of the home and homestead: for the transfer to the community,* by constitutional methods, *of all such industries as can be conducted socially: and for the establishment, as the governing consideration in the regulation of production, distribution and service, of the common good instead of private profit.*

The Society is a constituent of the Labour Party and of the International Socialist Congress: *but it takes part freely in all constitutional movements, social, economic and political, which can be guided towards its own objects. Its direct business is:* (a) *the propaganda of Socialism in its application to current problems;* (b) *investigation and discovery in social, industrial, political and economic relations;* (c) *the working out of Socialist principles in legislation and administrative reconstruction;* (d) *the publication of the results of its investigations and their practical lessons.*

The Society, believing in equal citizenship of men and women in the fullest sense, is open to persons irrespective of sex, race or creed, who commit themselves to its aims and purposes as stated above and undertake to promote its work.

The Society took the name of *Fabian* from the policy of temporizing it adopted, claiming to imitate that of the Roman dictator, Fabius Counctator, during his fight against Hannibal, whom he eventually defeated at Tarentum, 215 B. C.

Frank Podmore, well-known spiritualist and occultist, one of the founders of the Fabian Society, is quoted as saying to one of its earliest members: — "For the right moment, you must wait, as Fabius did most patiently, when warring against Hannibal, though many censured his delays, but when the time comes, you must strike hard, as Fabius did, or your waiting will be in vain and fruitless".

The Fabian Society waited forty years, striking a continual series of covert blows at the political, economic, social and religious structure of England, and in 1924 it came to power with the advent of the first Labour Government, which can be called the offspring of the Fabian Society.

The period had been fruitful, if long.

There is no gainsaying that the Fabian Society has been first and foremost a gathering of intellectuals — a rebellious Intelligentsia whose accomplishments seem the realization of Weishaupt's dream of Masonic Illuminism, cleverly combined with Moses Mendelssohn's dream of Jewish Illuminism (*Haskalah*).

Historically, it was founded in 1883 at the time when in the realm of philosophy and metaphysics, the political economy of John Stuart Mill, in England, and the Positivism of Auguste Comte, in France, had thrown perturbation into the minds of numerous thinkers and given abundant food to the Freethinkers of the epoch. Henry George's book on Socialism *Progress* and *Poverty* was in great vogue. The direct influence leading to the formation of the Fabian Society was, according to E. R. Pease, its historian, exercised by Thomas Davidson, the founder of *The Fellowship of the New Life,* which society culminated in *The Ethical Society of Culture* in New York. Considerable impulse was also given to the budding association by its assimilation of Robert Dale Owen's socialistic principles.

Among the intellectuals who joined The Fabian Society soon after its inception 1884 was the Irishman, George Bernard Shaw, who was elected a member in that year.

At that time, The Fabian Society had completely seceded from the *Fellowship of the New Life* and had formulated its own Socialistic programme. The following year, Sidney Webb, now Lord Passfield and ex-Minister of the Colonies, as well as Sydney Olivier, now Lord Olivier, who has held several Government appointments, were elected members of The Fabian Society. Soon afterwards, the late Mrs. Annie Besant, later head of the Theosophical Movement, also was elected a member.

Fabian Socialism, at the outset, groped its way along all the beaten paths of the Social Revolutionists who had preceded them. It also made incursions into Babouvism, Marxism, Bakounist Anarchism and the then existing various Social-Democratic groups. Being, however, mainly composed of intellectuals, bureaucrats, civil servants, journalists, etc., the Fabians, whose fundamental slogan was the righting of the wrongs of the working class, had no keen desire for riotous street manifestations and confined their earliest activities to drawing-room meetings.

It does not enter within the limits of the present sketch to retrace the history of the Fabian Society, but the point which should be regarded as of great importance is that out of the drawing-room meetings alluded to above, there emerged the truly Fabian tactics of temporizing and the decision taken and followed of penetrating into or, as Bernard Shaw himself expressed it, of *permeating* numerous existing societies with Fabian socialistic ideas and principles.

This method of penetrating into organizations, political and economic, and of boring from within, gave, in time, remarkable results. Fabians, mainly Civil Servants, easily found their affinities in Liberal circles and, moreover, owing to their loudly proclaimed socialistic profession of faith, obtained the confidence of the working classes. They were indeed sitting on both sides of the fence and recruiting the good-will of both Liberal and Labour organizations.

The study of Fabianism is one of almost unparalleled opportunism. Fabians seemed to have formulated no original creed of their own, but were animated by an unswerving resolve to get to the top and govern England. They accepted the creed or tenets of any camp into which they penetrated and, by degrees, converted its adherents to their own views. In this manner Fabian members secured their positions in political, industrial and educational fields. To suit even Anarchism, they formed a special Fabian branch which bore the name of The Fabian Parliamentary League.

No field of exploitation seems to have been overlooked by these socialist intellectual Illuminati:

I. POLITICS. — In Politics, their range of activities has been well defined by one of its leaders, Bernard Shaw, in a paper he read at a conference in 1892, at Essex Hall. The policy of "*permeation*" of the Fabian Society was clearly outlined and much stress laid upon the enumeration of results already achieved. Within a year of this conference, in January 1893, The Independent Labour Party was formed by the grouping of the local Fabian societies then in existence. These groups, under the leadership of Keir Hardie, Friedrich Engels (co-worker with Karl Marx) and Marx's daughter, E. Aveling, had accepted, as their code, Marxism thus summarised: — *To establish a Socialist State where Land and Capital will be held by the Community.* On such principles was Russia transformed into Soviet Russia in 1917.

The author of *The History of The Fabian Society* does not fail to point it out as the *Parent Society,* emphasizing the fact that the Marxist Independent Labour Party was but its offspring. Thus, leading, on the one hand, Marxist Socialism, and having, on the other, so permeated the Liberal party that they also practically ruled it, the Fabians were soon able to take part in local elections, and propose their own candidates for appointments on School Boards, Vestries, County Councils, Women's Liberal Federations, Liberal and Radical Unions, etc. They spared no pains in pushing forward the autonomy of municipalities as well as the various schemes for National Insurance, Old Age Pensions, Tariff Reform, Employers' Liability, Workmen's Compensation, etc.

Politically also, through their offspring The Independent Labour Party, they asserted their defeatist and anti-patriotic tenets during the Boer War of 1899-1902, when they expressed their wish "to see the Boers successful and the British Army driven into the sea".

By 1903, The Independent Labour Party, after 10 years of indefatigable efforts among the Trade Unionists, gave its parent, The Fabian Society, the opportunity and satisfaction of presenting England with a full-fledged Labour Party. Up to that time, Fabian candidates had contested and won seats in Parliament as Liberals. The practice of the policy of interlocking directorates had never better evidenced than by the tactics of Fabianism.

The outbreak of the War in 1914 furnished the Illuminati of Socalism with the opportunity of manifesting their anti-patriotic feelings much more openly than they had done during the Boer War. It was then that their policy of interlocking directorates bore abundant fruit. What one might call the "melting" property of The Fabian Society became more evident for, as such, it did not create a record of anti-patriotism. That particular task was entrusted to its members of the Labour Party *and* the Independent Labour Party who took a prominent part in the formation of the *Union of Democratic Control,* which counted the Zionist Jew Israel Zangwill amongst its leading band-masters.

The shameful defeatist, pro-German activities of the present Prime Minister of England, Ramsey Macdonald, Fabian and Labourite during the World War, and the open support given to Bolshevism by his Labour Party have for ever sullied the political honour of England and are a matter of history.

Yet another aspect of Fabianism is the great part it took in the formation and, later, direction of The League of Nations, which Bernard Shaw calls *an incipient international government.*

II. ECONOMICS. — In the realm of the Economic, Industrial and Financial life of England, The Fabian Society played no less a part than in politics. With its slogan of "Progressive Policy", [15] it invaded Agriculture, preaching the Nationalization of land, in other words, the confiscation of landed property.

The first blow to Industry was struck in Lancashire, the stronghold of English industry, in 1890, with the help of the late Mrs. Annie Besant as chief spokesman and agitator. Later, the Cooperative movement was captured and Fabianised and subsequently delivered over to the Independent Labour Party *and* Labour Party. It is due to the Socialists having been so successful in conquering industry that, during the World War, sabotage assumed such appalling proportions in the munition factories in England.

---

15. Compare the subversive "Conference for Political Progressive Action in America".

16. Supra, p. 221.

As to the financial "ideals" of The Fabians, whose basic principle is the ruin of Capitalism, they became realities when taxation of the people took undue proportions in the shape of income tax, super-tax, death duties, and are to be followed by *Capital Levy*. The promised benefits to the working class to be derived from such schemes as the National Health Insurance and Workmen's Compensation and Dole, Old Age and Widow's Pensions, have proved a myth. Yet they have gone a long way towards furthering the plans exposed in the *Protocols*, which aim at reducing to bondage the *Goyim*, rich and poor alike.

III. EDUCATION. — In the matter of Education, the Fabian Illuminati have followed a theory which is none other than that suggested by one of the souls of Bavarian Illuminism, Nicolaï, in the 18th century. Having secured posts on the School-boards of the country, it became very easy for Fabian socialists to instil their educational de-Christianized principles in the school curriculum. Their attack on religious teaching was subtle but deadly, as seen in the Education Act of 1902. They boasted openly of having in their ranks several Anglican bishops and divines, the list being headed by Bishop Headlam, one of the earliest Fabians. Eventually they won, having, as has always been their wont, resorted to intensive propaganda, generously distributing their tracts and leaflets.

Under Fabian educational schemes come the formation of the Educational Groups and of "The Nursery", the latter designed as a kind of training school for very young prospective Socialists. Women's groups were also formed, the members of which participated in all movements tending to a fuller feminist emancipation. But, by far, one of the most important steps taken by the Fabians along educational lines has been their inauguration in existing Universities of "University Socialist Societies", which in 1912 were finally grouped by Clifford Allen into "the Universities Socialist Federation". Fertile seeds of Fabian Socialism are also sown at the Summer Schools organized annually by the Society, which E. R. Pease rightly terms a "propagandist society". The culminating triumph of the Fabians, in the realm of education, was the creation of the London School of Economics and Political Science at the London University, where, today, one of the chief lecturers is the Jew socialist, Harold J. Laski, Member of the Executive Committee of the Fabian Society and Chairman of its Publishing Committee.

As has been suggested already, and as can be seen from the succinct *exposé* here given, Fabianism left no field unexplored or unexploited. For fifty years, it has treated England to doses of both pure and diluted Marxism, mostly diluted, as the English, by the very nature of their steady and conservative characteristics, are not easily aroused to excesses like those perpetrated by the Paris "Communards" of 1871. But, on the other hand, they have been thoroughly permeated and their poisoning has been one of long process.

The results are, to the naked eye, the history of England since the War, politically and economically.

Lloyd George's Coalition Government had been kind to Socialism, but the real harvest-time came when the Labour Party won the election in 1924 and its members governed, or rather *misgoverned*, England. It needed nothing short of the Bolshevist alliance which MacDonald wished to force upon the country to provoke the remaining sound reaction of the English people and prompt them to overthrow the Labour Government. But this show of resistance was ephemeral.

How pitiful it is to know that the return of the Labour Party to power, in May, 1929, is entirely due to the incompetence of a Conservative Government, in which the people trusted for the sane administration of the affairs of State. Yet, the Prime Minister, Leader of the Conservative Party, Mr. Baldwin, could not claim ignorance of the Judeo-masonic plans contained in the Protocols of the Wise Men of Zion. He found it easier deliberately to disregard them. Be it as it may, England is once more in the hands of the Labour Party with the inevitable and ubiquitous Ramsay MacDonald and, according to the latest report issued by the Society *"eight Fabians are members of the Cabinet and fourteen others hold offices in the Government without seats in the Cabinet"*.

From the Jew-led Fabian Society issue the chaotic words and deeds which are steadily wrecking not only general prosperity, but also combating with international forces drawn from all quarters of the globe any attempt at national readjustment such as the present movement in Germany.

The drawing-room meeting system described by E. R. Pease and which in America is known as "parlor-bolshevism", formed to gain well-to-do adherents, still functions, as witness the following article which appeared in the London *Evening Standard* of May 28, 1931:—

A 10-YEAR-PLAN FOR SOCIALISTS

HOUSE PARTY RESULTS IN CALL FOR CLEARER THINKING.

Mr. COLE GETS TO WORK

Open Mind on Empire Buying and Preference

From Our Political Correspondent.

The Government is to be presented with a brand new policy. Certain ministers are to take part in its preparation.

It is called a "long run" policy, and is planned "for ten years ahead."

To-morrow evening a group of Socialists and Trade Unionists will begin fashioning the new plan at a meeting to be held at Transport House [17]. The prime movers are Major C. R. Attlee (Postmaster-General), and Mr. G. D. H. Cole.

17. The premises of "The Labour Party".

Sir Stafford Cripps (the Solicitor-General), Mr. Ernest Bevin, and Mr. Noel Baker, M. P. -(Mr. Arthur Henderson's Parliamentary Private Secretary) are among those expected the invitation of Major Attlee and Mr. Cole at tomorrow's meeting.

AFTER THE WEEK-END PARTIES.

The new policy — or the plan for a new policy — had its origin in a series of house parties held last year at Easton Lodge (the Labour Chequers), [18] when Socialist politicians, economists and trades unionists foregathered at week-ends. Out of these meetings grew the new Fabian ResearchBureau (of which Major Attlee is chairman and Mr. Cole secretary), which received the official blessing of the Labour movement two months ago and is now established in premises in Abingdon street. [19]

It is with this new policy that we are presently concerned. Outside of England, the Fabians are affiliated with strong Socialist groups professing the same ideas in Denmark, South Africa, Canada and Australia, Japan, United States, Spain and Germany. Lectures by Fabians were also given in Paris at the *Comité d' Etudes Nationales*, founded and directed by the Jew Albert Kahn, and also at the *Club du Faubourg*, organized by the Jew Léo Poldès, as well as to the French Socialist Party, headed by the Jew Léon Blum.

On November 1, 1930, the *Evening Standard*, already quoted, contained the following lines:—

GOVERNMENT BY FABIANS

Many Labour members are talking about the dominance in the Government of that very academic body, the

18. Easton Lodge is the seat of Frances, Dowager Countess of Warwick. The Socialism of all "Parlor-Bolsheviks" reminds one of the Jew Isaac McBride's utterance: "We are going to milk the bourgeoisie and they will help us to keep (up) the struggle against themselves."

19. No. 23 Abingdon Street is the seat of the S. S. I. P. ("Society for Socialist Inquiry and Propaganda"); the new "Fabian Research Bureau": and the "Socialist League".

Fabian Society. I find that many people believed that this organization, through which many intellectuels entered the Socialist movement had ceased to exist. But is goes on with membership, small but influential, some 5,000.

Yet practically every recent appointment, either to high or low office, in the Labour administration has been made from the membership of the Society, the latest examples of which are the new Air Minister, Lord Amulree, and the new Solicitor-General, Sir Stafford Cripps. I am told that at least 90 per cent of the members of the Government are in the rolls of the Society, and that, contrary to regulations, so are a good many highly placed Civil Servants. The Civil Servants would probably defend themselves by saying that the Society is more intellectual than political.

This ascendancy is, of course, due to the all-powerful influence of Lord Passfield and his wife, Mrs. Sidney Webb, with whom the Fabian Society has been the passion of their lives.

If, on the one hand, the British Government is run by avowed Fabians, the present United States Government is in exactly the same position. The "brain trust" of Franklin D. Roosevelt is composed of several Jews, among them Bernard M. Baruch, Herbert Swope, Mordecai Ezekiel, James Warburg, Frank W. Taussig, Others like Swanson, Secretary of the Navy, [20] Arthur Bullitt, Louis M. Howe, Raymond Moley, Tugwell, George N. Peek, if not Jews, were closely connected with Jews and such radical organizations as the Conference for Progressive Political Action, the Rand School for Communism, the Friends of Soviet Russia, the League for Industrial Democracy.

The League for Industrial Democracy [21] is the American counterpart of British Fabianism. It runs parallel to the Ethical Culture Society, founded by the Jew Felix

20. See Whitney, "Reds in America", pp. 49, 58, 59.

21. Among the members of the Board of Directors of this League in 1926 figured Justice Wise, daughter of Rabbi Stephen Wise.

Adler, the Conference of Progressive Political Action, the Intercollegiate Socialist League, the Intercollegiate Liberal League, the American Civil Liberties Union, and countless other subversive groups. Under the heading "Other Fabian Organizations", mentioned in the Fabian Society's annual report for 1932, one reads:—

"Active relations are maintained between the "Fabian Society and the League for Industrial Democracy of America.... with the Public Ownership League of the U. S. A.".

Is not one forcibly reminded of the following sentence? "We appear on the scene as alleged saviours of the worker from this oppression, when we propose to him to enter the ranks of our fighting forces — Socialists, Anarchists, Communists — to whom we always give support in accordance with an alleged brotherly rule (of the solidarity of all humanity) of our *social masonry*". [22]

Not less than English Universities, have the American colleges been permeated with Fabian theories, and hardly any of them are without a branch of the National Student Forum (long headed by John Rothschild) or of the Intercollegiate Liberal League, [23] founded at Harvard in 1921. Particular attention must be drawn to the Rand School of New York, founded in 1905 which, ten years ago, was raided by order of the United States Government on account of its Communist teaching. [24]

The penetration of Fabianism in the church of America

22. Protocol No. 3.

23. Felix Frankfurter was one of its sponsors.

24. It is noteworthy that the Rand School received important financial support from the former Mrs. Willard Straight, née Dorothy P. Whitney, now the wife of Leonard Elmhurst who, according to Mr. Israel Sieff's statement, is Chairman of the agricultural group of the P. E. P. One of the lecturers at the Rand School who has come into recent prominence is Raymond Moley, personal adviser to President Roosevelt, and his special delegate to the London Conference, 1933.

is fully evidenced by the subversive activities of the Federal Council of Churches of Christ in America. [25]

As President Roosevelt's "brain trust" was recruited from such centres, it is clear that the composition of both the British and American Governments is similar. It is Jewish-radical or, to use plain language, Jewish-bolshevist. Both governments are run by men who are merely puppets in the hands of Jews highly placed in the secret councils of the central Jewish Kahal, the present-day Zionist World organization, whose object is the ultimate destruction of all our religious, social and industrial institutions and the annihilation of our freedom. It is therefore interesting to note that plans, evolved in the numerous bolshevist-socialist centres created by Fabians, Liberals and Socialists, are being executed in both the British Empire and the United States.

It is curious to compare these wonderful socialist economic plans with those which were to have been the basis of the ideal Jewish State in Palestine, after the Balfour Declaration. They were formulated in 1919 by Bernard A. Rosenblatt, a prominent Zionist, in his book *Social Zionism*. From it we cull only the following lines, not devoid of a certain interest:—

A. The Jew as a social force in history:

(1) The prophets of Israel as the preachers of political, social and economic democracy.

(2) The rabbis as the teachers in a democratic school of Jewish students.

(3) The Jewish figures in political history almost invariably the leaders in Liberalism, Labour and Socialism:

---

25. See Sanctuary, "Tainted Contacts" (New York, 1931).

(a) Examples: Karl Marx, Lasalle, Hess, Lasker, Bernstein, Joseph Fels, Brandeis, [26] Gompers. [27]

(b) Even unreasonable extremists like Trotzky show only the necessary evil involved in this Jewish tendency toward social justice. [28]

The press notice of Rosenblatt's book in the *American Jewish News* is headed "Will the Jews again lead the world?" [29]

The "experiment" of this ideal socialism having signally failed in Palestine, it is to be tried now in both England and America. In England, the centralization of all plans for the "new policy" has, for quite some time, been worked under the name of "Political and Economic Planning" or "P. E. P.", and in America it has taken the name of "N. R. A." (National Recovery Act). The plans of both are identical, only the method of execution is different. Whereas the English must be dealt with slowly, and as it were taken unawares, the American people, on account of the ignorance and the primitiveness of the masses, can be treated brutally, as is being done by Hugh Johnson [30] and other henchmen of President

---

26. Louis D. Brandeis, an active Zionist, formerly close personal adviser to President Wilson during the War, and who, since then, has been sitting as Justice on the Federal Supreme Court at Washington.

27. The late Samuel Gompers, President of "The American Federation of Labour."

28. If wholesale murder is practised by Trotsky (Braunstein) is only "the necessary evil involved on this Jewish tendency toward social justice", one hesitates to ask what evil would be necessary in order that the Jews might confer on us some "greater" social blessing.

29. The introduction to Rosenblatt's book is by Judge Julian W. Mack, U. S. Circuit judge, on "Juvenile Court", 1904-1917; member "Board of Inquiry on Conscientious Objectors", 1917-1918; President "Zionist Organization of America", 1921.

30. "In 1927, Baruch asked Johnson to join him in his New York office, and ever since, the General has been Baruch's

Roosevelt. In America, coercion is the order of the day; "freedom" is now a meaningless word: whereas the Englishman is asked to forego his freedom for the sake of patriotism, the American masses, aliens to the Anglo-Saxon race, are swayed only by cupidity and the promise of material prosperity. Both methods produce the same results: the concentration of all material resources in the hands of the Jews, the lowering of our standard of living, and complete physical and moral degradation. [31]

---

right-hand man.... During most of these years (after the War) Johnson was in touch with a man who was in the thick of many contests of finance, battles of Wall Street, and intrigues of international banking. This was Bernard Mannes Baruch, suave and rich New York capitalist, friend and supporter of the President, who gave Johnson to Roosevelt....... Another ace man on the Roosevelt staff here, George N. Peek, Administrator of the Farm Relief Act, was also a War Industries Board member, friend of Baruch, partner of Johnson in plow-making." Chicago Tribune, August 16, 1933.

31. "All people are chained down to heavy toil by poverty more firmly than ever they were chained by slavery and serfdom; from these, one way or another, they might free themselves, these could be settled with, but from want they will never get away." Protocol No. 3.

"The aristocracy which enjoyed by law the labour of the workers were wellfed, healthy and strong. We are interested in just the opposite — in the diminution, the **killing out of the goyim.** Our power is in the chronic shortness of food and physical weakness of the worker because, by all that this implies, he is made the slave of our will and he will not find in his own authorities either strength or energy to set against our will." Supra.

"The need for daily bread forces the "goyim" to keep silence and be our humble servants." Protocol No. 13.

EXCERPTS

from Congressman Louis T. McFadden's Radio Address of Wednesday Evening, May 2, 1934, as such appear in the Congressional Record of May 3, 1934, dealing with the P. E. P. Plan analyzed in "The Organization of British Slavery or Jew-Fabian Bolshevism."

"The country has recently been treated to the spectacle of the present administration's attempt to ridicule the idea that there is a definite new plan of government in process. Without attempting to comment in any manner whatever on the attempt to disarm the public, I desire now to refer briefly to a plan that was advocated as far back as 1918 when A. A. Berle had some very definite ideas regarding the establishing of a new State. Indeed, he wrote a little book on 'The Significance of a Jewish State' dedicated to his friend, Louis D. Brandeis. In it he regarded the Jew as 'the barometer of civilization at all times.' He recognized the inability of Christianity to avert war or 'to do a single thing towards mitigating its worst effects,' and seemed to think the Jews were the only power that could do anything about it. * * *

"An attempt to establish a political economic plan is now in operation under the leadership of a group, formerly connected with the Fabian Society in England. This, until the present, secret political economic plan was drawn up by Israel Moses Seiff, an Israelite, the director of a chain store enterprise in England, called 'Marks & Spencer', which house handles almost exclusively imports from

Soviet Russia, which enables them to undersell its competitors. * * *

"This political economic plan organization, now secretly operating in England, is designated 'freedom and planning', and is divided into many well-organized and well-financed departments, such as town and country planning, industry, international relations, transportation, banking, social service, civil division. It is already in operation in the British Government by means of the tariff advisory board. It has gathered all data statistics obtainable by governmental and private organizations in administrative, industrial, trade, social, educational, agricultural, and other circles. * * * Iron and steel and cotton industrials have been ordered by the tariff advisory board to prepare and submit plans for the reorganization of their industries, and have been warned that should they fail to do so a plan for complete reconstruction will be imposed upon them. This board has been granted default powers, and can, therefore, enforce its plan. * * * *

"That this political economic group practically control the British Government is indicated by the fact that Prime Minister MacDonald and his son and J. H. Thomas and other influential Britishers are officers of the group.

"An interesting sidelight is that some six months ago when the father of this plan, Israel Moses Seiff, was urged to show more activity by the members of his committee ,his answer was "Let us go slowly for a while and wait until we see how our plan carries out in America.' That statement indicates that a plan similar to theirs is being tried in America."

THE ORGANIZATION OF BRITISH SLAVERY
OR
JEW-FABIAN BOLSHEVISM

On March 29th, 1933, at a dinner given to the members of the P. E. P. Political Economic Plan, the Chairman of this group, the Jew Israel Moses Sieff made a speech on "Planning". The speech in itself already contained some leading lines as to the aims of the P. E. P. that can be summed up as the planned destruction of the existing order of our social, political and economic life and the erection of a structure based on centralization, standardization, expropriation and compulsion, leading to inevitable enslavement.

But in spite of having been somewhat rashly outspoken in his speech, Mr. Sieff did in reality show a certain amount of caution, for his *verbal* utterances were very mild compared to his written *expose* on the same subject. Entitled "Freedom and Planning" it was privately circulated some months ago.

The perusal of this document leaves the reader no room for doubting the sinister outcome of the present world economic and financial crisis as viewed by united Jews and Fabians.

The Jewish plans for the attainment of world domination have been clearly stated in the documents known as "The Protocols of the Wise Men or Elders of Zion" published in 1905 and subsequently in 1920. As to the Fabian subversive ideas, they have been and are still being expressed in the Fabian Societies' periodicals, pamphlets and meetings. The P. E. P. seems to be the central office wherein the propaganda for the schemes of the advent of the Jewish power is being prepared and sent forth by a group of Fabians headed by the Jew chairman Israel Moses Sieff, director of the chain stores of Marks and Spencer.

It is no wonder that as Fabianism is the power ruling England today, the members of the P. E. P. should be in close and constant contact with Mr. Ramsey MacDonald and his son. In fact it is rumored that the whole of the actual British government plans in the realm of economics issues from the offices of the P. E. P.

The document above referred to "Freedom and Planning" starts by giving a dark picture of: "Collapsing Civiliation". It fails however to point out that this fearful description is about the most sweeping indictment of what has been the Jewish capitalistic and democratic experiment of world government. For it would be a monstrous mistake for any intelligent citizen of whatever nation to close his or her eyes to the evident fact that for nigh sixty years, the Jews have surely and rapidly though almost *invisibly* climbed to the heights of government wherefrom the masses are ruled. Politically, financially and economically they have seized the reins of the governments of all nations and their invasion in the realms of social, educational and religious fields is not less important.

We are able to realize into what unfathomable abyss all organizations or our Christian civilization have been hurled to the great prejudice of all the populations of this earth and that is why the picture painted by the Chairman of the P. E. P. is in itself the condemnation of the Jewish method of government.

It is of course necessary for the reader to bear in mind the fact that in describing the woeful state of the world the Jew spokesman fails to ascribe it to the rule of the invisible Jewish government which as Disrael, a highly talkative if intelligent Jew, had so clearly shown had, allready in his time, penetrated all courts and parliments. (Refer to Coningsby published in London in 1844.)

Let us now quote excerpts from "Freedom and Planning";

"COLLAPSING CIVILIZATION"

"This generation is faced with the threat of a World collapse of modern civilization and the advent of a period comparable with the dark ages which followed on the collapse of the Roman Empire in the fifth century A. D.

We are apt to regard such statements as pleasantly sacrifying, pardonable exaggerations in the mouths of those who are trying to spur us to action against the very real ills of the times, but not meant quite seriously.

The threat is serious.

Chaos will overtake us if we cannot show intelligence enough to extricate ourselves.

For more than a year now nothing has enabled civilization to keep some sort of course and to ride out the storm except the immense momentum of ordinary economic processes and the inertia of habit and custom. It is the resisting power of these forces and not intelligence which has thus far staved off the collapse.

They can not bring us back prosperity, but they may suffice to carry the world through the immediate crisis. If so, we shall for a time be able to live on our capital, the capital stored up from past generations, the intellectual and moral capital of men and women trained for civilization and citizenship. By what chance will the next generation have, if half of them find no employment for their youthful energies, and all of them are living under the oppression of hopelessness and decay?

What forms collapse will assume no one can foresee. It may not come suddenly. More probably there will be a gradual decline with fleeting periods of revival.

"WORLD WIDE ECONOMIC DISTRESS"

Cracks are appearing everywhere. In China and in India economic distress is both aggravated and concealed by the social and political unrest of which it is the main root.

In South America revolution has become epidemic and all but one or two countries of the most solid are financially in default.

In Central and South Eastern Europe financial default is emminent, but that by itself is of little moment in comparison with the consequent social and political upheaval which will follow. It is open to question whether the populations of Germany and Central Europe can be fed and kept alive next winter and how long any organized government can control the situation in these countries.

In the U. S. A. loss of confidence is absolute. The strain of material suffering in a population, none too homogenous, accustomed for generation to rapidly increasing prosperity may lead to a breakdown of existing institutions and forms of government. The outcome is unpredictable but the consequences throughout the globe may be catastrophic.

World disorganization, famine, pestilence, and the submergence of our civilization are visible on the horizon. . .

"BRITAIN'S NEED OF A PROSPEROUS WORLD"

Britain cannot however prosper in a distressed world. Entirely dependent on external trade for her food and raw material Britain cannot escape world catastrophe by isolating herself.

Moreover that world wide loss of control of the machinery of civilization is all too visible in Britain and British institutions.

If Britain is to save herself and give the world that leadership which is urgently demanded, the first need is for complete reconstruction of our national life on lines fitted for the new needs of the twentieth century.

Here a fundamental difficulty must be faced. Economic nationalism is no solution. On the contrary it is among the main causes of the world's troubles. Recovery depends on building up afresh and extending even more widely than before the worldwide exchanges of goods and services which everywhere cross national and political boundaries.

The United Kingdom is far too small in area to form today an economic unit commensurate with the vast scale of modern commercial and industrial operations.

The aim must always be the widest possible international co-operation.

— — — — — We have allowed the members of our feeble minded to double themselves in the last twenty years.

We have watched the purchasing power of our currency fluctuate wildly and play havoc with our economic life, and have been powerless to help ourselves — — — — — — — Notorious unsuitable candidates "get themselves elected" (this is our habitual way of speaking of what happens) to Parliament and the Local Councils.

Prime Ministers get nervously worn out in the mere effort to grapple with the everyday business which faces them — — — — —

"THE FAILURE OF OUR POLITICAL AND ECONOMIC MACHINERY."

Our political and economic machinery is breaking down. The great fund of individual and corporate goodwill, greater probably than at any previous period in our history, goes to waste and all our wills are frustated for want of a large-scale plans on national re-organization.

Neither in politics nor in economics have we grasped that the first and urgent necessity is planning ahead.

Particular projects often of great political value are put forward in Parliament or elsewhere without any effort being made to relate them to each other or to a national plan, and they either break down or function imperfectly through needless friction engendered by absence of ordered planning.

Frequently where public opinion has become exasperated at its failure to get something done to remedy a defect which everyone recognizes as intolerable, our distracted legislators with unanimity unite to pass into law a compromise which is wanted by no one and merely aggravates the evil.

It is a common occurence for a government to be pursuing two or more mutually inconsistent policies at one and the same time.

*

Then follows the trend of the subtle insinuating ideas meant to induce and reconcile the British people to the voluntary abandonment of their freedom if thereby their country can be benefited. Thus are they meant to become the very victims of their genuine patriotism. The example they gave of sacrifice and self-discipline has been but one more tool in the hands of their double faced leaders. They already sacrificed their gold to comply with the plea that in so doing they would save their country. This is referred to in the document in the following lines:

"BRITAIN'S PLIGHT".

"Great Britain and some parts of the British Empire have in some degree improved their own position since last autumn. Absolutely the improvement in Great Britain has been small, though rela.ively in other countries it is striking.

'This achievement is of real value to the world, even though some part of it has been made at the expense of added difficulties for others.

It has been attained thanks to a remarkable demonsration of the self-discipline and well disposed spirit of public services and the sober imperturbability and reasonabliness of the British citizen in face of a crisis.

It is in this evidence of British character that the best hope for the future rests.

It is this high feeling that must be exploited and the next step is to show the people that their country's needs require of them the sacrifice of their individual freedom.

"Can we save our freedom?" — asks Mr. Sieff, and he advances the following line of arguments:

"CAN WE SAVE OUR FREEDOM?"

Mr. Bernard Shaw's mordant words pose directly the poignant question. Is the national reconstruction possible without sacrifice of the essentials of personal and political freedom?

For all their differences Bolshevism and Fascism have two outstanding features in common. Both stress the primary need for conscious forward planning on a national scale. Both repudiate the claims of personal and individual freedom.

In this country we hold fast to the concept of freedom as one of absolute validity.

We know in our hearts that we are in imminent danger of losing both our freedom and our material well-being if we go on drifting.

But if indeed national re-organization has to bought at the price of losing our freedom, many of us feel that it would be better for humanity to descend once again into the abyss of barbarism and struggle painfully back at some later epoch to a civilization capable of satisfying both its material and its spiritual aspirations.

Is the dilemma absolute? Can conscious forward planning of our economic life be reconciled with the essential and over-riding claim of freedom?

Is it true, that what we need is more government and a great encroachment on liberty?

Observe that it is in the sphere of our economic life, in the sphere of material things only, that conscious forward planning is demanded.

"May it not be that an unprejudiced re-examination of what we call freedom may reveal unexpected possibilities?"

* * *

In the realm of industry, the subversive opinion of the opinion of the P.E.P. is that to the doctrine of "laissez-faire" or competitive initiative should be substituted standardization, monopolies and trusts, all under the rule of what Mr. Sieff calls the *Planning Authority*. Whoever is acquainted with the Protocols of the Elders of Zion, knows that this 'planning authority' can have its directing center only in the councils of the supreme Jewish kahal where all "planning" and "conscious forward planning" have been done for centuries.

We quote further:

"A PLANNING AUTHORITY."

"Conscious planning leaves the consumer free but involves the substitution of some organized control over over-production and distribution on behalf of the community to take the place of that free play of supposedly automatic economic forces on which *laissez-faire* relied.

Control implies a controlling machinery. To the average man and woman among us there jumps to the mind at once the picture of a large number of new government departments and hordes of new officials attempting to take the place and do the work of the business man, the manufacturer, the farmer, the banker, the shopkeeper, or at least to tie them all up hand and foot and dictate to them in the management of their daily affairs. And we see further a glimpse of Parliment and Local bodies finally overwhelmed by the task of fulfilling their new duties and functions. — — — — —

"Is there not a middle way, or better still a new way of meeting the need for organizations and co-ordination of those economic tasks which the breakdown of *laissez-faire* is leaving unaccomplished?"

* * *

The 'new way' found by the subtle P. E. P. is the organization of 'Public Utility Bodies' fashioned somewhat on the pattern of the B. B. C., Central Electric Board, etc. and we are told that: — — — — "It is possible to envisage a considerable extension of this form of organization of the nation's business. A new picture begins to emerge in outline of industry, agriculture, transport, etc., enjoying, if not Dominion Status, at any rate wide powers of local self government, with the Cabinet, Parliament, and the Local Atuhorities liberated from duties to which they are not ideally suited and free to perform their essential functions on behalf of the community.

"THE ANALOGY OF THE ELECTRICITY GRID SYSTEM"

"The analogy of the Grid System of the Central Electricity Board, not itself undertaking the production of power nor the final distribution of electricity services to the consumer, but providing a co-ordinated system of carrying the electricity produced from the big generating stations to local distributing centers all over the country, can be suggestively applied to other services.

Imagine the dairy farmers of the country or of various regional divisions of the country as the milk generating stations, and the retailer of milk as the local distributing centers, with a Central Milk Board conducting the business of bulk marketing of milk as the milk Grid of Britain. Already under Agricultural Marketing Act there are signs of the coming of such a Milk Grid as a natural development to meet the needs of the day. An extension of the system with suitable adaptions to other agricultural products easily suggests itself, and even more directly as a method of dealing with the needs of modern transport by rail, road, water and air."

* * *

In the above qoutation we see the P. E. P. sketching a program of *distribution.* From the organized control of distribution to that of production, under any despotic rule, there is but one step and Mr. Sieff has inevitably taken it. Moreover, being one of many Jews who have of late years concentrated on the multiple shop and chain stores systems and the organizations of various cartels and trusts, Mr. Sieff could not refrain from dealing a blow at the independent retail stores which for centuries have been the mainstay of British trade. To paralize and thus eliminate the individual retail shopkeeper from trade has been one of the chief aims of Jewish "planning".

Let us now quote what is written on this subject:

"Organized Production"

"When we come to the organization of producers, agricultural, industrial and , the Central Electricity model becomes more difficult to follow. — — —

Methods of retailing can not indeed be left entirely unchanged in the face of twentieth century needs. The multiple shop and the chair store are already bringing about notable modifications. The waste involved in the 500,000 or more retail shops, one shop for every twenty households cannot be allowed to continue to block the flow of goods from producer to consumer. And re-organization of retail methods is necessary to achieve the adequate organization of production. — — — —

The development of an organized Grid System for the distribution of milk must, it is certain, lead to a profound modification of the traditional individualism outlook of the Dairy-Farmer. And so it will be in other producing industries. Cooperative organization of the business of distribution cannot fail to bring about conditions in which both the need and the will to organize themselves on a co-operative basis arise among the producers whether they be agriculturists, or producers of coal, or of iron from the mines, or manufacturers of steel, or of cotton, or of wool.

"Whether we like it or not — and many will dislike it intensely — the individualists manufacturer and farmer will be forced by events to submit to far-reaching changes in outlook and methods. The danger is that in resisting them because he regards them as encroachments on what he calls his freedom, he will make things much worse for himself and for the community. Resistance is likely to play into the hands of those who say that thinkering is useless and that full blooded socialism or communism are the only cure. Or he may be tempted to flirt with Fascist ideas. In either case he loses his cherished freedom, and it is only too probable that Fascism and Communism alike would be but short stages on the road to barbarism."

* * *

It would be difficult to imply threats in a more outspoken manner and Mr. Sieff goes on to state that:

. . . . . . "It is idle to deny that some at least of the changes required when conscious forward planning extends into the field of production are of a revolutionary character.

It is all important that we should appraise them soberly and without prejudice and distinguish clearly between unavoidable alterations of methods or economic organizations and fundamental attacks on our personal and political freedom — — — —

Without entering more deeply into details than space here allows, the position of the farmer and manufacturer under a system of planned production can only be sketched in broad outlines.

He may be conceived of as remaining in full control of all the operations of his farm or factory, but receiving from the duly constituted authorities instructions as to the quantity and quality of his production, and as to the markets in which he will sell. He will himself have had a voice in setting his constituted authority and will have regular means of communicating with it and of influencing its policy. He will be less exposed than at present to interference from above, that is from Government Departments and local Bodies and their inspectors. He will be less free to make arbitrary decisions as to his own business outside the region of day to day operation of the plant or farm.

It must be presumed that the constituted authority will be armed by enabling legislation Act of Parliment and by a majority decisions of its own members, presumably elected by votes of those minorities in clearly specified cases.

All this is not very different from what already occurs in particular organized industries, but must be conceived of as applying generally to most, if not all, of the major fields of production, and as part of a conscious and systematically planned agricultural and industrial organization."

* * *

Having thus given out the basis principles upon which the Judeo-Fabian new structure of British economic life is to be erected, an outline of the organization which will direct the functioning of the plan is given:

"A NATIONAL PLAN IN OUTLINE."

"An outline of the organization contemplated would be somewhat as follows:

"A National Planning Commission, with advisory not exective functions, subordinate to the Cabinet and the Parliament, but with clearly defined powers of initiative and clearly defined responsibilities, its personal representative of the nation's economic life.

A National Council for Agriculture, a National Council for Industry, a Steel Industry Corporation, a Milk Producers Corporation, organized on the lines of Public Utility Concern, serving at least to federate, and in suitable cases to own the plants, factories, etc., engaged in production.

A series of Public Utility Corporations dealing with distributive services, e. g. the Central Electricity Board. the National Transoprt Board (or a number of Regional Transport Boards): the National Milk Marketing Board.

In the constitution of these bodies provision would naturally be made for suitable representation of interests, including organized Labor, and for their due co-ordination by means for example of the election by various corporations of some of their members to serve on the National Councils. To all of them Parliament would delegate considerable powers to regulate the affairs of their particular industries."

* * *

So far so good. Any ideologist or cracked brain human being can devise some kind of utopia, in fact most of the inmates of lunatic asylums have been interned for that very reason. However, they are usually pronounced dangerous for society from the moment that they attempt to work out their fancy into reality.

Plans for the realization of Mr. Sieff's wierd ideas have already been made. They are summed up in two words: COMPULSION and EXPORTATION.

Reading the following quotations, one is forcibly reminded of the tenets preached in New York at the Rand School and meetings of the "Friends of Soviet Russia."

"From the standpoint of encroachments upon freedom apart from the denial of the tenets of individualism, the most obvious target for attack are perhaps the proposed grant of powers to compel minorities and (point not yet mentioned) the probable necessity for drastic changes in the ownership of land.

Powers of compulsion or minorities are not unknown under present conditions and will probably not arouse very violent antagonism on the ground of high principle.

The question of private ownership of land is one which never fails to encounter deep rooted passions. It is also one which arises immediately in almost every aspect of consciously planned reconstruction.

The conclusion seems to be unescapable that whether in the field of Town and Country Planning or in that of Agricultural (or Rural) Planning or in the organization of Industry, it is not possible to make reasonable progress without drastic powers to buy out individual owners of land.

This is not to say that land nationalization in the ordinary sense of the term is either necessary or desirable, far from it. Nothing would be gained by substituting the State as landlord. What is required, if only with a view to equitable treatment of individuals, is transfer or ownership of large blocks of land, not necessarily of all the land in the country, but certainly of a large portion of it into the hands of the proposed Statutory Corporations and Public Utility Bodies and of Land Trusts.

In many cases, all that would be needed, would be the conversion of rights of ownership of land into rights of participations as share holders in the new corporations or in Land Trusts. It would be possible further in a large number of cases to leave management undisturbed, together with the enjoyment of the amenities which at present go with ownership, subject to the transfer of title to the Corporations or Trusts.

Here again, limits of space preclude fuller treatment of the subject. All that is here relevant is the inevitable conclusion that the planned economy which the nation needs to meet the demands of the twentieth century must clearly involve drastic inroads upon the rights of individual ownership of land as at present understood."

* * *

As to *Finance* and the right of citizens to deal freely with their money, Mr. Sieff's kind solicitude for the property of others has prompted him to formulate the following point of view so worthy of paternal bolshevism:

— — — "Stable money cannot be secured without the considerable extension of control on behalf of the community over free flow of investment and the uses to which the individuals makes of his capital.

While as consumer he can retain full freedom of choice as to competing wants he will satisfy, there are real difficulties in leaving him entirely free to invest his savings in any way he chooses.

"It is probable that many of these difficulties can be solved on the one hand by extension of the system of insurance, on lines to which recent developments of the motoring law again supply suggestive analogies and, on the other hand, by means which while leaving the small capitalist untrammelled will so canalize the flow of both long term and short term investment of the large sums which are at the disposal of banks and financial institutions as well as funds in the hands of large insurance companies as to ensure that adequate capital is available for the big industrial, agricultural and distributive corporations already envisaged."

Then comes the discussion of the problem of Labour which points out the future uselessness of the present Trade Unions who still labour under the delusion that they have achieved the nec plus ultra of good conditions for workmen! — — The P. E. P. will reorganize them.

Social Services, a P. E. P. organization will, among other things, "call for a big change in the organization of the Medical Profession which has, at present, too often a vested interest in disease".

Needless to add that "Imperial Planning" and "International Planning" have also been the object to Mr. Sieff's careful attention. Suffice it to quote the conclusive words of his scheme: "The only rival world political and economic system which put forward a comparable claim is that of the Union of Soviet Republics."

* * *

The conclusion is almost naive but far from surprising when we know that the "plans" for the disruption of Russia and enslavement of the Russian people were made in the councils of the Jewish Kahal of which Mr. Sieff is a prominent member.

Let us now see what is to be the fate of this British Constitution of which every Britain is so justly proud:

"Nevertheless our first plan is to replan Britain — — Effective planning on the economic side and even the introduction of desirable reforms in detail has become impossible without a drastic overhauling both of Parliament and the Central Government and of the machinery of Local Government. Political and economic planning are complemetary and supplementary to each other and must be carefully inter-related. We need new economic and political institutions to match the new social adjustments which applied science has created and a new technique both in politics and industry to enable us to find intelligent methods of surmounting new difficulties and complexities. — — —

"It has been suggested more than once in the course of this essay that devolution of powers to statutory bodies will be an important feature of the new order and that in the result Parliament and the Cabinet will be relieved of some part of their present duties and set free to the great advantage of themselves and of the nation for their proper tasks of directing and guiding public policy.

"Big consequent changes will follow in the machinery of government" — — —

* * *

And to anyone inclined to criticize Mr. Sieff's marvelous scheme of destruction of all existing social, political and economic order, the following answer is given:

"One possible answer is of course to refer our critic to what was said at the outset as to the imminence of catastrophe if we continue to drift — — Reluctance to embark on a doubtful adventure deserves a less negative treatment.

"The dangers which our critics fear are real dangers — — Our statutory Corporations and Public Utility Boards may easily become unadventurous obstacles to progress, determined enemies to all new ideas. It may be indeed that one of the lessons we have to learn from our present distress is that scientific invention itself requires some planning in its application to the economic structure of the nation.

"The problem of progress is no longer the problem of getting enough chance to prevent routine from deadening effort, but the problem of preventing change from destroying both routine and all social stability.

"This however is no justification of institutions which deaden effort.

"Or proposals must rather be defended by the claim that they will liberate the spirit of initiative and not deaden it, in that they will provide means by which the energetic man of business may escape from the dishearteninging frustrations and failures which are caused by the complexity of the machine, and will give him scope for serving his generation in a larger kingdom than *the narrow field of competition* with rivals in particular industrial or commercial pursuits.

"Though organized on public utility lines with MONOPOLISTIC privileges, the GREAT INDUSTRIAL CORPORATIONS will find ample room for energy and initiative in performing their primary task of combining maximum with minimum costs of production. The executive heads of particular factories will not lack the spur of competition" — —

Lastly we need to be told that:

— — — "Experience alone can prove the justice of our claim that economic freedom will not be fatally shackled by the effort of conscious forward planning. Experience too will be needed to make clear the boundaries of the province within which individualistic effort can best be relied upon to secure the highest national dividend" — — — —

* * *

How forcibly one is here reminded of the words of the apostless and disciples of Lenin and Trotsky-Bronstein who so loudly proclaimed that the imposition of Bolshevism in Russia was but a great experiment! Is a five year plan of enforced labor to be imposed also upon the British people?

Silence surrounds the results of the same experiments in Mexico, Spain and the South American States because it is the policy of the destructors of our Christian civilization to muzzle the press that they own, but England, though ruled by the chosen of the Kahal namely, the revolutionary Fabian Group is given a warning in time and can therefore frame a line of defense.

The justification of the "Conscious forward planning" scheme is given as the final part of Mr. Sieff's masterpiece.

The inrony of calling destruction a "CONSERVATIVE EVOLUTION" will not escape the reader.

"CONSERVATIVE EVOLUTION"

"Indeed the Socialist or Communist will condemn our planning as mere tinkering with the outworn machine of capitalism. To him it will appear a hopelessly conservative and anaemic attempt to stave off the red blooded revolution which alone would satisfy him.

"Our plan is, we claim, conservative in the truest and best sense. It is constructive, not destructive, and builds solidly upon the present and the past. It faces the issue boldly and it not afraid to challenge vested interests and deeply cherished habits of thought and action.

"It does not however propose to expropriate anyone and in requiring the application of compulsion in a limited sphere it is not doing more than extend and make explicit and give systematic application to tendencies and practices already at work — Such sketch, in the broadest outlines of the lines which reconstruction might take as has been given here, must inevitably raise more questions in the mind of the attentive reader than it answers."

* * *

It does!

Mr. Sieff's document is as clear an expose of a policy calculated to kill human initiative and the spirit of competition which means progress as is given in the "Protocols of the Wise Men of Zion".

Will the British people allow themselves to be further bamboozled by those who have already got the best of their fine spirit of patriotism and intend to exploit is still more?

Yes the political, economic and spiritual needs of England require as much scope of freedom today and in the future as they ever did in the past.

The foregoing quotations have given but a very succinct expose of "conscious forward planning" as given out by Israel Moses Sieff.

The analogies between his utterances and the contents of the document known under the title of the Protocols of the Wise Men of Zion first published in 1905 are very striking indeed. We quote but a few taken from the edition of the Protocols published by Small & Maynard of Boston, Mass., U. S. A. in 1920:

ANALOGIES WITH THE PROTOCOLS:

P. 26. 5th Pr. — "*There is nothing more dangerous than individual initiative*: if it had a touch of genius it can accomplish more than a million people among whom we have sown dissensions. We must direct the education of the Goy societies so that arms will drop hopelessly when they face every task where initiative is required. The intensity of action resulting from the individual freedom of action dissipates its force when it encounters another person's freedom. This results in heavy blows at morals, disappointments and failures."

P. 27. 6th Pr. — "We will soon begin to establish huge monopolies-reservoirs of huge wealth, upon which even the large fortunes of the Goys will depend to such an extent that they will be drowned, together with the governmental credits, on the day following the political catastrophe."

P. 27. 6th Pr. — "*The aristocracy of the Goys, as a political force is dead. We do not need to take it into consideration: But as landowners they are harmful to us because they can be independent in their sources of life. For this reason we must deprive them of their land at any cost.*

P. 34. 10th Pr. — "For this reason our plans must be strongly and clearly conceived. . . . . These plans will not immediately upset contemporary institutions. They will only alter their organization, and consequently the entire combination of their development, which will thus be directed according to the plans laid down by us."

P. 44. 13th Pr. — To divert the over-restless people from discussing political problems, we now make it appear that we provide them with new problems namely, those pertaining to industry. Let them become excited over this subject as much as they like" — — —

CONCLUSION

On re-reading the foregoing pages before sending them to press, the writer is painfully aware of their inadequacy. The subject is too vast and too unfamiliar to the general public to permit of successful treatment in a small volume. It has been necessary to compress, at the risk of fatiguing and even antagonizing the reader by excessive brevity and abrupt transitions.

At the same time the author has had to take counsel of prudence in the selection of material, for the Jews have always counted on the fact that, if the whole truth were told in one comprehensive utterance, no one would believe it. Thus, bigots and minds bursting with the discoveries they have made, have never been feared by the Jews. People are incapable of believing or receiving certain knowledge which runs counter to their habitual manner of thinking: facts are not accepted on proof, but on understanding.

Yet the problem is of such pressing interest and the lurking evil so destructive, that silence is complicity. In daily life, the serpent of Judah lies in wait in every bypath for its Gentile victims, and few are those cunning enough to escape its fangs. In social and political circles, in business and art, wherever one probes, Zionism raises its ugly head — *surgit atrox et spinosa* — and suddenly reveals itself ubiquitous and all-powerful. But its power is magnified because concealed, — just as a venomous snake is more dangerous hidden in the grass, than exposed on a **broad, level road.**

It is therefore very encouraging to note, each year and in nearly every country, the issue of new publications [1] devoted to the defense of local and national interests against "bad cosmopolitanism and bad finance" [2]. These books and periodicals reach the public as the result of exceptional perseverance and sacrifice [3] on the part of the authors and publishers. Nor are the vigorous campaigns of the older patriotic groups [4] in England, Canada, and the United States, — to mention only three English-speaking countries — a matter of less satisfaction.

These signs indicate the growth, during the past ten years, of a small but intelligent minority, determined to fight to the last ditch, and learning to wield its single weapon, publicity, with increased skill and effectiveness.

For the cardinal fact is this: once the screen of secrecy has been removed, once Zionism has been dragged into the open, the peoples of the earth will know how to deal it the death-blow. In Palestine there have been Zionist movements since the days of Nehemiah: they have always ended in failure, because their success depended on secrecy, and it was impossible to keep the secret from their own race for long. This world-Zionism has gone incomparably farther, because for generations the Jews have maintained secrecy among themselves as against the *goyim*.

No organization with a predetermined aim, such as Zionism, can achieve success without secrecy: its programme, elaborated in the course of centuries, is necessarily

---

1. E. g. **Le Patriote** of Montreal.
2. The words of Sir Mark Sykes, **supra**, p. 55.
3. In addition to the difficulty and expense of publication, authors and editors are constantly faced with the alternative of paying heavy fines or serving a term in gaol.
4. As for instance, in London, "The Britons", and the group that publishes the admirably-edited weekly, **The Patriot**.

rigid in its main features; it will not bend or ply to suit circumstances, but everything must be ground to fit the mould. This is possible if people are led, little by little, to adopt each feature of this programme, to regard it as their own choice, and thus put the heavy yoke on their own necks. But if the people should realize that this yoke of iron which the *Kahal* has been so long in forging, is now being imposed on them, they would have none of it. Such is the problem in its broader aspect.

From the outlook of the individual, on the other hand, it is clear that a serious study of the whole question is richly rewarded. Beneath the changing surface of things, the new names and the specious promises, it is easy to recognize the old issue, the real movers behind the scenes, and their definite aims. After a year's study, the observer should be able to follow all the big moves in the Jewish game and predict, with amazing accuracy, the course which Zionism will take under given circumstances and the one along which it will seek to guide the world at large. The one thing Zionists cannot do is change their secret programme: it binds them, as they would bind the world. It is therefore essential to master all the points of this programme, in order to recognize each under its manifold disguises. The man who has done this, holds in his hand a lever with which to pry Zionism out of its concealment. If he is discreet and courageous, he need fear nothing. In his ears will sound the words:

"Behold, I give unto you power to tread on serpents and scorpions, and over all the power of the enemy: and nothing shall by any means hurt you." [5]

Zionism risks more by attacking such a man then he by attacking Zionism, against which new enemies spring up every day from the least-expected quarters of the globe.

---

5. Luke x, 19.

Our concern is therefore not so much for the ultimate survival of free Gentile nations, as for the national freedom and culture of our own and the next succeeding generations. Now is the time to resist in ourselves, and to stir others to resist that subtle, hypnotic current drawing towards the East to slavery and sensuality, to Babylonian pomp and spiritual desolation. The beauty of Greece, the freedom and courage of the North, the Christianity of Western Europe, these are our heritage: their spirit lives in us, and it is our duty and privilege to defend it.

June, 1934.

APPENDIX

A Protocol of 1860

We take this Protocol from the *Morning Post* of September 6th, 1920:—

"A correspondent writing in reference to the hidden peril draws, attention to a Manifesto issued in 1860 to the 'Jews of the Universe,' by Adolphe Cremieux, the founder of the Alliance Israelite Universelle, and the well-known member of the Provisional Government of 1871. Adolphe Cremieux, while Grand Master of the French Masonic Lodges, offered 1,000,000 francs for the head of William I. of Germany. On his tomb he requested the following sole inscription to be inscribed: —

'Here lies Adolphe Cremieux, the founder of the *Alliance Israelite Universelle.'*

THE MANIFESTO

Emblem: *On top — the tablets of Moses, a little lower — two extended hands clasping each other, and as basis of the whole — the globe of the earth.*

Motto: *"All Jews for one, and one for all."*

The union which we desire to found will not be a French, England, Irish, or German union, but a Jewish one, a Universal one.

Other peoples and races are divided into nationalities; we alone have not co-citizens, but exclusively co-religionaries.

A Jew will under no circumstances become the friend of a Christian or a Moslem before the moment arrives when the light of the Jewish Faith, the only religion of reason, will shine all over the world.

Scattered amongst other nations, who from time immemorial were hostile to our rights and interests, we desire primarily to be and to remain immutably Jews.

Our nationality is the religion of our fathers, and we recognize no other nationality.

We are living in foreign lands, and cannot trouble about the mutable ambitions of countries entirely alien to us, while our own moral and material problems are endangered.

The Jewish teaching must cover the whole earth. Israelites! No matter where fate should lead — though scattered all over the earth, you must always consider yourselves of a Chosen Race.

If you realize that the Faith of your forefathers is your only patriotism —

— if you recognize that, notwithstanding the nationalities you have embraced, you always remain and everywhere form *one* and *only* nation —

— if you believe the Jewry only is the one and only religious and political truth —

— if you are convinced of this, you, Israelites of the Universe —

— then come and give ear to our appeal and prove to us your consent! . . . . . .

Our cause is great and holy, and its success is guaranteed. Catholicism, our immemorial enemy, is lying in the dust, mortally wounded in the head.

The net which Israel is throwing over the globe of the earth is widening and spreading daily, and the momentos prophecies of our holy books are at last to be realized.

The time is near when Jerusalem will become the house of prayer for all nations and peoples, and the banner of Jewish mono-deity will be unfurled and hoisted on the most distant shores.

Let us avail ourselves of all circumstances.

Our might is immense — learn to adopt this might for our cause.

What have you to be afraid of?

The day it not distant when all the riches and treasures of the earth will become the property of the Children of Israel.

A Protocol of 1869

THE FATAL DISCOURSE OF RABBI REICHHORN

In its issue of October 21, 1920, (No. 195), La Vieille France published an extremely important Russian document in which the following passage occurs:

"There is a striking analogy between the *Protocols of the Elders of Zion* and the discourse of the Rabbi Reichhorn, pronounced in Prague in 1869 over the tomb of the Grand Rabbi Simeon-ben-Ihuda, and published by Readcliffe, *who paid with his life for the divulgation;* Sonol, who had taken Readcliffe to hear Reichhorn, was killed in a duel some time afterwards. The general ideas formulated by the Rabbi are found fully developed in the *Protocols.*"

In its issue of March 10, 1921, (No. 214) *La Vieille France* gives the version of this funeral oration which was published in *La Russie Juive*. It is perfectly clear that the funeral oration and the *Protocols of the Elders of Zion* come from one and the same mint. Both are prophetic; and the power which made the prophecies has been able to bring about their fulfilment. This oration is so important that we append to it an account of the fulfilment, of each of the sections. There can no longer be any doubt as to whose is the power which is disturbing the world, creating World unrest, and at the same time reaping all the profits. Jewry is enslaving all Christian peoples of the earth. There IS a Jew World Plot and it now stands finally and completely unmasked.)

1. *Every hundred years, We, the Sages of Israel, have* been accustomed to meet in Sanhedrin in order to examine our progress towards the domination of the world which Jehovah has promised us, and our conquests over the enemy — Christianity.

2. This year, united over the tomb of our reverend Simeon-ben-Ihuda, we can state with pride that the past century has brought us very near to our goal, and that this goal will be very soon attained.

3. Gold always has been and always will be the irresistible power. Handled by expert hands it will always be the most useful lever for those who possess it, and the object of envy for those who do not.

With gold we can buy the most rebellious consciences, can fix the rate of all values, the current price of all products, can subsidise all State loans, and thereafter hold the states at our mercy.

4. Already the principal banks, the exchanges of the entire world, the credits of all the Governments, are in our hands.

5. The other great power is THE PRESS. By repeating without cessation certain ideas, the Press succeeds in the end in having them accepted as actualities. The theatre renders us analogous services. Everywhere the Press and the Theatre obey our orders.

6. By the ceaseless praise of DEMOCRATIC RULE we shall divide the Christians into political parties, we

shall destroy the unity of their nations, we shall sow discord everywhere. Reduced to impotence, they will bow before the LAW of OUR BANK, *always united,* and *always* devoted to our Cause.

7. We shall force the Christians into wars by exploiting their pride and their stupidity. They will massacre each other, and clear the ground for us to put our own people into.

8. The possession of the land has always brought influence and power. In the name of social Justice and Equality we shall parcel out the great estates; we shall give the fragments to the peasants who covet them with all their powers, and who will soon be in debt to us by the expense of cultivating them. Our capital will make us their masters. We in our turn shall become the great-proprietors, and the possession of the land will assure the power to us.

9. Let us try to replace the circulation of gold with paper money; our chests will absorb the gold, and we shall regulate the value of the paper which will make us masters of all the positions.

10. We count among us plenty of orators capable of feigning enthusiasm and of persuading mobs. We shall spread them among the people to announce changes which should secure the happiness of the human race. By gold and by flattery we shall gain the proletariat which will charge itself with annihilating *Christians* capitalism. We shall promise workmen salaries of which they have never dared to dream, but we shall also raise the price of necessities so that *our profits will be greater still.*

11. In this manner we shall prepare Revolutions which *the Christians will make themselves* and of which we shall reap the fruit. . .

12. By our mockeries and our attacks upon them we shall make their priests ridiculous then odious, and their

religion as ridiculous and as odious as their clergy. Then we shall be masters of their *souls.* For our pious attachment to our own religion and the superiority of our souls.

13. We have already established our own men in all important positions. We must endeavor to provide the *Goyim* with lawyers and doctors; the lawyers are *au courant* with all interests; doctors, once in the house, become confessors and directors of consciences.

14. But above all let us monopolize Education. By this means we *spread ideas that are useful to us,* and shape the children's brains as suits us.

15. If one of our people should unhappily fall into the hands of justice amongst the Christians, we must rush to help him; find as many witnesses as he needs to save him from his judges, until we become judges ourselves.

16. The monarchs of the Christian world, swollen with ambition and vanity, surround themselves with luxury and with numerous armies. *We shall furnish them with all the money their folly demands,* and so shall keep them in leach.

17. Let us take care not to hinder the marriage of our men with Christian girls, for through them we shall get our foot into the most closely locked circles. If our daughters marry *Goyim* they will be no less useful, for *the children of a Jewish mother are ours.* Let us foster the idea of free love, that we may destroy among Christian women attachment to the principles and practices of their religion.

18. For ages past the sons of Israel, despised and persecuted, have been working to open up a path to power. They are hitting the mark. *They control the economic life of the accursed Christians;* their influence preponderates over politics and over manners.

19. At the wished for hour, fixed in advance, *we shall let loose the Revolution,* which by ruining all classes of

Christianity will *definitely enslave the Christians to US.* Thus will be accomplished to the promise of God made to his People.

A Protocol of 1919

A Russian newspaper, *Prizyv,* of 5th of February 1920, published in Berlin, contained an interesting document in Hebrew, dated December, 1919, which was found in the pocket of the dead Jew Zunder, the Bólshevic Commander of the 11th Sharp-shooter Battalion, throwing light on the secret organizations of Jewry in Russia. In extenso it ran as follows:—

SECRET. — To the representatives of all the branches of the Israelite International League.

Sons of Israel! The hour of our ultimate victory is near. We stand on the threshold to the command of the world. That which we could only dream of before us is about to be realized. Only quite recently feeble and powerless, we can now, thanks to the world's catastrophe, raise our heads with pride.

We must, however, be careful. It can surely be prophesied that, after we have marched over ruined and broken altars and thrones, we shall advance further on the same indicated path.

The authority of the, to us, alien religious and doctrines of faith we have, through very successful propaganda, subjected to a merciless criticism and mockery. We have brought the culture, civilization, traditions and thrones of the Christian nations to stagger. We have done everything to bring the Russian people under the yoke of the Jewish power, and ultimately compelled them to fall on **their knees before us.**

We have nearly completed all this but we must all the same be very cautious, because the oppressed Russia is our arch-enemy. The victory over Russia, gained through our intellectual superiority, may in future, in a new generation turn against us.

Russia is conquered and brought to the ground. Russia is in the agony of death under our heel, but do not forget — not even for a moment — that we must be careful! The holy care for our safety does not allow us to show either pity or mercy. At last we have been allowed to behold the bitter need of the Russian people, and to see it in tears! By taking from them their property, their gold, we have reduced this people to helpless slaves.

Be cautious and silent! *We ought to have no mercy for our enemy.* We must *make an end of the best and leading elements* of the Russian people, so that the vanquished Russia may not find any leader! Thereby every possibility will vanquish for them to resist our power. *We must excite hatred and disputes between workers and peasants.* War and class-struggle will destroy all treasures and culture created by the Christian people. But be cautious, Sons of Israel! Our victory is near, because our *political and economic power and influence* upon the masses are in rapid progress. We buy up Government loans and gold, and thereby we have controlling power over the world's exchanges. The power is in our hands, but be careful — place no faith in traitorous shady powers!

Bronstein (Trotsky), Apfelbaum (Zinovieff), Rosenfeld (Kameneff), Steinberg — all of them are like unto thousands of other true sons of Israel. Our power in Rus sia is unlimited. In the towns, the Commissariats and Commissions of Food, House Commissions, etc., are dominated by our people. But do not let victory intoxicate you. Be careful, cautious, because no one except yourselves will protect us!

Remember we cannot rely on the Red Army, which one day may turn its warfare on ourselves.

Sons of Israel The hour for our long-cherished victory over Russia is near; close up solid your ranks! Make known our people's national policy! Fight for eternal ideals! Keep holy the old laws, which history has bequeathed to us! May our intellect, our genius, protect and lead us!

Signed, The Central Committee of the Petersburg Branch of the Israelite International League.

www.ingramcontent.com/pod-product-compliance
Lightning Source LLC
Chambersburg PA
CBHW020942310726
48980CB00001B/18

* 9 7 8 1 5 8 5 0 9 5 9 1 9 *